THE COUNTER-
REFORMATION
IN THE VILLAGES

THE COUNTER-REFORMATION IN THE VILLAGES

Religion and Reform in the
Bishopric of Speyer, 1560–1720

MARC R. FORSTER

CORNELL UNIVERSITY PRESS · Ithaca and London

First published 1992 by Cornell University Press.

International Standard Book Number 0–8014–2566–2
Library of Congress Catalog Card Number 91-55564

Printed in the United States of America

*Librarians: Library of Congress cataloging information
appears on the last page of the book.*

♾ The paper in this book meets the minimum requirements
of the American National Standard for Information Sciences—
Permanence of Paper for Printed Library Materials, ANSI Z39.48–1984.

FOR GISELA AND HORST

Contents

Contents

Acknowledgments

It is impossible to thank the many people and institutions who made this book possible. The Fulbright-Hays Foundation and the Harvard University History Department funded research trips to Europe. The R. F. Johnson Faculty Development Fund of Connecticut College provided support in the final stages of this project. Most of the research was done at the Badisches Generallandesarchiv in Karlsruhe and the Landesarchiv in Speyer, and I especially thank the staffs of those archives for their help. I also thank the staffs of the Archives départementales du Bas-Rhin (Strasbourg), the Stadtarchiv Speyer, the Hauptstaatsarchiv Stuttgart, the Archivum Romanum Societas Jésu (Rev. Francis Edwards, S.J.), and the Stadtarchiv Mainz.

Many people gave me advice and criticism along the way, including Robert Bireley S.J., Thomas A. Brady, Jr., Mark Edwards, Joel Harrington, Benjamin J. Kaplan, Hans-Joachim Köhler, Jeff H. Lesser, David Luebke, Mark Peterson, Simon Schama, Laura Smoller, and Bruce Venarde. Carol Betsch and Elizabeth Holmes of Cornell University Press, with the assistance of Andrew Lewis, saved me from many serious errors and inconsistencies. Steven Ozment provided support, counsel, and suggestions at all stages of the project. His contribution is much greater than he would ever admit. I have benefited enormously from both the personal and professional assistance of my parents, Elborg and Robert Forster. They read every page of the manuscript and gave both parental support and invaluable editorial advice.

Acknowledgements

The greatest thanks goes to my wife, Tina, and daughter, Sara, for their patience and company throughout the years of work on Speyer. This book is dedicated to my aunt and uncle, Gisela and Horst Cyriax, who gave me the appreciation of the German language, culture, and history without which the book would never have been written.

M. F.

Glossary and Abbreviations

Units of Measure

Malter measure of grain equal to 1.5 hectoliters or approximately 4.2 bushels

Morgen measure of land equal to 32 to 36 ares or approximately three-quarters of an acre

Fuder measure of liquid, usually wine, equal to 1,000 to 1,200 liters

Abbreviations in the Notes (Sources indicated are cited in full in the bibliography.)

Archives

ADBR Archives départementales du Bas-Rhin (Strasbourg)
ARSJ Archivum Romanum Societas Jésu (Rome)
GLAK Badisches Generallandesarchiv Karlsruhe
HStA.St. Hauptstaatsarchiv Stuttgart
LASp. Landesarchiv Speyer
St.A.MZ Stadtarchiv Mainz
St.A.Sp. Stadtarchiv Speyer

Published References

Duggan   Lawrence Duggan, *Bishop and Chapter: The Governance of the Bishopric of Speyer to 1552*

Duhr   Bernhard Duhr, S.J., *Geschichte der Jesuiten in den Ländern deutscher Zunge vom 16. bis 18. Jahrhundert*, vols. I, II/1, II/2, and III.

Remling II   Franz Xavier Remling, *Geschichte der Bischöfe zu Speyer*, vol. II.

Remling, *UB*   Franz Xavier Remling, ed., *Urkundenbuch zur Geschichte der Bischöfe zu Speyer*, vol. II.

Stamer   Ludwig Stamer, *Kirchengeschichte der Pfalz*, vols. II, III/1, and III/2.

THE COUNTER-
REFORMATION
IN THE VILLAGES

Introduction

In 1560 the people in the villages around Speyer considered themselves to be Christians. By 1720 those villagers who lived under the rule of the bishops of Speyer had become self-consciously Catholic Christians. In the sixteenth century there had been a relaxed coexistence of Protestants and Catholics in this religiously fragmented region; by the eighteenth century there were two distinct and often mutually hostile confessional cultures.[1] Even today local people recall religious confrontations in the years before the Second World War. Brawls between Protestants and Catholics were common. Protestants worked openly on Catholic holidays, and Catholics intentionally sent their religious processions through Protestant villages. The establishment of these confessional cultures, which distinguished German life from the eighteenth century until the migrations of the post-1945 period, was the most important religious development of the early modern period. This book focuses on one

---

1. "Confession" is a general term referring to the three Christian religions in Germany after the Reformation, that is, Roman Catholicism, Calvinism, and Lutheranism. Modern Americans might call these "denominations." Before the Thirty Years' War religious groups lived together peacefully in many German cities and in confessionally mixed rural regions like the Palatinate, Baden, Swabia, and Alsace. See Etienne François, "De l'uniformité à la tolérance: Confession et société urbaine en Allemagne, 1650–1800" *Annales E.S.C.* 37, no. 4 (1982): esp. 783; Paul Warmbrunn, *Zwei Konfessionen in einer Stadt. Das Zusammenleben von Katholiken und Protestanten in den paritätischen Reichstädten Augsburg, Biberach, Ravensburg, und Dinkelsbühl von 1548 bis 1648* (Wiesbaden: Franz Steiner Verlag, 1983); R. Po-chia Hsia, *Society and Religion in Münster: 1535–1618* (New Haven: Yale University Press, 1984); Hans-Christoph Rublack, *Gescheiterte Reformation. Frühreformatorische und protestantische Bewegungen in süd- und westdeutschen geistlichen Residenzen* (Stuttgart: Klett-Cotta, 1978). Both Hsia and Rublack attribute the end of religious coexistence to the Counter-Reformation.

aspect of this development, the growth of Catholic consciousness in the Bishopric of Speyer.[2]

In this region, as elsewhere in Germany, confessional divisions were a long-term consequence of the Protestant Reformation. By the mid-sixteenth century, cities such as Speyer and Worms and several smaller territories had become Lutheran, and the most important territory in the middle Rhine valley, the Electoral Palatinate, was Calvinist. The people of the region, however, were slow to accept the religious practices and modes of behavior promoted by official churches. The Catholic villagers of the region, most of whom lived in the territory of the bishops (the *Hochstift* Speyer) began to develop a distinct Catholic lifestyle and religious culture only after 1650.

The rise of Protestantism created religious division, but the Catholic confessionalism of the Bishopric of Speyer was, in some sense at least, also a consequence of the Counter-Reformation, the broad-ranging reform of the Catholic Church set in motion by the Council of Trent (1545–63). However, neither the institutional reforms nor the new models of piety favored by the Tridentine Church gained a strong hold in Speyer. The popularity of Catholicism in the countryside in the eighteenth century was instead the consequence of a non-Tridentine process of Catholic renewal. Building on popular forms of piety and traditional forms of ecclesio-political organization, especially the communal control of rural parishes, the local Catholic Church successfully adjusted to the post-Reformation situation. The Church reformed the worst abuses of the clergy, but did not emphasize disciplining the laity, which in other places aroused strong resentment. This limited policy was possible because here there was no state firmly intent on using the Church to help discipline its subjects.

In many ways the Catholic Church succeeded in the Bishopric of Speyer because of the moderation of the Counter-Reformation there. This moderation, in turn, was a consequence of the divisions within local Catholicism. Tridentine reform had few supporters in Speyer, and the bishopric resisted outside influences at many levels. The powerful Cathedral Chapter and five smaller aristocratic chapters hindered all attempts to centralize the bishopric in order to defend their traditions and privileges. Catholic authorities were unable and often reluctant to follow the guidelines of Trent and impose new

2. The Bishopric of Speyer included much of the southern Palatinate (Pfalz) and northern Baden and stretched in the east into Württemberg. In the Napoleonic period, the bishopric lost all its jurisdictions on the right (or east) bank of the Rhine. Today, the Bishopric of Speyer covers all of the southern Palatinate.

religious practices on the Catholic population. The rural population and traditionalist upper clergy favored traditional Catholic piety, with its local and regional particularities.

The example of Speyer challenges and thus helps us to refine general interpretations of the Counter-Reformation. The development of a popular Catholic consciousness in a region without a strong Catholic state calls for an adjustment of the so-called confessionalization thesis. As presented by Ernst W. Zeeden, Heinz Schilling, and Wolfgang Reinhard confessionalization is, to quote Zeeden, "the intellectual and organizational hardening of the diverging Christian confessions . . . into more or less stable church structures with their own doctrines, constitutions, and religious and moral styles."[3] By focusing on the organizational similarities rather than the theological differences between the confessions, this thesis emphasizes the parallels between the three official religions during this process. All confessions in Germany tried to bring "true religion" to the mass of the population. Educational measures, especially catechism classes, and disciplinary measures such as visitations of rural parishes, were all designed to cause people to internalize the new religion, whether it was Lutheranism, Calvinism, or reformed Catholicism. Although this program suffered setbacks, these historians argue that by 1618 "confessionalization" had profoundly changed religious life in much of Germany.[4]

More important, confessionalization was closely tied to the emerging territorial state. As princes and bureaucrats worked to expand their authority, rationalize government, and centralize their states,

3. Quoted in Robert Bireley, S.J., "Early Modern Germany," in John O'Malley, ed., *Catholicism in Early Modern Europe: A Guide to Research* (St.Louis: Center for Reformation Research, 1988), 11. See also Ernst W. Zeeden, "Grundlagen und Wege der Konfessionsbildung in Deutschland im Zeitalter der Glaubenskämpfe," *Historische Zeitschrift* 185 (1958): 249–99; idem, *Die Entstehung der Konfessionen. Grundlagen und Formen der Konfessionsbildung im Zeitalter der Glaubenskämpfe* (Munich: R. Oldenbourg Verlag, 1965); Wolfgang Reinhard, "Gegenreformation als Modernisierung? Prolegomena zu einer Theorie des konfessionellen Zeitalters," *Archiv für Reformationsgeschichte* 68 (1977): 226–52; Heinz Schilling, "Die Konfessionalisierung im Reich. Religiöser und Gesellschaftlicher Wandel in Deutschland zwischen 1555 und 1620," *Historische Zeitschrift* 246 (1988): 1–45. Hans-Joachim Köhler, *Obrigkeitliche Konfessionsänderung in Kondominaten. Eine Fallstudie über ihre Bedingungen und Methoden am Beispiel der baden-badischen Religionspolitik unter der Regierung Markgraf Wilhelms (1622–1677)* (Münster: Aschendorff, 1975).

4. Bernard Vogler, *La vie religieuse en pays rhénan dans la seconde moitié du XVIe siècle (1556–1619)*, 3 vols. (Lille: Service des reproductions des thèses, 1974); idem, *Le clergé protestant rhénan au siècle de la Réforme (1555–1619)* (Paris: Ophrys, 1976); idem, "Die Ausbildung des Konfessionsbewußtseins in den pfälzischen Territorien zwischen 1555 und 1619," in Horst Rabe et al., eds., *Festgabe für Ernst Zeeden zum 60. Geburtstag* (Münster: Aschendorff, 1976). Vogler argues that Protestants in the Palatinate (which is around Speyer) developed a "confessional consciousness" by 1619, at least among an elite.

they also strove to create religious unity. In addition, they used the parish network, which was an effective administrative link to the countryside, to govern in the villages. Although the close ties between the new states and the churches were most apparent in the new Protestant territorial churches, they were also important in Catholic areas of Germany, especially in Bavaria and the Habsburg lands. Thus, according to the confessionalization thesis, the Protestant Reformation (at least after 1525) and the Counter-Reformation were essentially programs in the development of the early modern state.[5]

The Catholic population of the Bishopric of Speyer developed a confessional culture without being confessionalized. This evolution does not, of course, contradict the confessionalization thesis, for the lack of strong state institutions certainly slowed the pace of the Counter-Reformation and may have delayed the development of confessionalism until after 1650. Yet even in regions with strong state institutions, confessionalization occurred in the second half of the seventeenth century.[6] Perhaps the role of the state in the growth of confessional allegiances has been overestimated; certainly large parts of Catholic Germany lacked strong states yet still developed vibrant Catholic cultures.[7]

The decades after 1650 were decisive for the development of confessionalism and for the major achievement of the Counter-Reformation in Speyer, the placement of reformed priests in the parishes. In this

5. Volker Press, *Calvinismus und Territorialstaat. Regierung und Zentralbehörden der Kurpfalz, 1559–1619* (Stuttgart: Ernst Klett, 1970); Peter Blickle, *The Revolution of 1525. The German Peasant's War from a New Perspective* (Baltimore: Johns Hopkins University Press, 1981); idem, *Gemeindereformation. Die Menschen des 16. Jahrhunderts auf dem Weg zum Heil* (Munich: R. Oldenbourg Verlag, 1985).

6. Confessionalization proceeded slowly even in Bavaria (Dieter Albrecht, "Gegenreformation und katholische Reform" and "Die Barockzeit," in Max Spindler, ed., *Handbuch der bayerischen Geschichte*, vol. 2 [Munich: C. H. Beck, 1988], 714–35). In Tirol confessionalism took hold in the 1640s (Jürgen Bücking, *Fruhabsolutismus und Kirchenreform in Tirol (1565–1665). Ein Beitrag zum Ringen Zwischen "Stadt" und "Kirche" in der frühen Neuzeit* [Wiesbaden: Franz Steiner Verlag, 1972]). In Alsace the period of confessional cultures was after 1650 (Louis Châtellier, *Tradition chrétienne et renouveau catholique dans le cadre de l'ancien Diocèse de Strasbourg (1650–1770)* [Paris: Ophrys, 1981]). For German cities see François, "De l'uniformité à la tolérance," esp. p. 783; Warmbrunn, *Zwei Konfessionen in einer Stadt.*

7. Although my analysis is based on one bishopric, its conclusions suggest a model of Catholic reform applicable to large parts of Catholic Germany. The political and religious fragmentation, division of authority, and weakness of ecclesiastical and state institutions, as well as the popular traditional Catholicism that characterized the Bishopric of Speyer, existed in much of southwest Germany, Switzerland, parts of Franconia, and the Rhineland. There have been few studies of the Counter-Reformation outside the great principalities of Bavaria, the Habsburg lands, and the prince-bishoprics of Mainz, Würzburg, Trier, and Münster.

sense, the confessional age continued through and beyond the Thirty Years' War, instead of ending in 1618 or 1648. The traditional periodization reflects the political conflicts of the second half of the sixteenth century, rather than the process of popular religious differentiation, which accelerated after 1650. Furthermore, German historians of Catholicism have insisted on a break between the Counter-Reformation (or Catholic Reformation) and baroque Catholicism, a distinction that has little validity for the Bishopric of Speyer.[8] The continuities across the whole period of this book are much more pertinent than the changes brought by the Thirty Years' War. This fact has long been recognized by French historians of the Counter-Reformation, who emphasize that Tridentine reforms began to make an impact in French dioceses only in the late seventeenth century.[9]

The history of Catholicism in Speyer, then, challenges the proponents of the confessionalization thesis to consider the smaller territories and the "individualized country" of the old Reich, and to examine the process over a longer period.[10] It is also a major theme of this book that religious reform, and especially Catholic reform, was not imposed exclusively from above. The beliefs, practices, and modes of behavior of the Catholic population of Speyer changed and developed through a dynamic relationship between Catholic reform and popular reaction.[11]

One of the weaknesses of the acculturation thesis of Jean Delumeau and John Bossy is that it does not account for the local development of religious reform. Delumeau and Bossy argue that the Counter-Reformation (and the Protestant Reformation) was above all an attack on traditional popular religion and popular culture. Delumeau asserts provocatively that medieval Christianity was essen-

---

8. Some historians recognize a "second wave" of Tridentine reform in the 1650s, 1660s, and 1670s. After this, the period of baroque Catholicism starts. See for example Albrecht, "Die Barockzeit," pp. 733–34; Manfred Becker-Huberti, *Die tridentinische Reform im Bistum Münster unter Fürstbischof Christoph Bernhard v. Galen 1650 bis 1678* (Münster: Aschendorff, 1978).

9. Jeanne Ferté, *La vie religieuse dans les campagnes parisiennes, 1622–95* (Paris: Librarie Philosophique J. Vrin, 1962). Louis Pérouas, *Le diocèse de la Rochelle de 1648 à 1724: Sociologie et pastorale* (Paris: S.E.V.P.E.N., 1964); Alain Lottin, *Lille, Citadelle de la Contre-Réforme, 1598–1668* (Lille: Westhoeck, 1984). Alain Croix, *La Bretagne aux 16e et 17e siècles. La vie, la mort, la foi* (Paris: Maloine SA, 1981).

10. See Mack Walker, *German Home Towns: Community, State, and General Estate, 1648–1848* (Ithaca: Cornell University Press, 1971), 1–2.

11. Historians of early Protestant movements have always been aware of the importance of popular involvement in, pressure for, and reaction to, the Reformation. See, for example, Lorna Jane Abray, *The People's Reformation. Magistrates, Clergy, and Commons in Strasbourg, 1500–1598,* (Ithaca: Cornell University Press, 1985); Suzanne Karant-Nunn, *Zwickau in Transition, 1500–1547: The Reformation as an Agent of Change,* (Columbus: Ohio University Press, 1987).

tially "pagan." The goal of the Counter-Reformation was to "chris-
tianize" Europe by attacking popular "superstitions" and "excesses"
and encouraging the proper practice of religion. Bossy objects to some
of what he has called Delumeau's "gratuitous assumptions" about
the nature of medieval Christianity and argues that medieval Christianity was a successful family-based and community-oriented religion. In general, however, Bossy accepts the acculturation thesis.
Both historians emphasize the Catholic Church's struggle to impose
elite religion on the population of Europe. The people often resisted
these reforms and, especially in France, resistance led to an aliena-
tion of the population from the Church, strong peasant anticlericalism, and the "collapse of popular religion."[12]

In Speyer the Catholic villagers did not simply accept or resist
changes. The people supported some Tridentine reforms, for example
the requirement that priests reside in the parishes, and resisted others, especially efforts to limit popular festivities and reorganize parish administration. Furthermore, some reforms, such as the new
marriage regulations, were manipulated by groups within the peasantry, in this case village elders and parents, for their own benefit.[13]
The relationship between the reforming Church and the Catholic
people was characterized by compromise and cooperation as much as
by conflict and resistance.

This dynamic is nowhere more apparent than in the relationship
between the parish priests and their parishioners, which is a primary
focus of this book. It is increasingly apparent that the clergy was the
pivotal group in any attempt to reform popular religion. Both Bernard
Vogler, in his study of Protestantism in the Rhine Palatinate, and
Philip Hoffman, in analyzing the Counter-Reformation in Lyon, have
emphasized the role of the clergy in implementing religious change
in the countryside.[14] The Counter-Reformation caused important
changes in the character of the Catholic clergy in the Bishopric of
Speyer as well. The late sixteenth-century "peasant-priests" with
their concubines were very different from the celibate, educated, and

12. John Bossy, "The Counter-Reformation and the People of Catholic Europe," *Past and
Present* 47 (1970); idem, *Christianity in the West, 1400–1700* (London: Oxford University
Press, 1985); Jean Delumeau, *Catholicism between Luther and Voltaire: A New View of the
Counter-Reformation* (London: Burns and Oates, 1977); Philip Hoffman, *Church and Com-
munity in the Diocese of Lyon, 1500–1789* (New Haven: Yale University Press, 1984).

13. For other examples of this process see Thomas Robisheaux, *Rural Society and the
Search for Order in Early Modern Germany* (Cambridge: Cambridge University Press,
1989), esp. chap. 4.; Hermann Rebel, *Peasant Classes: The Bureaucratization of Property
and Family Relations under Early Habsburg Absolutism, 1511–1636* (Princeton: Princeton
University Press, 1983).

14. Vogler, *Le clergé protestant rhénan*; Hoffman, *Church and Community*.

sometimes militantly Catholic priests of the early eighteenth century. I have found, however, that even the latter clergymen were not "agents of the Counter-Reformation" as Hoffman would have it. When caught between the desires of Church reformers and the needs of their parishioners, the priests generally acted as mediators. At the same time, the parish clergy was not passive. Reformed priests educated in seminaries all over Germany dominated religious life in the bishopric after 1700. Although they were unable to foster new forms of piety, they did much to support and encourage a traditionalist Catholic revival during the period from 1700 to 1720.

Acculturation also requires a unified elite, or at the very least, a dominant group within the elite, possessing a unified program. In Speyer no such group existed. The conservative upper clergy generally resisted Tridentine reforms, which they correctly saw as a threat to the *Reichskirche*, which reserved its benefices for the aristocracy. In the absence of a strong state to force their compliance with the decrees of the Council of Trent, conservative canons functioned as a brake on the acculturation of the laity by reform priests and religious orders.[15] Divisions within the clerical elite make the standard distinction between reforming elite and traditionalist population very problematic. The cathedral canon in Speyer may have been as much a part of the clerical elite as the Jesuit father, but in religious culture he often had more in common with the local peasant.

Another emphasis of this book is the interplay between local Catholicism and the international Church. The Counter-Reformation in Speyer depended on outsiders for its leadership. Jesuits, above all, but also ecclesiastical officials trained elsewhere, and reforming priests educated in seminaries outside the bishopric formed the elite that brought Tridentine Catholicism to Speyer. The traditions of local religious life, anchored above all in lay and clerical institutions, constantly hindered the activities of the reformers.

Naturally the upper clergy in the chapters played a major role in weakening the Counter-Reformation. More significant for Catholicism in the countryside, however, was the village communes' control of the rural parishes. Peter Blickle has focused attention on the importance of rural communes (*Gemeinden*) in German religious life, arguing that the communes supported the Protestant Reformation in the early sixteenth century. In addition to favoring the Protestant insistence on the authority of Scripture, many peasants (and

---

15. The French, Spanish, Austrian, and Bavarian states often forced the ecclesiastical hierarchy to comply with Tridentine decrees.

townspeople) understood the Reformation as an opportunity to increase local control over the Church.[16] This hope ended with the
defeat of the Peasants' War (1525) and the development of the Protestant territorial churches. In Speyer, however, the communes found
the decentralized and disorganized Catholic Church receptive to
many of the ecclesio-political ideals of the "communal church" (Gemeinde Kirche). In the late sixteenth century, indeed throughout the
early modern period, these communes maintained and expanded
their considerable control over the local parish churches. They managed the finances of the parish, organized local religious life, and
wielded significant influence over the appointment and disciplining
of parish priests.

As the confessional consciousness of the Catholic inhabitants
grew, it remained linked to the communes. Catholicism became an
important part of the communal identity of these villages in this
predominantly Protestant region. This Catholic identity was especially important after 1650, when the villages had to absorb large
numbers of immigrants as they recovered from decades of war.
Catholicism performed an important integrative function in these
villages especially because a close tie already existed between the
commune and the parish and between the villagers and traditional
Catholic practices.

In several important ways then, the communal church, which
Blickle argues lost its significance in the early sixteenth century,
thrived in the Catholic villages of the Bishopric of Speyer into the
eighteenth century. Furthermore, there is little evidence that the
communes came to be dominated by a peasant elite, who manipulated the gemeinde's control of the parish for its political or financial
benefit.[17] The absence of a strong state or a local nobility allowed the
people meaningful influence in their own religious lives.

 The nature of the transition from traditional Christianity to self-
conscious Catholicism in Speyer determined the character of local
Catholic culture. The strength of local institutions, the weakness of
Tridentine reform, and the tenacity of popular religion meant that
Catholicism at the end of our period remained more traditional than

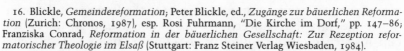

16. Blickle, Gemeindereformation; Peter Blickle, ed., Zugänge zur bäuerlichen Reformation (Zurich: Chronos, 1987), esp. Rosi Fuhrmann, "Die Kirche im Dorf," pp. 147–86;
Franziska Conrad, Reformation in der bäuerlichen Gesellschaft: Zur Rezeption reformatorischer Theologie im Elsaß (Stuttgart: Franz Steiner Verlag Wiesbaden, 1984).

17. R. Po-chia Hsia, Social Discipline in the Reformation: Central Europe 1550–1750
(New York: Routledge and Kegan Paul, 1989), 64–69; Rebel, Peasant Classes; Franz Ortner,
Reformation, katholische Reform, und Gegenreformation in Erzstift Salzburg (Salzburg:
Universitätsverlag Anton Pustet, 1981).

Tridentine. The forms of Counter-Reformation piety, which emphasized frequent confession and communion, individual prayer, and austere self-discipline, had little resonance in the countryside.[18] Instead, the villagers favored a community-oriented piety with a focus on weekly religious services, the Mass, processions, and local pilgrimages.

An older generation of German Catholic historians recognized the traditional foundations of baroque Catholicism, with its ornate churches, enthusiastic public piety, and ostentatious public religion.[19] Some recent studies have also emphasized the connections between traditional Christianity and Tridentine Catholicism. Tridentine reform, especially in southwest Germany, caused an evolution in popular religion but also allowed traditional forms of piety a vital role.[20] In Speyer, Catholicism experienced a popular revival precisely because a limited Counter-Reformation allowed traditional religion to keep its vitality in the villages.[21]

The traditional nature of Catholicism in the Bishopric of Speyer helps explain the renowned piety of the Germans in the eighteenth century, a piety that contrasted with widespread anticlericalism and religious indifference in much of the French countryside.[22] This is a reminder that regional and national differences within Catholicism remained important, even as the Tridentine Church sought to centralize the Church and regularize the experience of Catholics throughout the world.

The Bishopric of Speyer in the Sixteenth Century

The Bishopric of Speyer straddled the Rhine river in a prosperous and densely populated part of Germany. This was an agricultural

18. Bossy, "The Counter-Reformation and the People of Catholic Europe"; idem, *Christianity in the West*; Louis Châtellier, *The Europe of the Devout: The Catholic Reformation and the Formation of a New Society* (Cambridge: Cambridge University Press, 1989).

19. The classic formulation of this viewpoint is Andreas Ludwig Veit and Ludwig Lenhart, *Kirche und Volksfrömmigkeit im Zeitalter des Barock* (Freiburg: Verlag Herder, 1956).

20. Châtellier, *Tradition chrétienne et renouveau catholique*, part 4, chap. 5; idem, *Europe of the Devout*; Hsia, *Social Discipline in the Reformation*, p. 90.

21. Here I disagree with the older view, which sees the revival of popular Catholicism as a direct consequence of Tridentine reforms. See Stamer III/1 and III/2 and Andreas Ludwig Veit, *Kirche und Kirchenreform in der Erzdiözese Mainz, 1517–1618* (Freiburg: Herdersche Verlagshandlung, 1920).

22. Timothy Tackett, *Priest and Parish in 18th Century France: A Social and Political Study of the Curés in the Diocese of Dauphiné, 1750–1791* (Princeton: Princeton University Press, 1977).

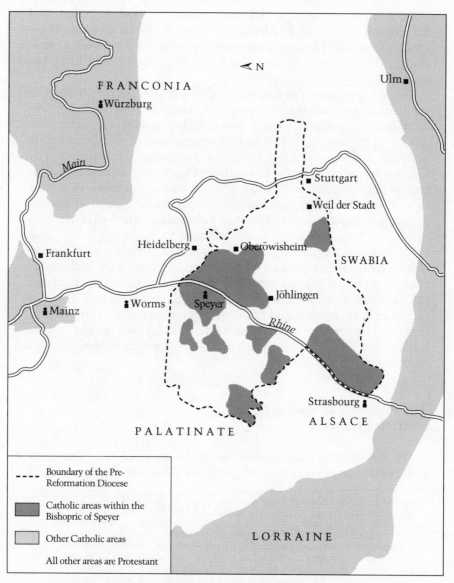

The Bishopric of Speyer, 1600

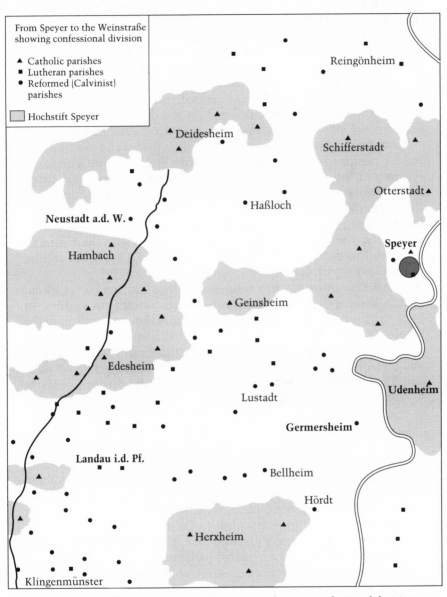

From Speyer to the Weinstraße
showing confessional division

▲ Catholic parishes
■ Lutheran parishes
● Reformed (Calvinist)
  parishes

▨ Hochstift Speyer

Reingönheim

Deidesheim

Schifferstadt

Otterstadt ▲

Haßloch

Neustadt a.d. W. ●

Speyer

Hambach

▲ Geinsheim

Edesheim

Lustadt

Udenheim

Germersheim ●

Landau i.d. Pf.

● Bellheim

Hördt

▲ Herxheim

Klingenmünster

The Palatinate, 1600. From Speyer to Weinstrasse showing confessional divisions

region of small towns and large villages. The peasants, whether they lived in grain-growing villages in the Rhine plain or in the wine villages at its edges and in the smaller valleys of the Kraichgau, produced for the market. The rural population had commercial links with the imperial cities of Speyer and Worms and with Heidelberg, the capital of the Electoral Palatinate, as well as with such smaller towns as Landau, Weißenburg, Bruchsal, and Durlach.[23] This area was urbanized and commercialized, exposed to cultural and economic developments but also to invading armies and the plague.

Economic and social conditions tied the villages and towns of the region together, just as political conditions divided them. This was a region with a hodgepodge of tiny principalities, free imperial cities, and ecclesiastical states typical of southern and western Germany at that time. Within the boundaries of the diocese of Speyer were parts of six major principalities, four imperial cities, and several smaller territories, domains of imperial knights and independent monasteries.[24] The bishop of Speyer himself governed a scattered secular principality which lay on both sides the Rhine.

The Reformation further compounded the fragmentation of authority and localization of power that characterized the region. Between 1530 and 1560, Protestantism captured about two-thirds of the diocese, greatly reducing the effective spiritual authority of the bishops. Even within the remaining Catholic areas, princes, magistrates, and powerful ecclesiastical institutions all claimed extensive powers. These conditions would profoundly limit the progress of Catholic reform in the Bishopric of Speyer.

The Diocese of Speyer

In the late Middle Ages, the bishops of Speyer claimed ecclesiastical jurisdiction over a diocese that stretched from the Pfälzerwald in the west to the Neckar river in the east and contained over three hundred parishes. By the middle of the sixteenth century, however, the spread of the Reformation meant that the bishops exercised real authority only over those villages under their direct secular authority, an area of fewer than a hundred parishes.

Protestantism made steady progress in the middle Rhine region

23. Erich Keyser, ed. *Städtebuch Rheinland-Pfalz und Saarland* (Stuttgart: Kohlhammer Verlag, 1964), 124–25.
24. States: Electoral Palatinate (*Kurpfalz*), Pfalz-Zweibrücken, Baden-Baden, Baden-Durlach, Württemberg, *Hochstift* Speyer. Imperial cities: Speyer, Landau, Weil der Stadt, Weißenburg.

after 1520. Luther had popular support in the cities of Speyer and Worms long before those cities officially broke with the Catholic Church in the 1540s. The leading principality of the region, the Electoral Palatinate, followed a more tortuous path to Protestantism, but in 1563 Elector Frederick III published a Reformed (i.e., Calvinist) church ordinance, beginning a period of aggressive anti-Catholic policy by the government of the Palatinate.[25] In the various territories, Protestant princes removed Catholic priests, secularized monasteries, and established territorial churches.

The Reformation changed the political as well as the religious situation in the region. The traditional alliance between the bishops of Speyer and the Palatinate became difficult to maintain, exposing the bishops' small and vulnerable principality to the real danger of "mediatization" by one of its powerful neighbors. The bishopric also faced financial difficulties from the loss of income from fees and fines that had accrued from the jurisdictional rights of the bishops. Yet the financial impact of the Reformation should not be overestimated. Protestant and Catholic officials worked out methods of dealing with financial disputes. The Protestant Electors Palatine, for example, held the patronage and tithe in several villages in the bishop of Speyer's territory, but installed and paid the Catholic priests appointed by the bishop. The bishop did the same in Palatine villages where he held patronage rights. In this way, a general modus vivendi was established.

The Catholic position in this region was politically weak, a condition most apparent in areas where the bishops shared secular authority with Protestant princes (the *Gemeinschaften*). In the 1570s, the Electoral Palatinate removed the Catholic priests from all twenty-one villages in the two gemeinschaften of Landeck and Altenstadt. The bishop protested half-heartedly and appealed to the people "to stay with the Church and not take up the Calvinist teachings." At the same time, both the bishop and the Cathedral Chapter feared that too strong a protest might cause trouble with the Electoral Palatinate. In the end, these areas became firmly Protestant.[26] In territories of shared or disputed authority, political power was decisive, and in the sixteenth century the Catholic Church was on the defensive.

Protestantism did not have the popular appeal in the countryside that it had in the cities of the region. Protestant authorities struggled to impose new religious practices in their villages, and there were a

---

25. Press, *Calvinismus und Territorialstaat*.
26. Stamer III/1, pp. 51–52; GLAK 61/10942, pp. 516–20.

few Protestants in officially Catholic villages. The first episcopal visitation of the Catholic villages of the bishopric in the 1580s revealed very few active Protestants, except perhaps in the villages right outside the city of Speyer.[27] There were, however, resilient communities of Anabaptists throughout the bishopric. After about 1570 these people emigrated to Moravia in a steady stream.[28]

Several Catholic territories lay within the diocese of Speyer but outside the bishop's secular principality. Here the authority of the bishops over spiritual matters, and especially over the clergy, was formally recognized but in practice rarely exercised. The margraves of Baden-Baden, the city council in Weil der Stadt, and the von Gemmingen family, a family of free imperial knights, all insisted on their right to discipline the clergy within their territories, often refused to recognize the patronage of rural parishes by ecclesiastical institutions, and never recognized episcopal authority over marriage cases.

Religious and political fragmentation was most profound in the city of Speyer itself, where the official religion varied from house to house. The imperial city became Lutheran in the 1540s, but there was an important Catholic presence throughout the early modern period. In the sixteenth century, between 13 and 17 percent of the population of about 7,500 were Catholic clergy and their dependents.[29] A treaty with the city (the *Rachtung*) regulated the rights of the clergy and gave them economic privileges and legal exemptions. There were also several hundred members of the Imperial Chamber Court (*Reichskammergericht*) residing in Speyer, most of whom were Catholic. These divisions led to some tensions, but surprisingly few conflicts erupted between the Lutheran townsmen and Catholic residents—partly because the *Bürger* and the clergy had a variety of common interests, including a desire to keep the bishop out of the city, which they had done successfully since the fifteenth century. At the same time, the staunch Lutheranism of the magistrates and the city population deeply affected the consciousness of the ecclesiastics living in Speyer. Local churchmen developed an awareness of Catholic weaknesses, a sense of the limits of Church reform, and a realistic understanding of the strength of Protestantism in the region—all of which would deflate their enthusiasm for the Counter-Reformation.

27. Stamer III/1, pp. 104–5.
28. Ibid., pp. 135–36; GLAK 61/11494, 11495, and later. The property of Anabaptists who had left for Moravia was confiscated by the bishopric.
29. Willi Alter, "Von der konradinischen Rachtung bis zum letzten Reichstag in Speyer (1420/22–1570)," in Stadt Speyer, *Geschichte der Stadt Speyer* (Stuttgart: Kohlhammer Verlag, 1983), 554, 555, 584.

The *Hochstift* Speyer

This book focuses on the villages within the principality governed by the bishops of Speyer, a medium-sized territory containing in the late sixteenth century over eighty villages, three towns, and a population of about thirty thousand.[30] Not an "enclosed" principality, it consisted of four large enclaves and several smaller ones.

Nor was the Hochstift a centralized principality with strong state institutions. The bishops did not pursue a policy of state-building. Instead, a bewildering variety of social, political, and juridical conditions constantly limited the authority and freedom of action of the ruling bishop. The geographical and territorial fragmentation of the Hochstift, the institutional power of the Cathedral Chapter, and the local power of the village communes together perpetuated this situation throughout the early modern period.

The nucleus of the Hochstift was the area around the town of Bruchsal. The bishop's authority was almost unchallenged in the more than twenty villages of this region. Here he was the only lord, held all judicial rights, was the patron of most of the parishes, and was a major landowner. Most of the peasants were his serfs (*Leibeigene*). Outside this region, however, the situation became more complicated. Perhaps the richest villages of the Hochstift were along the Palatine *Weinstraße* on the left bank of the Rhine. Here the bishop's authority was more circumscribed. The Cathedral Chapter held most of the tithes and the patronage of the village churches, and many of the serfs in these villages belonged to the Elector. Furthermore, these villages were located in a series of enclaves surrounded by Palatine territory and located on the other side of the Rhine from the episcopal capital in Udenheim (Philippsburg). The episcopal administration often had practical problems asserting the prince-bishop's authority in these villages.

The village of Jöhlingen is a good example of the extent to which power was fragmented even within the villages of the Hochstift Speyer. The secular lordship of Jöhlingen belonged to the Cathedral Chapter in Speyer, as did the patronage of the village parish. Many, although not all, of the peasants were serfs of the chapter, and the chapter held the power of low justice. The canons exercised this power by sending two of their number and a secretary to Jöhlingen twice a year to judge civil and minor criminal cases on the spot. Most of the cases of this *Vogtsgericht* concerned brawls, financial and property disputes, and family conflicts. The bishop held the power of high justice in Jöhlingen, and all witchcraft and murder cases were

---

30. Duggan, pp. 7, 193–97.

forwarded to his court. The Cathedral Chapter, however, always investigated these cases before sending them on. In general the Cathedral Chapter, not the bishop's government, dealt with most matters of government, including tax assessments and the quartering of soldiers. The rights of the neighboring Electoral Palatinate, which had the power to collect certain tolls and imperial taxes in the village, and which claimed some jurisdiction over Palatine serfs living in Jöhlingen, also limited the chapter's authority. The margraves of Baden-Durlach, princes of the other neighboring villages, claimed similar, although less extensive, rights.

On a day-to-day level the kind of fragmentation of authority that existed in Jöhlingen was unimportant. Economic relations with neighboring villages and within the village proceeded without disruption, taxes were collected, and criminals were punished. The villagers, however, adeptly played different authorities off against one another. This tactic proved most effective when it came to obstructing new taxes or new statutes. In religious affairs it allowed the villagers to resist changes ordered by reformers. The existence of conflicting jurisdictions also meant that Church authorities could not enforce new laws until complicated jurisdictional disputes had been resolved.

At a higher level, the bishops of Speyer had to share political power with the Cathedral Chapter. Lawrence Duggan has argued that the chapter took a leading role in the government of the bishopric in the Middle Ages. The canons based their power on canon law, which gave them the sole right to elect and advise bishops and govern during vacancies. As a result, "the bishop was obliged to consult with his canons and to obtain their consent to a whole range of acts."[31] Duggan equates the role of the Cathedral Chapter with that of a parliament. By the sixteenth century, the bishop needed the approval of the chapter for new taxes, for many important appointments, and for major political decisions. In many ways the Cathedral Chapter "remained the center of stability in the see of Speyer."[32] Of course the canons were far from selfless in their interest in the bishopric. The noblemen from the Kraichgau and the Rhine valley who dominated the Cathedral Chapter preserved Church benefices and government positions for members of their families.[33]

The government of the bishops of Speyer was small and rather

31. Ibid., p. 187.
32. Ibid., p. 187.
33. Volker Press, "Das Hochstift Speyer," in Volker Press, ed., *Barock am Oberrhein* (Karlsruhe: Kommissionsverlag G. Braun, 1985), 252–54.

ineffectual. The central administration, headed by the chancellor, was located at the bishop's palace in Udenheim. Until the eighteenth century, there was no integrated or centralized bureaucracy, a situation that circumscribed the ability of the bishops to enforce their will in the countryside.[34] The local administrators were the *Amtmänner*, of whom there were about eight in the sixteenth century. These officials took advantage of the scattered territorial situation and their distance from central authority to operate fairly independently, and, in fact, the village communes (gemeinden) provided the day-to-day administration of the villages.

Although the communes were administrative units of the Hochstift, they were also autonomous, self-governing institutions, especially in weakly administrated territories.[35] The *Schultheißen* (or headmen) acted as the bishop's bailiffs in the villages but also served as members of the village gemeinde. In petitions to the bishop, the schultheißen almost always appear together with the locally elected members of the village councils, the *Dorfmeister* (or *Bürgermeister*) and the *Gerichtsmänner*. The schultheiß, together with the village council (the *Gericht*) governed in the villages, assessed taxes, adjudicated disputes, and represented the village before the bishop's government. There was always the potential for conflict between the schultheißen, who were appointed, and the other members of the village council, who were elected by the commune, yet such disputes were rare. The schultheißen were local men and seem to have worked together with the villagers on all issues of importance.

The rural communes around Speyer, as in much of southwest Germany, had strong traditions of resistance to outside authority.[36] Furthermore, in Speyer, in the absence of a rural nobility or a strong state, the communes could go beyond resistance and actually pursue their own goals, in religious as well as political matters. Most communes also had the financial resources to maintain local autonomy. They owned property and collected rents as well as a variety of fines and dues and used this money to hire lawyers as well as shepherds, policemen, and schoolteachers.

The power of the communes varied. Communal institutions in the wine-growing villages on the left bank of the Rhine and in the more

---

34. Duggan, pp. 152–57; Press, "Das Hochstift Speyer," pp. 260–62.

35. Peter Blickle, *Landschaften im Alten Reich: Die staatliche Funktion des gemeinen Mannes in Oberdeutschland* (Munich: C. H. Beck, 1973), 124–26.

36. On communes see Blickle, *The Revolution of 1525*, and *Gemeinde Reformation*; Heide Wunder, *Die bäuerliche Gemeinde in Deutschland* (Göttingen: Vandenhoeck und Ruprecht, 1986).

isolated villages on the edges of the Kraichgau (such as Neipsheim and Jöhlingen) seem to have been quite strong, probably because these villages were far from the secular power of the bishops. The villages in the Rhine valley and around Bruchsal, especially where the prince-bishop was the only landlord, had weaker communes and therefore less influence over political and ecclesiastical affairs. Most appeals to the various Church authorities came from the "Schultheiß, Gericht, *Juratoren*, Dorfmeister, und die ganze Gemeinde" (the headman, the council, the elders or wardens, the mayor, and the whole commune). Certain powerful individuals could, and often did, dominate communal institutions. Yet in Speyer, the gemeinden maintained their autonomy and were never integrated into the state apparatus.[37] The influence of the communes meant that a localization of power characterized the secular government of the bishopric as it did the political framework of the region.

This fragmentation of authority extended to ecclesiastic administration as well. The various chapters in Speyer and in the countryside exercised extensive patronage rights in the villages. Furthermore, the provosts of the four chapters were also archdeacons of the diocese, theoretically giving them a power to discipline the rural clergy parallel to that of the bishop. These powers limited the bishop's vicar general, who was the chief spiritual official of the bishopric. The vicars general in the sixteenth century were assisted by several ecclesiastical judges and a small staff. The vicars occupied a difficult position, especially in relation to the Cathedral Chapter. Most of these men, although officials of the bishops, held benefices in the cathedral in Speyer and were therefore beholden to the canons. The position of vicar general had neither status nor clearly defined powers, and even the most activist vicars general were obliged to recognize the limits of episcopal power, even within the Hochstift.

The conditions examined here evolved between 1560 and 1720, the most important political development being the growth in importance of French power along the Rhine, especially after the Thirty Years' War. At the local level and within the Catholic Church, however, the essential fragmentation of authority and localization of power remained a decisive factor in local religious life into the eighteenth century and were crucial determinants in the evolution of Catholic reform.

37. Wunder, *Die bäuerliche Gemeinde*, chap. 5, esp. pp. 80–82.

I

The Traditional Church and the Resistance to Reform

The structures of political and religious life in the Bishopric of Speyer limited the impact of the Counter-Reformation there. We appreciate this especially when we look at the nature and function of the Catholic Church in the middle decades of the sixteenth century, before Tridentine reforms had a significant effect on the bishopric.

When examining Catholicism in Speyer, one must confront two assumptions of all previous studies. The first premise dates back to the sixteenth century. Most churchmen at the time, and Church historians since, have held that the pre-Tridentine Church was in terrible condition, especially in the countryside. The clergy was professionally incompetent and morally bankrupt, Church finances were in disarray, and the people badly "infected" with Protestantism. Given these conditions, the population naturally welcomed the effort to reform the Church.[1]

The second, in many ways contradictory, assumption is that of modern historians, who argue that the common people of Europe defended traditional religion and resisted all religious reform.[2] These historians tend to see rural populations as above all conservative and predisposed to resist change from outside. In this view, the villagers necessarily reacted negatively to all reform.

1. The best example of this school is Stamer, III/1 and III/2. Stamer's study is, however, often very thoughtful and excellently grounded in the sources. See also Veit, *Kirche und Kirchenreform*. For sixteenth-century views, see Chapter 2.
2. Especially, Bossy, "The Counter-Reformation and the People of Catholic Europe"; idem, *Christianity in the West*; Delumeau, *Catholicism between Luther and Voltaire*.

These assumptions do not accurately explain conditions in the Bishopric of Speyer between the 1560s and the 1580s. The sources indicate that the Catholics of the bishopric had problems with the Church, but were in general content with their priests and with the overall operation of rural Catholicism. The villagers even favored those reforms which improved the quality of local religious services. The innovations they resisted were those that threatened the "communal Church." Beginning in the fifteenth century, village communes had widened their domination of rural parishes, a process that accelerated in Speyer in the sixteenth century as ecclesiastical organization disintegrated under the impact of the Reformation.[3] From the 1560s to the 1580s, the villagers of the Bishopric of Speyer fought to maintain or even increase their control over the local Church.

The ecclesiastical elite of the bishopric responded to the Counter-Reformation with equal ambivalence. Not surprisingly, many ecclesiastics feared that reform jeopardized the nobility's control of rich benefices in the collegiate chapters and positions in the episcopal administration. Nevertheless, the Protestant Reformation threatened the very survival of Catholicism in the region and forced the hierarchy to take some action. The decrees of the Council of Trent were a further impetus to action, although German churchmen remained skeptical of reform and accepted papal commands with a certain selectivity.

If we examine the structures of Catholicism in the Bishopric of Speyer in the mid-sixteenth century, both in the villages and at the upper levels of the Church, we can see the obstacles faced by anyone trying to implement the ambitious program of the Council of Trent. Catholic reformers were never allowed to forget that village communes controlled the rural Church and the aristocracy dominated the ecclesiastical hierarchy. Ultimately, all reform had to come from outside the local Church. Under these conditions imposing such reform was to be an uphill fight.

The Clergy and the Rural Parish, 1560–1585

In 1583, twenty years after the Council of Trent, the bishop of Speyer ordered the first visitation of the Catholic villages of his diocese. The visitors found that the rural Church was essentially under the local control of village communes, which expected the parish priest to live according to community rules, regulated a large

3. Fuhrmann, "Die Kirche im Dorf."

part of the financial resources of the parish, and exercised consider-able influence over the appointment, disciplining, and removal of parish priests. This situation resulted partly from the weakness of higher authority, both political and spiritual, and partly from long-standing traditions of village government and Church organization.

The visitation also revealed that each village had a resident parish priest, the primary concern of villagers. The priest was clearly a member of the community and obeyed its rules. Generally he lived with a concubine, farmed his fields, and dressed like a peasant. The villagers expected the priest to perform regular church services, to baptize children, to lead processions, and to give his blessing at burials. Village communes generally procured parish priests they liked and got rid of ones they found unacceptable. But although they were happy with their priests, the villagers protested forcefully against the financial exactions of the upper clergy. The aristocratic chapters in Speyer, Weißenburg, and Bruchsal absorbed such a large part of the resources of the village churches, that the priests often found their benefices too small to support themselves and their families.

The villagers were mostly good Catholics, at least in the sense that they attended Mass regularly and received communion annually. The Protestant Reformation had disrupted the patterns of local re-ligious life to some extent. Protestant authorities forbade proces-sions that had traditionally linked the villages together from passing through Protestant territory, and they reduced the financial re-sources of the local churches. Protestantism itself had a limited appeal within the villages; few peasants traveled to neighboring vil-lages for Protestant services. The villagers had no interest in confes-sional politics, per se. But to prevent unwanted changes in their traditional practices and further financial exactions, they defended a community-based church against the incursions of all outside au-thorities.

Although episcopal authorities had tentatively begun to introduce reforms in the 1560s, the rural Church reflected in the minutes of the visitation of 1583–88 was essentially pre-Tridentine. Attempts to eradicate clerical marriage and institute catechism classes, however, are signs of a growing gap between the goals of reform-minded churchmen and the interests of the villagers of the Bishopric of Speyer.[4] Above all, the authorities expected and demanded a rural

4. Much of the following section is based on the minutes of the visitation of 1583–88, which are in GLAK 61/11262 and LASp. D2/306/10. For discussion of visitation records as historical sources see Gerald Strauss, *Luther's House of Learning: Indoctrination of the Young in the German Reformation* (Baltimore: Johns Hopkins University Press, 1978);

clergy that would perform the sacraments regularly, as required by the statutes of the diocese, enforce the ordinances of the bishop, and maintain the property of the church. Episcopal officials had also begun to emphasize the everyday behavior of the parish priests, who were supposed to avoid involvement in local conflicts, be sober, moral, and above all celibate. These concerns, which reflect the decrees of the Council of Trent, were not shared by the people in the villages. Celibacy, for example, was not important to them, nor did it bother them if their priest had a drink in the village inn. They did, however, want a priest who resided in their village and was an active member of the community.[5] The visitation indicates clearly that most rural priests met the expectations of the villagers better than those of the ecclesiastical authorities.

Clerical Marriage and Concubinage

The enforcement of clerical celibacy was a major, if not dominating, concern of sixteenth-century Catholic authorities. Historians of the region have emphasized the prevalence of clerical marriage and concubinage in the Bishopric of Speyer in the late sixteenth century and have frequently cited this as a sign of the sad state of the Catholic Church in the countryside.[6] It is true that twelve of the twenty-two *Pfarrer* visited in 1583 and 1584 were living with women, although none seemed to have gone so far as to marry his companion.[7] In fact, the ongoing efforts of the bishops and their officials to prevent rural Catholic priests from marrying had been effective. In 1563 the priest in Deidesheim, Ulrich Meyer, apparently promised to marry his housekeeper and was subsequently imprisoned.[8] Ten years later, the pfarrer in Deidesheim (perhaps the same man) was relieved of his functions for having married. This case apparently caused scandal in the bishopric.[9] It served to make it clear to the rural clergy that they could not marry their lifelong companions (often the mothers of their

---

James Kittelson, "Successes and Failures in the German Reformation: The Report from Strasbourg," *Archiv für Reformationsgeschichte* 73 (1982); Ernst W. Zeeden and Hans-Georg Molitor, eds., *Die Visitation im Dienste der kirchlichen Reform* (Münster: Aschendorff, 1967).

5. Hoffman, *Church and Community in the Diocese of Lyon*, chap. 2; Bossy, "The Counter-Reformation."

6. Remling II, pp. 374–75; Stamer III/1, pp. 90–95; Hans Ammerich, "Formen und Wege der katholischen Reform in den Diözesen Speyer und Straßburg. Klerusreform und Seelsorgerreform," in Volker Press et al., eds., *Barock am Oberrhein* p. 298.

7. GLAK 61/11262; LASp. D2/306/10; Stamer III/1, p. 91–92.

8. Remling II, pp. 374–75. Remling incorrectly identifies this priest as Ulrich Mai.

9. Stamer III/1, p.40.

children). Enforcing clerical celibacy, of course, was much more difficult. During the episcopate of Bishop Marquard (1560–81), a quarter of the rural priests who were imprisoned by the bishop's officials were prosecuted for simple concubinage.[10] Yet the visitation of 1583–88 shows how ineffective these disciplinary measures had been.

Concubinage was apparently more widespread in the Bishopric of Speyer than in many other Catholic dioceses in Europe. More than half of the priests investigated in the 1580s lived with concubines. By contrast, in 1570 in the neighboring Archbishopric of Trier about one-third of the rural priests were living with women.[11] The overall percentage of priests with concubines in Speyer may actually have been somewhat lower than indicated by the visitation, since the visitors probably concentrated on a region where abuses were more prevalent. Nevertheless, the records show that the efforts of the bishops to eradicate the widespread and open concubinage among the rural clergy had failed.

The unstable and unclear confessional situation of the period from 1530 to 1560, when various territories in the region (especially the Electoral Palatinate) reversed their positions on Protestantism several times, may have contributed to confusion among the clergy, as may have the apologists for clerical marriage within the Catholic Church itself. As late as 1564, after the Council of Trent had clearly forbidden concubinage, there was correspondence between the bishop of Worms and the Cathedral Chapter in Speyer on the desirability of clerical marriage.[12]

The most likely explanation for this phenomenon, however, is the fact that by living with a concubine a parish priest was conforming to the standards of his village. The visitors questioned the church wardens, the villagers responsible for managing parish property, about concubines and found that the peasants had no objection to the

---

10. GLAK 67/423. This figure is based on a review of the *Urfehden* (*Urpheden*), oaths sworn by the priests when they were released from prison, usually promising not to return to their evil ways.

11. Hansgeorg Molitor, *Kirchliche Reformversuche der Kurfürsten und Erzbischöfe von Trier im Zeitalter der Gegenreformation* (Wiesbaden: Franz Steiner Verlag, 1967), chap. 4. Clerical concubinage was apparently universal in rural Switzerland (Johan Georg Mayer, *Das Konzil von Trent und die Gegenreformation in der Schweiz*, vol. 2 [Stans: Hans und Matt, 1901], chap. 1). Concubinage was more prevalent in parts of the Bauland region of the Bishopric of Würzburg than in Speyer (Helmut Neumaier, *Reformation und Gegenreformation im Bauland unter besonderer Berücksichtigung der Ritterschaft* [Würzburg: Bohler Verlag, 1977], pp. 223–24.

12. GLAK 61/11494, pp. 75v–76r. The Lutheran example and the confusion over Catholic policy may have led to increased concubinage after 1550 (Neumaier, *Reformation und Gegenreformation im Bauland*, p. 222).

priests' companions.[13] Most wardens responded to the visitors' questions in a matter-of-fact manner. In Hainfeld, for example, one warden said that the pfarrer, Michael Krailin, "behaves well, in that he and his current housekeeper (*kochin*) have brought up four children." Another added, "He leads a pious life, lives with his housekeeper, with whom he has four children, as it is customary among priests." One of the visitors added a *"nota bene"* in the margin of the minutes next to that statement. In Venningen, the wardens seemed somewhat more concerned about their priest's concubine. "He has a maid with whom he has a child, [but] otherwise he has been a fine servant (*thiener*) for almost thirty years." "He behaves well and lives frugally, the only thing is that he has a little child by his servant."[14] In most villages the reactions of the laity to the priests' concubines fell somewhere between indifference and mild discomfort, the latter reaction probably more a result of the insistent questioning on this subject.

When the villagers expressed dissatisfaction with the pfarrer's lifestyle, they usually had quite normal objections that could have been leveled at any member of the community. In Weyer unter Rietburg a church warden reported complaints about the priest, Joachim Röser, for constantly quarreling loudly with his housekeeper and his two sons. Family quarrels were not unusual in early-modern villages. What had shocked the wardens in this case was the cause of the disputes: the concubine and the two children had directly disobeyed Röser's orders in the "family."[15] Perhaps the villagers hoped that the visitors would help straighten out the situation, since the pfarrer's special status precluded direct legal intervention by the usual village authorities.

The parishioners in Kirrweiler suspected their parish priest, Theodor Schobman, of a much more serious transgression. The sacristan explained that the priest had three maids, one who worked the fields, a second, an elderly woman, who was the mother of his child, and a third—the problem—"who comes from Landau and is the daughter of a cleric." The older woman had "been heard to say in their house that he plans to get rid of her and go to Speyer and openly marry the maid from Landau."[16] There is good reason to suspect that this story was only rumor or perhaps an effort to discredit Schobman, since he had several influential enemies in the village and, moreover, had

13. The visitors asked pointed questions, but also allowed the wardens to respond at length. The responses seem open and honest.
14. LASp. D2/306/10, pp. 423r, 426r, 263r, 265v.
15. Ibid., pp. 341r, 343r.
16. Ibid., p. 136r.

been the pastor in Kirrweiler since at least 1561 without causing problems.[17] Nevertheless, it is clear that the villagers judged their priests by the same standards as their other neighbors: having a long-term partner was acceptable, but discarding an elderly woman in favor of a younger one was not.

The behavior of Johann Fischer (Vischerius), pfarrer in Hambach and dean of the rural chapter, was the cause of scandal throughout the region. As early as August 1582, the Cathedral Chapter in Speyer, the patron of the parish, had discussed the removal of Fischer, on the grounds that he was "very neglectful and had a scandalous life."[18] In the summer of 1583, the visitors found Fischer's behavior not only well known in the large and wealthy village of Hambach, but common knowledge also among the other parish priests in the area. The villagers accused him of womanizing. Like Schobman in Kirrweiler, he had abandoned a long-time companion and her children in favor of a younger servant. Then he compounded the problem by getting a third woman pregnant. As a result, Fischer had lost the respect of his parishioners. One church warden lamented that there were many disobedient parishioners, a result of the pfarrer's "scandalous domestic life" and neglect of his duties. "Many hesitate to receive the sacraments from him."[19]

Other priests, some of whom had concubines themselves, also found Fischer's behavior reprehensible. Although the visitors asked each priest to report on the other priests in the region, most hesitated to comment on their colleagues' domestic arrangements. Only Fischer's name came up repeatedly. Herr Schobman from Kirrweiler, himself suspected of having two women, remarked that Fischer's conduct had caused great public scandal and added "no one should do this sort of thing." The pfarrer in St. Martin discussed Fischer's failings at great length. According to the villagers, Fischer had several other faults, including a tendency to drink too much and a passion for gambling. Many other parish priests had these weaknesses, but in most places the parishioners did not mind too much. In Hambach, the priest's domestic situation served to turn Fischer's lesser failings into part of a general pattern of behavior of which his neighbors disapproved. As one warden said, "He drinks with us, but all the trouble is due to the [pregnant] maid."[20] Of all the priests discovered

---

17. GLAK 61/10947, pp. 171r, 171v; GLAK 67/425, p. 49 (Investiture of Theodoricus Schobman).
18. GLAK 61/10945, p. 892.
19. LASp. D2/306/10, pp. 55v–56v.
20. Ibid., pp. 125v, 226v, 59v.

to have concubines, only Fischer had violated the local standards of acceptable behavior to the extent that his parishioners questioned the efficacy of the sacraments received from him.

The people of the bishopric demanded only that their priests behave as members of the community and seem to have found some of the visitors' inquiries strange, if not amusing, an example being their interest in the priests' clothing. The wardens almost invariably responded that the priest wore his black coat to services and otherwise dressed like a peasant. The villagers clearly considered this normal and proper. Drinking was another concern of the ecclesiastical authorities that the villagers did not share. "He does what other people do, he drinks himself full of wine." In a wine-growing region this was accepted, as long as it did not interfere with the priests' duties. Even fighting was not a major offense. A warden in Harthausen admitted that the parish priest "had gotten into fights several times in [the neighboring village of] Heinhofen, but, he thought, with good reason."[21]

Some priests were hard-working and ambitious farmers. Johann Sielius, pfarrer in Niederlauterbach, was a careful manager of the village church's property, and a wealthy man in the village in his own right. Not only did Sielius keep careful track of all tithes and dues owed to him, but he was also a successful winegrower. In 1583, a good year, he earned over 200 gulden on wine alone, and was able to invest 270 gulden of his own money on repairs and improvements on the parsonage. The villagers reacted to his success with envy mixed with admiration. He was a "good neighbor," but there were also references to the usual village disputes in which Sielius was a party. "[Sielius] has been here a while and produces rather abundantly. . . . [There are no problems with his behavior] except that there have been some disputes with him because of his cows, which he lets run free and which do a lot of damage. [He also] has a big belly and can put away four *maß* [of wine?] before it has any effect on him." In addition to his success as a farmer, Sielius was a proud paterfamilias. He had seven surviving children, apparently all by the same woman, to whom he was planning to pass on his fortune. He did not hesitate to display his wealth. "He held a baptism [for his own child] as if it were a church festival. Everyone has to have a triumph."[22] While it is perhaps true that Sielius was not necessarily well liked by all his neighbors, it is obvious that they saw no conflict between his activities as family man and peasant and his position as a priest.

21. Ibid., pp. 54r, 520v.
22. GLAK 61/11262, pp. 259, 276, 294, 290, 264.

In his sense of family, his desire to pass his hard-earned wealth on to his children, and his need to demonstrate his position and status in the community, Sielius was no different from any other wealthy and influential villager. Nor is this surprising. Like the clergymen in the neighboring Protestant territories, Catholic priests were often good fathers and family men. Unlike the homes of Protestant pastors, however, the parsonages in Catholic areas were not "seats of culture" or islands of a new morality in a traditional village.[23] As part of the village community, the pfarrer differed very little from their neighbors and shared their interests. It was more difficult for Catholic priests than for Protestant pastors to pass benefices and status on to their children, but there do seem to have been priestly "dynasties" in the cities, where sons followed their fathers into the clergy. This was not as frequent in the countryside. Some indication, however, of the social position of a priest's family can be found in one of the few clerical wills that survive from the sixteenth century.

In 1592 Johann Merckell, the former priest in Jöhlingen, dictated a detailed will while in retirement in Bruchsal. After paying the bishop the usual fees, and willing his library to the church in Jöhlingen, Merckell left all his property to his nine grandchildren. Unlike priests in the eighteenth century, he funded no masses for his soul. The will specifically required that his two children be passed over and that the property be administered for the grandchildren until they married or took clerical orders. Merkell's daughter was married to a citizen of Jöhlingen, and his son seems to have been resident there as well. Merckell's family was rooted in the village where he had served; like any good father, Merckell in his old age was concerned with the welfare of his descendants.[24]

If there was one difficulty the parishioners had with their parish priests, it was that they were often "foreigners." More than half of the priests who appear in the minutes of the visitation, were not natives of the Bishopric of Speyer. Most of these outsiders came from the Bishopric of Constance, although there were individuals from as far away as Merseburg (in Saxony) and Cologne. It was an old tradition for priests to come down from the mountainous and perennially overpopulated region of Swabia (most of which was in the huge Bishopric of Constance) into the wealthier bishoprics of the Rhine valley (Basel, Strasbourg, Speyer, Worms). The percentage of non-native priests in Speyer was apparently rising in the second half of the sixteenth century. In a group of parishes investigated in 1556, only

23. Vogler, *Le clergé protestant rhénan*, chaps. 4 and 5.
24. GLAK 42/2491.

about one-third of the priests could be categorized as "foreign," and most of these were from the neighboring Archbishopric of Trier.[25] The villagers viewed "foreign" priests with suspicion, but in the sixteenth century most seem to have worked hard to assimilate into the community.

The Duties of the Parish Priest

An important purpose of the visitation of 1583–88 was to determine if the parish priests were fulfilling their pastoral duties properly. The visitors focused their attention in three areas, all of which had been given new emphasis by the Council of Trent: preaching, the administration of the sacraments, and the teaching of the catechism. The laity, by contrast, had less interest in preaching and the catechism than the ecclesiastical officials. Furthermore, the lay people ignored the sacraments of Confirmation and Extreme Unction. They wanted a priest who lived in the village and gave weekly services. Here again, the concerns of the village community dominated conditions in the rural parishes.

By the 1580s the sermon had become, in Catholic as well as in Protestant areas, the central event of the Sunday service. All the rural parish priests in the Bishopric of Speyer preached in the vernacular at the end of the service. The visitors were generally satisfied that the sermons took place, although reports on their quality and impact are rare. The church wardens usually commented on the method used by the pfarrer. Some used notes, some read from books (especially the Bible), and others preached from memory. The most common observation was that the priest "preached as his duty required."[26] The documents suggest that the sermons neither particularly impressed, nor deeply moved the people. A warden in Diedesfeld quite tolerantly, but tellingly, said that the parish priest "preaches as well as he can, but he [the warden] has certainly heard better, [also] has never heard an Our Father from him, and does not believe he can [say one]."[27]

While most priests preached in the fashion of the pfarrer in Diedesfeld, there were a few sermons that caught the attention of the listeners. Johann Fischer, the pfarrer in Hambach, preached a full

25. Francis Rapp, *Réformes et Réformation à Strasbourg: Eglise et société dans le Diocèse de Strasbourg (1450–1525)* (Paris: Ophrys, 1974), 313, for the tradition of Swabian priests in the Rhine valley. For conditions in 1556 see LASp. D2/306/8.

26. GLAK 61/11262 and LASp. D2/306/10.

27. LASp. D2/306/10, p. 194v.

hour on the subject of the Passion, but given his general unpopularity, one doubts that he impressed the villagers positively. The priest in Edesheim was especially diligent, preaching and praying more than required by the ecclesiastical authorities.[28] This was exceptional. Most of the parish priests fulfilled their preaching duty in a mechanical and unimaginative way.

In their investigation of the administration of the sacraments, the visitors found that the impact of recent changes in sacramental practice had barely penetrated into the villages. Extreme Unction remained unknown, as did Confirmation. Most of the parish priests argued that this was not their fault. They all claimed to have the necessary oil and instructions to perform last rites, but no one ever requested it. The situation with Confirmation was similar. The pfarrer in Kirrweiler did claim to teach the sacrament, but this was rare. Typical was the comment of the priest in Steinfeld: "He says [that] of course he believes that Confirmation is a sacrament, but the practice is not taught."[29] There is absolutely no comment from the lay people concerning either of these two sacraments. They were not interested.

The priests were also closely questioned about baptism, especially concerning godparents. Most claimed that they obeyed the regulations allowing only one godparent of each sex, which may have been the tradition in many of these villages anyway. Some were more flexible. One pfarrer admitted to allowing two or three godparents of each sex if the poor people (*pauperi*) requested it.[30] Almost all the priests were satisfied that their parishioners fulfilled their penitential duties by confessing and taking communion at Easter. The visitors, however, expressed concern that some of the priests heard group, rather than individual, confessions. Most of the priests denied this charge, although in the far southwestern corner of the diocese the practice of group confession seems to have survived. A few of the priests also collected money for administering some of the sacraments, always claiming that this was a traditional practice and freely offered by the parishioners.[31]

Just before the visitation, Bishop Eberhard had published a new marriage ordinance to implement the reforms in marriage practice ordered by the Council of Trent. Although the changes in the Church's marriage law were not extensive, the Church now required

28. Ibid., pp. 59r, 60v, 376r.
29. GLAK 61/11262, p. 603.
30. Ibid., p. 287.
31. One example of this was in Salmbach (GLAK 61/11262, p. 406). See also Stamer III/1, pp. 90–100.

advance publication of the intent to marry (the posting of banns). Furthermore, priests had to keep a marriage register. Since the new ordinance had only recently been published, the visitors were most interested in finding out if the priests were properly publicizing it from the pulpit. In every case the priests claimed to be doing their duty, a claim confirmed by the church wardens.[32]

Although the visitation of 1583–88 showed that there had been an effort by the rural clergy to conform to new episcopal regulations, it is also clear that they were still serving their parishes in a "traditional" way. The parish priests did not try to force any new sacramental practices on their parishioners, nor did they seem particularly committed to these new practices themselves. Reflecting this disinterest was the continued use of the Speyer Agenda of 1512. This book, which prescribed liturgical practices, was in use in about half of the parishes visited in the 1580s, although it had officially been superseded in the 1560s by the Mainz Agenda of 1551. There were several cases where the priest had both at his disposal, but used the older Speyer one by preference. In doing so he may have stayed closer to local traditions, but he failed to benefit from the new *exhortationes (Ermahnungen)* in the Mainz Agenda, passages designed to encourage the "simple" parish priests to emphasize the sacramental teachings of the Church in their sermons.[33] Sacramental practices in the Bishopric of Speyer, by preference of both the laity and the rural clergy, had changed little since the early sixteenth century.

The teaching of the catechism was the innovation *par excellence* of the Reformation era. At various times in the 1570s the bishops of Speyer had ordered the priests to begin catechism lessons. In the 1580s, however, few of the priests were in fact complying with these orders. Only five of the twenty-two parish priests investigated even claimed to be catechizing. Most of the others said that they had stopped the classes during the plague of the previous year and had not gotten around to resuming them. Other pfarrer blamed their failure to teach on the unwillingness of the village youths to attend the catechism class. Catechism classes were not very popular among the

---

32. *Collectio processuum synodalium et constitutionem ecclesiarum diocesis Spirensis ab anno 1397 ad annum 1720* (Bruchsal, 1786), 385; Stamer III/1, p. 101. Parish registers, with records of baptisms, marriages, and burials rarely survived the destructive wars of the seventeenth century. Where they exist, marriage and baptism records begin in the late 1580s and 1590s. See the Parish Register Collection of the Church of Jesus Christ of Latter Day Saints, especially Films 0367712 (Hochdorf), and 1049306 (Waibstadt).

33. Alois Lamott, *Das Speyerer Diözesanrituale von 1512 bis 1932. Seine Geschichte und seine Ordines zur Sakramentliturgie* (Speyer: Verlag der Jaegerschen Buchdruckerei, 1961), 58–59.

villagers either. In Hainfeld the wardens thought that the priest was doing a good job, "although he had not taught the catechism since the previous bishop died." In Gleißweiler the villagers also reported that the pfarrer neglected the catechism.[34] The local people had no interest in receiving instruction from their pfarrer on the rudiments of the faith or the efficacy of the sacraments. As far as they were concerned, the duties of their priests were to perform baptisms, marriages, funerals, and Sunday services—and no more.

The most important event of rural religious life was, of course, the Sunday service. Generally this ceremony included the Mass followed by a sermon. Many of the church wardens used the visitation as an opportunity to criticize their parish priests' performance of these services. Although many parish priests were complimented for continuing traditional practices (*alte Bräuche*), a comment perhaps directed against both neighboring Protestant clergy and reforming Catholic authorities, the villagers reproached some pfarrer for infrequent services. They accused the unpopular pfarrer in Hambach, Johann Fischer, of failing to hold services every Sunday, of not preaching on feast days, and of holding the required Saturday services only three times the previous year.[35] Some villagers pushed for more frequent masses. In Niederlauterbach, for example, villagers went out of their way to protest that their priest preached regularly but did not hold Mass every week.[36] In general, however, the laity seemed satisfied with the weekly services. There were no complaints of long, boring ceremonies, as there were in neighboring Protestant areas in this period.

Only one parish priest protested that his parishioners did not remain until the end of his sermons. This complaint came from one Michael Tonsoris, a very diligent priest who had been sent out to Edesheim from Speyer three years earlier and still returned to the Jesuits in Speyer regularly for confession. Tonsoris also found his parishioners less than satisfactory in their paying of tithes and in their charitable offerings. He seems to have been one of the first of the "reformed priests" in the countryside.[37]

Although the rural clergy and their parishioners were in general agreement on the duties of the priests, this does not mean that the lay

34. LASp. D2/306/10, p. 423r, 459r.
35. Ibid., p. 56r.
36. GLAK 61/11262, p. 260.
37. For Protestant areas see Vogler, *La vie religieuse en pays rhénan.* For conditions in Edesheim see LASp. D2/306/10, pp. 374v and 370v. Concerning Tonsoris's appointment to Edesheim see GLAK 61/10945, pp. 361–62.

people in the Bishopric of Speyer were completely happy with how the parish clergy had performed those duties. In almost every village the wardens complained that the priests had fled the village during the previous year's plague. Their absence had serious ramifications for two reasons. The villagers expected their priests to comfort the sick and hear the confessions of the dying. Perhaps more important, the parish priest was needed to participate in the processions that the villages organized in an attempt to appease God and ward off the plague. "During the plague he did not want to do his duty by the poor sick and instead went to Speyer and stayed away several days," one warden reported. The rural clergy were not the only offenders. The Franciscan monks who were acting as parish priests in Heiligenstein were unwilling to come out of the city during the plague.[38] Priests who fled to Speyer, which in the peasants' opinion was full of useless and parasitic clergymen, during the plague drew the ire of their parishioners for their lack of loyalty to the village community. Some priests performed better, if not perfectly, during the plague. The pfarrer in St. Martin was apparently unwilling (or afraid) to visit the sick and the dying, but he did encourage the people to come to him for confession *before* they fell ill so they would not die in a state of sin. He, at least, seems to have remained in the village during the plague. A few parish priests actually received compliments from their parishioners for their behavior during the plague.[39]

In end effect, the local people expected certain services from their parish priest and saw the episcopal visitation as an opportunity to voice complaints and seek improvements in the quality of that service.

The Deterioration of the Benefice System

In a wide-ranging and detailed study of the Bishopric of Strasbourg in the fifteenth and early sixteenth centuries, Francis Rapp shows how the temporal, especially the financial, concerns of the clergy hampered the efforts of pre-Reformation Church reformers. One of the greatest problems, particularly in the countryside, was a "deterioration of the benefice system." In the Middle Ages many parishes had been incorporated into ecclesiastical institutions (mostly *Stifter* or chapters, but sometimes monasteries as well). This process siphoned off resources to pay wealthy aristocratic canons and, at times, episco-

---

38. LASp. D2/306/10, p. 131v. For Heiligenstein see Stamer III/1, p. 100.
39. LASp. D2/306/10, pp. 232r, 340r.

pal administrators. The income of the rural benefices shrank considerably. Economic conflicts brought on by the reliance of much of the clergy on income derived from loans to the peasantry exacerbated the deteriorating relations between the Church and the people. In periods of economic growth this system functioned fairly well, but during the repeated agricultural crises of the early sixteenth century many peasants defaulted on their loans, leaving the parish priests impoverished. These priests were forced to accumulate several benefices. They often circumvented the Church regulation against holding two benefices *cum curo* (i.e., benefices charged with care of souls) by holding one benefice *cum curo* and one (or more) benefice *simplex*. The latter, mostly chaplaincies, only required the fulfillment of certain services. Economic problems not only made the clergy less sympathetic to the efforts of Church reformers, which threatened to eliminate such practices; they also meant fewer clerics in each parish, which led to general popular disaffection with the Church.[40]

To be sure, conditions in the Bishopric of Speyer in the late sixteenth century were somewhat different from those in Alsace eighty years earlier. The most important difference was that two-thirds of the parishes in Speyer had become Protestant, a situation that had financial as well as religious consequences. Nevertheless, Catholic priests (and the Church reformers) in Speyer also faced the threat of a complete breakdown of the benefice system, a threat caused by many of the same problems that existed in Strasbourg at the beginning of the century. Incomes were small; many priests held several benefices at once; and the laity complained constantly about the resulting decline in the number of priests and the quality of services.

In 1556, as part of the process of creating a Protestant territorial church, the officials of the Electoral Palatinate investigated conditions in thirty-seven villages on the left bank of the Rhine. Catholic priests still held benefices in these villages and still peformed Catholic services. The purpose of this investigation was to inspect the economic condition of the benefices in order to prepare for the installation of new Protestant clergymen. Although strongly and openly anti-Catholic, the report presents a clear picture of the financial difficulties faced by the rural clergy in the pre-reformed Church.

The most important issue was that of vacant benefices. Several parishes were too poor to support their own priest and had to share a priest with another village. In several villages benefices had re-

---

40. Rapp, *Réformes et Réformation à Strasbourg*, esp. book 3, chap. 2, "La détioration du système bénéficiale," and p. 317.

mained vacant for long periods, while the patrons (usually in this area the Cathedral Chapter) collected the income. In the village of Zeiskam, the pfarrer preferred to live in the nearby town of Germersheim. He had not been to his parish in ten years, and left the services up to a poorly paid substitute.[41]

The villagers reserved their strongest complaints for the higher clergy in Speyer. They felt they were served by poor-quality priests because most of the income of the churches went to Speyer. The villagers in Bellheim said that theirs was a wealthy parish, but that most of the tithe went to Speyer and, as a result, they got a "bad person" as a priest. They would prefer a married priest over the "temporary priests" they had been sent. In Wolmersheim the villagers complained that they paid a very large tithe, but that the priest's income was small, and as a result only young and uneducated priests were willing to serve the parish. In Rohrbach the priest was forced to live on the money from endowed masses, endowments that were losing value owing to inflation and difficulty in collecting debts.[42] In addition, most of the chaplaincies were either vacant or held by nonresident priests in monasteries or in the city.

It was frequently suggested that these funds be used to help the poor. There were strong strains of anticlericalism in some villages: "The poor people complained in this way about the priests, as they do in many places, [saying] that it is a pity above all [that] in the cities, where the fewest people are, the priests lie about in great idleness, while [the parishes] in the countryside, where most of the people are, are completely abandoned [although they] support the cities, the princes, and the clergy."[43] In a similar vein, the Gemeinde of Edesheim, when warned in 1572 to pay the tithe, said that the clergy (*Pfaffen*, a derogatory variant of pfarrer) had enough wine, whereas the villagers needed to get bread for their children.[44]

Complaints by parish priests about their income were, of course, endemic. The Cathedral Chapter, where many of the priests registered their complaints, was not unsympathetic. In 1568, after repeated complaints by the new pfarrer in Deidesheim (one of the best-endowed parishes in the bishopric), the canons admitted that the parish had a small income. One proposal was to incorporate a chaplaincy to improve the priest's situation. A few years previously the pfarrer in Geinsheim rather pitifully requested that he be allowed to

41. LASp. D2/306/8, pp. 16v, 17v, 18r, 18v, 24r–25r.
42. Ibid., pp. 23r, 23v, 27v–28v, 40v, 41r.
43. Ibid., p. 30v.
44. Stamer III/1, p. 41.

continue to use a garden that belonged to the primissary in the village. His financial situation was especially desperate after two straight years of poor grain and wine harvests.[45] In the years around 1570 the Cathedral Chapter reacted positively to quite a few requests for increases to parish incomes.

Even the wealthiest parish priests could complain bitterly about the financial sacrifices they were forced to make in the Bishopric of Speyer. This was the case of Georg Hennenberg, who in 1571 was the newly appointed parish priest in the episcopal residence town of Udenheim (later Philippsburg). Although Hennenberg's income of over 250 gulden per year was probably considerably greater than that of any other parish priest in the diocese, he found it insufficient to support his household and quite a bit smaller than that of his previous post. He suggested that the bishop find another priest for this parish, someone who had a smaller household. What is most apparent from this case is that the bishops of Speyer did not have the resources to hire good priests away from other dioceses, even to fill their best benefices.[46]

The village communes often supported their priests in these requests for more income. In Rot im Bruhrein, in 1564, the gemeinde asked the bishop to improve the income of the parish, perhaps by giving the pfarrer an additional benefice. The priest had threatened to leave. The local episcopal official was ordered to negotiate with the priest, but the Bishop's Council warned that this could set a bad precedent. "The pfarrer should be told to be happy with this [improvement], and not come back next year and ask for another raise." Nevertheless, in 1573 a similar request from Rot was forwarded to the bishop, and the priest was once again given a raise, apparently for the second year in a row.[47]

The parish priests and the villagers usually knew exactly how much money, grain, and wine the village had paid in tithe and what part of it was returned to the priests as income. In 1565 the pastor in Kirrlach complained that the patron of the village, the Chapter of St. German in Speyer, took the tithe for itself, "and gave him, as the one who did the work, the smallest part." The village gemeinde sent along a petition supporting the priest. The bishop was sympathetic and wrote to the chapter, requesting that the canons increase the pfarrer's income, adding that he did not like to see priests changing

---

45. GLAK 61/10941, pp. 845, 854, 858, 876, 145, 146, 115, 156, 214, 215.
46. GLAK 218/237.
47. GLAK 61/11494, pp. 3r, 3v; GLAK 61/11494a, p. 1r.

parishes so frequently. They should be paid enough to remain in one place for more than a few years. The bishop was very hard with St. German, probably because it was widely known that the urban chapters habitually stinted their parish priests.[48]

St. German was certainly not the only offender. The Cathedral Chapter, which held the patronage of over thirty parishes, collected large tithes from these villages and paid only a small portion of this income to support the rural clergy. The village of Geinsheim, for example, paid the chapter 180 *Malter* of grain in 1577. During the same period the parish priest received about 50 malter.[49] In general the parish priests received about a third of the tithe, an amount that often left them impoverished, even in wealthy villages.[50]

The poor incomes of the parish clergy concerned both the laity in the villages and the episcopal authorities. A major reform of the benefice system would require confronting many entrenched institutions in the Church. No sixteenth-century bishop of Speyer was willing, or indeed able, to challenge the privileged chapters that derived the greater portion of their income from the patronage of parish churches. This problem would continue to plague Catholic reformers for quite some time to come.

Local Church and Communal Control

The village of Riedseltz is located on the southern edge of the Bishopric of Speyer. In the sixteenth and seventeenth centuries its secular lord was the Order of Teutonic Knights. Although surrounded by Protestant territory, the village remained Catholic. Ultimate ecclesiastical authority in the village was held by the Bishop of Speyer, but immediate control in religious matters was exercised by the chapter in Weißenburg, a few kilometers away. In 1573, the commune complained to the representative of the Teutonic Knights (also in Weißenburg) that the Catholic people of Riedseltz had been living without a parish priest for many years. For this they blamed the chapter, which, although it held the patronage of the village church and collected the tithe, refused to install a priest. The canons argued that the village church was only a "filial" (or branch) church and that the Riedseltzers were supposed to go to the neighboring village of Steinseltz for services.

48. GLAK 61/11494, pp. 177v, 178r.
49. A *malter* in Baden was 1.5 hectoliters, or about 4.2 bushels.
50. For Geinsheim, and tithes collected by the Cathedral Chapter in 1577, see GLAK 67/484. Concerning the pastor's income, see LASp. D2/306/10, p. 188r. There are many complaints about insufficient income in the minutes of the Cathedral Chapter.

The village commune responded with an articulate statement of the villagers' understanding of the role of the gemeinde in Church affairs. Above all, the commune had to ensure that the village was properly served by a resident priest. Going to Steinseltz was an unacceptable solution, for the pastor there was not a Catholic and gave sermons that were hostile to the Catholics. It was of apparently equal importance that the church at Steinseltz was so small that the Riedseltzers often had to stand outside in the rain and snow. The space problem notwithstanding, the villagers, fearing brigands and fire, did not like the idea of leaving Riedseltz empty every Sunday and holiday. Without a resident pfarrer, the villagers lived without the sacraments, especially those of baptism and communion, and no priest visited the sick and the dying. Children in need of baptism were carried from village to village, and the parents had to beg the neighboring priests to baptize them. The proposal that a priest resident in a nearby village do services in Riedseltz was also rejected, on the grounds that he could neither provide regular services nor come to the village on demand.

Not only did the villagers of Riedseltz make it clear what they expected of a priest, they also took the initiative in securing one. Emphasizing that the village had grown considerably in the previous years and paid a tithe easily sufficient to support a resident parish priest, the villagers withheld the wine tithe in the fall of 1572. The chapter in Weißenburg responded by promising to appoint a priest, a promise they reneged on as soon as the tithe was paid. Next, the commune attempted to appoint and pay a pfarrer itself, a solution that was both expensive and only marginally successful, since what the village could afford to pay was too small to keep a priest for any length of time. What the villagers really wanted, as one representative of the Teutonic Knights astutely reported to his superiors, was to have the tithe left to them and let them support their own pfarrer. The Teutonic Knights supported the villagers, and, with the mediation of the bishop's officials, a compromise was reached in 1580 whereby the chapter contributed about half of the tithe for the support of a priest. The knights also contributed the income of a chaplaincy in the village, and the villagers rounded out the cost of a priest's benefice with a significant contribution of their own.[51]

Although the primary concern of the villagers of Riedseltz, the appointment of a resident priest, was a practical one, this dispute also reflects the conflict between two views of ecclesio-political organiza-

51. ADBR 19 J 395, nos. 24, 32, 35, 36; ADBR 19 J 396, no. 20.

tion. By appointing their own priest, withholding the tithe from the chapter in Weißenburg, and demanding its use for the support of a resident cleric, the villagers demonstrated their belief that the commune should administer the parish church, evidence of the existence of what Peter Blickle has called the "communal church" (gemeinde kirche). Blickle argues that, in the early sixteenth century, German peasants worked to "communalize" village churches. Rosi Fuhrmann has found evidence of this process occurring in the Bishopric of Speyer as early as the fifteenth century. In the ecclesio-political sphere this communalization had several consequences. Villagers wanted resident clerics, control of the tithe, the right to elect the priest, an "equitable church" (wohlfeile Kirche, where priests were not allowed to charge for sacraments), and the abolition of many ecclesiastical jurisdictions. These ideas remained current in the later sixteenth century. All the elements mentioned by Blickle as being important in the early 1500s (except the last) can be seen in the demands of the Riedseltzers in the 1570s. In asserting their desire to remain Catholic, however, these villagers did not link these ecclesio-political ideas with an appeal to Scripture or Protestant theology, which Blickle argues did occur in the early Reformation period.[52]

The peasants of Riedseltz had no reason to make their communal church Protestant. The villagers could see how the Protestant territorial churches functioned in neighboring villages. In this part of Germany Catholicism was more disorganized, fragmented, and decentralized than the Calvinist and Lutheran state churches. Village communes like the one in Riedseltz exploited this situation to exercise decisive influence over rural Catholicism, which enabled them to retain a relative independence their Protestant neighbors did not enjoy.

The peasants also had religious reasons to remain loyal to Catholicism. If, as Blickle argues, Protestant theology had appealed directly to rural populations in the 1520s, by the later sixteenth century educated pastors and administrators brought the new religion to the parishes.[53] In Calvinist areas, like the Palatinate, Protestantism meant the suppression of local religious traditions. By contrast, the kind of pre-Tridentine Catholicism that prevailed in the Bishopric of Speyer was more tolerant of local religious traditions. This lent strength to what might be called "Catholic communalism."

52. Blickle, Gemeinde Reformation, esp. pp. 52–61; Fuhrmann, "Die Kirche im Dorf."
53. Blickle, Gemeinde Reformation; Conrad, Reformation in der bäuerlichen Gesellschaft.

In the mid-sixteenth century, rural communes had considerable influence over the appointment of new parish priests. They usually exercised this influence indirectly, since no village commune had the patronage of its own parish church.[54] Nevertheless, it was an accepted tradition, especially in the wealthy wine villages, for the patron of the village to send applicants out to the villages for a "trial sermon" (*probe Predigen*), which would give the gemeinde a chance to form an opinion of the priest's suitability. At times the villagers even recommended priests to the Cathedral Chapter or other patron. Most of the ecclesiastical authorities had little interest in forcing an unpopular priest on an unwilling community and therefore paid close attention to the opinions and recommendations of the gemeinde.

Even though no village commune had the patronage of the parish church, some did control the patronage of the smaller benefices (a chaplaincy or primissary). This was true in Langenbrücken, where the village *Gericht* (court or council) had the right to appoint the primissary. In this case the income of this secondary benefice was assigned to the parish priest, which gave the villagers some voice in his appointment.[55]

When a village gericht recommended a priest to fill a vacancy in its church, it usually named a priest from a neighboring parish. This option was open only to the wealthier villages, where the income was large enough to lure a priest away from a poorer parish. The Protestant Reformation had also made this practice more difficult by reducing the number of Catholic parishes, and therefore the number of priests. Nevertheless, the ecclesiastical authorities were generally pleased to have a priest recommended by the commune. In 1566, for example, the Gemeinde of Hainfeld asked that the current priest in Weyer unter Rietburg, Valentin Becker, be appointed to their parish. The Cathedral Chapter did appoint Becker, rather than another priest who had applied to the chapter in person, because the village had requested him. Sometimes a priest seeking a benefice went straight to a village with a vacancy to give a "trial sermon," in the hope that the villagers would recommend him to the patron. This strategy succeeded in Hambach in 1569, when an unnamed pfarrer was ac-

---

54. The commune of Hainfeld claimed alternate patronage of its parish church with the Cathedral Chapter. It is unclear if the village exercised this right in the sixteenth and seventeenth centuries (LASp. D2/306/10, p. 420v). See also Fuhrmann, "Die Kirche im Dorf," pp. 181–82.

55. GLAK 229/57747 (Langenbrücken), p. 1; Fuhrmann, "Die Kirche im Dorf." Fuhrmann demonstrates that many of these secondary benefices had been created by the gemeinden in the fifteenth century to improve the religious services available in the villages.

cepted by the Cathedral Chapter on the strength of the parishioners' recommendation.[56]

The ecclesiastical authorities took the "trial sermons," and the villagers' opinions of them, seriously. In 1571 a priest who had done a bad job during his probation period in Ruppertsberg was sent packing; a priest who had given a very good "trial sermon" in the smaller and less well endowed parish of Niederkirchen replaced him.[57] In 1576 the parish of Bauerbach was vacant, and the Cathedral Chapter had two applicants. Both were sent out to the village to give sermons on consecutive Sundays. Even before the sermons had taken place, the canons explicitly promised to leave the final choice between the two candidates to the commune, a promise they kept. The Cathedral Chapter, of course, could reject a village's candidate, as it did in Ruppertsberg in 1575, saying that the proposed priest was "a most frivolous person whose conduct is bad."[58] Before the 1580s, however, this occurred very rarely. It was in the interest of everyone involved that the villagers be happy with their parish priest, and the patrons usually had no reason to reject their choice.

The villagers had perhaps even more influence over the removal of unsatisfactory clergymen than they did over the selection of new priests, because the ecclesiastical authorities themselves were divided on the question of who had the authority to make such decisions. In theory the bishop, or his vicar general, had the power to discipline all members of the secular clergy. While it appears that no one questioned this power, the patrons (especially the Cathedral Chapter) also claimed the power to remove unsatisfactory priests. This situation of competing and overlapping jurisdictions gave the rural communes considerable room for maneuver. Unsuccessful appeals to one authority for the removal of an unsatifactory priest could be followed by a petition to another.

Objections to parish priests varied. The pfarrer in Neipsheim in the late 1560s was rather generally disliked. One complaint was that he "behaved totally inappropriately, and, in addition, he was impossible to understand." After over two years of complaints, during which time the Cathedral Chapter repeatedly promised to remove the offending priest, the pfarrer himself begged to be given another parish since the villagers were making life miserable for him in Neipsheim.[59] More often it was the everyday behavior of the priest that

56. GLAK 61/10941, pp. 263, 275; GLAK 61/10942, p. 143.
57. Ibid., p. 463.
58. GLAK 61/10943, pp. 467–68, 474, 228–28.
59. GLAK 61/10941, p. 552; GLAK 61/10942, p. 74.

raised the ire of his neighbors. The pfarrer in Venningen, Viax Fileman, did his priestly duties well, but was unable to get along with the villagers, especially when he drank too much.[60] The villagers often complained forcefully about priests who considered themselves above the rules that all members of the community had to obey. In St. Martin in 1564, a new priest claimed exemption from several taxes and tried to take the profits from the sale of several barrels of wine that belonged to the parish but had been harvested before he had taken over the benefice. The bishop's officials intervened, with specific instructions to pacify the gemeinde, if possible without curtailing the priest's income too severely. In the end the disputing parties made real concessions on both sides to reach a compromise.[61] In all cases, Church authorities respected the complaints of the villagers. Rarely were unpopular parish priests left in their villages, even when the authorities were sympathetic to the priest's plight. A frequent policy was to transfer the offending cleric to another parish, preferably at some distance from the village where he had had trouble.

The church wardens, as representatives of the village, had considerable control over the financial resources of the parish. While this control often came with responsibilities, such as the upkeep of part of the church, it also gave the village influence over the priest. The minutes of the visitation of 1583–88 show clearly that the wardens were the ones who knew where the various funds of money were invested, how much income they were getting, and how this income was to be dispensed. The parish priest was not consulted on these issues, although he usually received some of his income from these funds.

The needs and desires of the villagers, working through the communes, dominated rural Catholicism in the Bishopric of Speyer. Furthermore, this communalism remained the focus of local Catholicism throughout the early modern period. The villagers strove to preserve the communal church as a barrier against the full implementation of Tridentine Catholicism. This weakness in Catholic reform, however, did not hurt local Catholicism. During the two centuries after the Council of Trent, the rural population remained loyal to Catholicism; but this loyalty was usually to this traditional communal Church, rather than to the Catholic Church as a whole.

---

60. GLAK 61/11494, pp. 138r, 145v. Fileman (Pileman) was also beaten up outside of Venningen the previous year (in 1564), an incident that the authorities blamed on Protestant youths from a neighboring village in the Electoral Palatinate (GLAK 61/11494, pp. 74r–74v).
    61. Ibid., pp. 31v, 65r, 65v, 70r.

The Traditional Church

Marquard von Hattstein (1560–1581):
A Pre-Tridentine Bishop

Although the Protestant Reformation threatened its incomes, status, and authority, the upper clergy of the Bishopric of Speyer did not rush to embrace the Counter-Reformation. Perhaps nowhere else in the empire was the traditional aristocratic Church more entrenched than in the bishoprics of the Rhine valley. In the Bishopric of Speyer, as in the rest of Catholic Europe, noble canons and abbots consistently defended their ancient privileges. The political fragmentation and regional particularism of Germany, however, gave this opposition to reform a specific character. Even bishops often hesitated to advocate reform, despite the extensive new powers the Council of Trent had given them, for the Tridentine Church threatened to eliminate the privileges their families had enjoyed, and, in its dogmatic rigidity, to foreclose any chance for compromise with the Protestants.[62]

Bishop Marquard von Hattstein was a leading member of this "traditional" party, and his personal background, his Church career, and his policies as prince-bishop of Speyer provide a window on the kind of Church the reformers sought to change. Men like Marquard were entrenched in the most influential institutions of the Rhenish bishoprics. The most important and powerful of these in the Bishopric of Speyer were the collegiate chapters in Speyer, Weißenburg, and Bruchsal. The canons of Speyer, however, unlike those of many Cathedral Chapters in Germany, did not consistently oppose reform. By the 1560s the chapter had come to be dominated by a reform party that constantly urged a reluctant Bishop Marquard to implement the decrees of the Council of Trent.[63]

Marquard, who ruled from 1560 to 1581, was in many ways a prince-bishop of the "old school." A younger son of one of oldest noble families on the Rhine, Marquard began his Church career at the age of fifteen. In the 1550s he rose rapidly within the hierarchy, a consequence only in part of his family connections and good breeding. Apparently well educated, he was especially known for his business talents and political abilities. In 1557 Marquard represented the archbishop-elector of Mainz at the Reichstag and in 1569 became a

---

62. Zeeden, Entstehung der Konfessionen, pp. 122–23.
63. In Trier the Cathedral Chapter tended to be a brake on the bishops' efforts to reform the diocese, although few of the canons openly opposed reform (Molitor, Kirchliche Reformversuche, chap. 2).

judge at the Imperial Chamber Court (*Reichskammergericht*).[64] Marquard's career was not altogether unusual for a talented, hardworking young nobleman, but his success had nothing to do with his personal piety or a commitment to Church reform.

Many contemporaries suspected Marquard of being a secret Protestant, and one modern scholar has argued that he was a supporter of the radical Schwenkfeldian movement.[65] Whatever his personal opinions, Marquard tolerated a variety of religious views in his court. He was also a personal friend of the aggressively Calvinist *Pfalzgraf* (and later Elector Palatine) Johan Casimir and even hosted the Huguenot leader Condé at his palace. Finally, Marquard had a concubine, a fact that was apparently common knowledge in the region, although the Cathedral Chapter tactfully did not mention her in its ongoing disputes with him.[66]

Marquard was most comfortable as a territorial prince, and to enhance his status his first project was to expand the episcopal palace. Soon after his election, Marquard made an extensive tour (in grand style) of his principality in an effort to underscore his position as secular ruler. The purpose of this journey was to receive oaths of allegiance from his subjects. In the process he managed to get in some good hunting. In Bruchsal, for example, he went straight to a shooting contest after Sunday services. After this expedition Marquard took a business trip to Mainz, putting off for months his ceremonial entry into Speyer, his ordination as priest, and his elevation as bishop.[67] Clearly this was a man who enjoyed the role of a Renaissance prince.

Stamer considers Marquard's performance as bishop to have been "ambiguous"; he acknowledges Marquard's effectiveness as a politician, but condemns his failure to reform the Church.[68] In fact, Marquard pursued a self-conscious and consistent policy both as a prince and as bishop. Although the Cathedral Chapter and some modern historians accused him of being "remarkably passive" in the face of the pressures put on his bishopric by the Electoral Palatinate, he actually cultivated a friendship with the powerful (and Protestant)

---

64. Stamer III/1, pp. 16–17; Remling II, pp. 358–359.

65. Heinz-Peter Mielke, "Schwenkfeldianer im Hofstaat Bischof Marquards von Speyer (1560–1581)," *Archiv für mittelrheinische Kirchengeschichte* 28 (1976): 77–82.

66. Stamer III/1, p. 21; Mielke, "Schwenkfeldianer," p. 79.

67. Remling II, pp. 361–64, 392; Stamer III/1, p. 17. Stamer refers to Marquard as a "baufreudiger Kirchenfürst," while Remling considered his building a sign of his greatness. By avoiding ordination, Marquard, like most aristocratic churchmen kept open the option of inheriting the family estate should his older brothers die without heirs.

68. Stamer III/1, pp. 16–23: "Die zweispältige Haltung des Bischofs Marquard von Hattstein"

Palatinate with the purpose of preserving his principality's independence. This friendship was no more than a continuation of the long-
standing tradition of friendly ties between the *Kurpfalz* and the Bishopric of Speyer, ties that many contemporaries found uncomfortably
close. As confessional tensions rose, Marquard was suspected of
cooperating in a Palatine plot to secularize the bishoprics of Speyer
and Worms and turn them into hereditary principalities, perhaps
with himself remaining as prince in Speyer.[69] Such a plot would not
have been out of character for Marquard, if only to keep "his" principality in the family. As it was, Marquard helped his family as best
he could, appointing at least eight of his kinsmen to lucrative positions in the administration of the bishopric.[70]

In religious politics, Marquard represented an important strand
within the Catholic Church in Germany, a group that still hoped to
reach a compromise with the Protestants to create a truly German,
Imperial Church. This group had had considerable influence in the
1540s, when Protestants and Catholics came close to real compromise. After the Peace of Augsburg in 1555, Germany became increasingly polarized along confessional lines, but even then many
German Catholics were slow to support the reforms of the Council of
Trent. They believed, correctly, that a reformed and militant Catholicism would not only eliminate any chance for compromise with the
Protestants in Germany, but would also require loyalty to an international and authoritarian Church that would not recognize their particular traditions. The aristocratic members of this traditionalist
group, of course, were also very interested in protecting their centur-
ies-old dominance of the German Church, a position threatened by
the Tridentine reforms. Marquard was influenced by all of these
considerations.

Bishop Marquard consistently pursued a policy of compromise and
conciliation. In 1578 he severely reprimanded Conrad Fürer, the
priest in Bruchsal, for refusing to bury a Lutheran burgher in the
town graveyard, and for having a second Lutheran arrested. Marquard
explained that, as a Catholic prince, he wanted nothing more than to
uphold the Catholic Church, and its decrees and canons. To do so,
however, was not always possible. As he explained it:

69. Press, "Das Hochstift Speyer," pp. 262, 252; Stamer III/1, pp. 19–23, for secularization,
see esp. p. 21. See also GLAK 65/626, p. 264a (handwritten addition to the *Chronik des
Bistums Speyer* by Philip Simonis [1608]). Simonis says that the Domdekan Andreas von
Oberstein persuaded Marquard to reject the Palatine proposal.
70. Remling II, p. 383.

His lordship [the bishop] does not have an enclosed principality as others do, and [he] is not as strong and powerful as some other Catholic [princes], but instead is surrounded on all sides by electors, lords, and nobles of other religions. . . . [F]or the time being, unfortunately, it is necessary to remain good neighbors. . . . [A]nd in such cases one must proceed and negotiate with care.

Considerations of practical politics, and the bishop's understanding of the Peace of Augsburg in 1555 clearly informed Marquard's policy in this case. The "Religious Peace" protected both religions in the Empire, at least "until a general council can bring both sides to a unified understanding." Meanwhile, it was in the interest of the Bishopric of Speyer to respect the treaty, especially since it protected Catholics (and, he implies, sources of Church income) in Protestant territories.[71] Overzealous priests like Fürer must be kept under control.

Although he avoided confrontation with his Protestant neighbors, Marquard was active in the organizational and financial affairs of the Church. He ordered several surveys of the benefices in the bishopric, apparently for the purpose of bringing order to the financial and jurisdictional confusion of his domain.[72] Marquard also promulgated two tithe decrees, in 1562 and 1575, apparently in response to widespread resistance to the tithe in the countryside. These decrees required the bishop's secular officials to take a greater role in enforcing the payment of the tithe.[73] These measures are typical of Marquard's traditionalist view of Church administration, which emphasized the financial exploitation of the Church's resources for the benefit of the upper clergy.

Bishop Marquard and his officials made a modest effort to discipline the clergy. Ecclesiastic courts prosecuted and punished both parish priests and members of the lower collegiate clergy. In the synod recesses, published twice a year and in theory read to the rural clergy at the meetings of the rural chapters, Marquard regularly admonished the priests to improve their morals, perform their pastoral duties correctly, and resist the temptations of the world. In both content and emphasis, however, these admonitions were neither original nor innovative.

71. GLAK 61/11494b, pp. 59r–60v.
72. GLAK 67/425, pp. 31r–41r; GLAK 61/11494b, p. 16r.
73. GLAK 67/425, pp. 42r–44r; *Sammlung der Hochfürstlichen-Speierischen Gesetze und Landesverordnungen* (Bruchsal, 1789), part 1, p. 32ff.

The synod recesses (*Processus synodalis*) of Marquard's episcopate are typical of his attitude to the problems of the Church in Germany. In Marquard's view, the lax morals of the clergy had led to the rise of Protestantism. A return to "temperance, justice, truth, sobriety, chastity, and the other virtues of the clerical estate" will bring the people back to the Catholic Church.[74] Marquard never went beyond such formulaic censure to recommend institutional, doctrinal, or pastoral reforms. Throughout the 1560s and 1570s, the synod recesses continued to maintain that the elimination of clerical abuses (especially concubinage) would be sufficient to end the Protestant threat. Beyond making some vague references to the pastoral duties of the clergy, he said little in his synod recesses to improve the clergy.

Marquard had more direct ways of disciplining the clergy. Although most of the records of the ecclesiastical courts have been lost, a series of oaths (*Urpheden*) sworn to by clerics who had been punished by the vicar general do survive. These also show that, while Marquard's episcopate was not lax, it was very traditional. Marquard's vicars general backed up the warnings of the synods by punishing clerics who were caught with concubines or overindulged in the fine wines of the region. They focused their efforts on the urban clergy. Between 1560 and 1583, forty-seven clerics from the four chapters in Speyer (and one from the chapter in Weißenburg) were punished. Only twenty rural parish priests were arrested. The vicars general most frequently disciplined the lower urban clergy, often for minor offenses such as drunkenness and brawling. This reflected Marquard's interest in maintaining good relations between Protestants and Catholics within the Lutheran Imperial city, and his relative lack of concern about the less visible and politically less explosive situation in the Catholic villages. Furthermore, in most cases the punishments were light, consisting of minor fines and short imprisonments. Only two of the twenty parish priests punished were forced to resign their benefices.[75]

Marquard and the supporters of the traditional Catholic Church did not share the Tridentine Church's image of the ideal cleric. This was nowhere more evident than in the bishop's choices for the post of vicar general. The *Vicarius in Spiritualibus* was the most important ecclesiastical official in the bishopric, for he was charged with disciplining the clergy. Obviously, a person with such a responsibility should be above reproach. When the position fell vacant in 1566,

74. *Collectio processuum synodalium*, p. 355.
75. GLAK 67/423.

Marquard recommended a Dr. Jacob Imhaber from Freiburg in Breisgau to the Cathedral Chapter. The chapter, exercising its considerable powers, rejected the candidate, pointing out that he was well known in Freiburg as the father of a "bastard."[76] The bishop then recommended Steffan Pummelin, who had a young concubine and had been the cause of great scandal in Speyer. His sermons (he was one of the priests in the Cathedral) were also suspicious: "He had been heard to say publically [that] if he were vicar [general], he would want to allow everyone to have a concubine." Despite these objections, the bishop's candidate was accepted. The Cathedral Chapter was not happy with his performance, and five months after his appointment the canons called him in for a severe reprimand. Within a year after his appointment he was removed from office.[77]

Overall, Bishop Marquard was neither negligent nor passive. He was a hard-working and practical politician and as prince-bishop he was effective, if conservative. From the 1560s on, however, Marquard also had to deal with a reform-minded party within the Catholic Church in Speyer. Marquard responded to this pressure in the same way that he responded to the Protestant threat—with conciliation and passive resistance.

In 1566, Pope Pius V ordered Marquard to visit his diocese and to improve the discipline of the clergy under his jurisdiction. The pope was aware of the difficulties faced by Catholics in the Bishopric of Speyer and feared for the survival of the Church in the region. At the same time, he was also well informed of the abuses of the Catholic clergy and argued that the first step in combating Protestantism had to be the reform of the clergy. This process could be most effectively started by an episcopal visitation. The pope even pointed out that the emperor also favored a visitation. He ended his letter with lines obviously directed at Bishop Marquard himself: "A warning to those who could remove [abuses], [but who instead] sanction the negligence and approve the hiding of so much scandal."[78] No visitation, however, actually took place as a result of the pope's letter. Marquard regularly claimed that "various inconveniences had come up that had made it impossible for such work to be carried out."[79]

The arrival of the Jesuits in Speyer in the 1560s forced Marquard into a difficult position. He seems to have disliked them intensely.

76. GLAK 61/10941, pp. 182, 185.
77. GLAK 61/10961, pp. 288–89, 472, 772.
78. Remling *UB*, pp. 615–17.
79. GLAK 61/10942, pp. 36–37. Also see Chapter 2.

The Lutheran city council in Speyer quoted him as saying that, "he would happily see that the bloodthirsty . . . Jesuits, as many as are here, be dissolved, and he said to the Burgher Hans Weick on the 30th of October, 1573, [that] he wished that the devil would take all Jesuits."[80] The city council shared this view. For nine years (1566–75) Marquard resisted the efforts of the Cathedral Chapter to install a permanent Jesuit College in Speyer.[81] This attitude was perfectly consistent with his long-term political and religious policy.

Officially Bishop Marquard supported bringing in the Jesuits (as he wrote the Cathedral Chapter in 1566), and he admitted that they would no doubt increase the quality of teaching and preaching in Speyer. He had, however, misgivings (Bedenken). First, he complained of the expense. Unlike the wealthy archbishoprics of Trier, Mainz, and Augsburg, the "poor Bishopric of Speyer" could not afford to support a college. This was especially true since the bishop had already committed himself to the rebuilding of his palace in Udenheim. Because of a shortage of money, the bishop was unable to fill the positions of vicar general and ecclesiastical judge. Most important, the bishop had heavy political expenses for the Reichstag, for ongoing suits in the courts, and for taxes to the emperor.[82]

Marquard also argued that the Jesuits would bring the bishopric into serious conflict with its Protestant neighbors.

> Since we do not have full jurisdiction in the city [of Speyer] and already the [City] Council and the citizens, since they are followers of the Augsburg Confession, have appointed preachers, it might well happen (since not everyone likes to accept everything with tolerance), especially if it were a [whole] College, [that] they [the Jesuits and the Lutheran preachers] will lead each other to disputation and other troubles, and this might cause all sorts of divisions and hostility.[83]

The Jesuits would also increase the belligerence of the Calvinist theologians at the University of Heidelberg. Marquard hinted darkly that this could mean "unneighborly behavior" against the bishopric by the Electoral Palatinate and the possible breakdown of the religious peace in the region. Ultimately, Marquard recommended that

80. St.A.Sp. 1A/408/1, pp. 1v, 2r.
81. See below, Chapter 2, for a more complete discussion of the founding, financing, and activities of the Jesuit college.
82. LASp. D2/905, pp. 20r–22r.
83. Ibid., pp. 22v, 23r.

the chapter wait until after the next meeting of the Reichstag, where all such issues should be discussed.[84]

Although Marquard could not, in the end, prevent the Cathedral Chapter from installing the Jesuits in Speyer, his dislike of them places him firmly in the mainstream of "traditional" German Catholics in the sixteenth century. A great part of this distaste was probably temperamental, cultural, and personal. The Jesuits were outsiders, with little respect for local traditions or local elites. They were also well educated and faultless in their personal morality and consequently a constant affront to traditionalist clergymen. Yet Marquard's objections, at least as he expressed them to the Cathedral Chapter, were mostly political. Fearing for the safety of his small ecclesiastical principality, Marquard consistently opposed religious reforms that threatened political conflicts with neighboring Protestant powers.

The Collegiate Chapters

Men like Bishop Marquard continued to dominate the Catholic Church in the Bishopric of Speyer for much of the sixteenth century. It was only in the years after 1570 that reformers gained the upper hand, and with the election of Eberhard von Dienheim in 1581 they took over the most powerful office in the bishopric. This victory did not mean that the more conservative elements in the local Church lost all influence. Many tradition-minded members of the regional nobility continued to seek ecclesiastical careers in Speyer, especially in the collegiate chapters, which remained basically unaffected by the Counter-Reformation and functioned as institutional bases for the traditionalists.

Although at times reformers could gain control of some chapters— as they did of the Cathedral Chapter in the late sixteenth century— in general Tridentine reform was perceived as a threat by the chapter canons. Episcopal centralization ordered by the Council of Trent jeopardized the chapters' privileges and exemptions, new disciplinary measures attacked the aristocratic lifestyle of the canons, and the Tridentine emphasis on the pastoral role of the clergy challenged the central role of the chapters.[85]

84. Ibid., pp. 23r, 23v.
85. The Council of Trent did reaffirm the role of cathedral chapters in electing bishops, but this only confirmed the status quo in German bishoprics.

In addition to the Cathedral Chapter, there were three collegiate chapters in the city of Speyer, St. German, St. Guido, and Allerheiligen, with together over a hundred benefices. Even more aristocratic and privileged than these were the two large rural chapters, the *Ritterstift* in Bruchsal and the chapter in Weißenburg. Two smaller chapters, in Sinsheim and Landau, declined to insignificance in the sixteenth century, mostly because of pressure from the Protestant powers. The monasteries no longer had a significant role in the bishopric. Protestant princes had secularized most of them in the middle of the century, although those in the city of Speyer survived (reduced in size and influence).

The Cathedral Chapter, with its extensive powers and considerable wealth, was by far the most important ecclesiastical institution in the bishopric. Many of the canons held benefices in other Cathedral Chapters, and as a result it was less local in character than the smaller chapters. New trends within Catholicism often reached the Bishopric of Speyer through the cathedral canons. In this way, a strong reformist party developed within the chapter in the 1560s.[86]

All the chapters were organized on the pattern of the Cathedral Chapter. The Cathedral Chapter in Speyer had fifteen canons, five of whom held "dignities." The most prestigious of these offices was that of provost (*probst, praepositus*). In the sixteenth century this office was almost always held by an absentee canon. The day-to-day leader of the chapter was the dean. The other dignities were cantor, custos, and scholaster. Below the canons were a group of thirteen *domicellarii* (young canons in training). To become a canon one had to prove at least four quarterings of nobility, a requirement that, during the sixteenth century, was gradually stiffened to eight quarterings.[87] A large group of vicars did most of the work of the chapter, performed the required services in the Cathedral, and managed the chapter's property. In the fifteenth century over one hundred clerics were attached to the Cathedral in Speyer. The other chapters were smaller. St. German, for example, had fourteen canons and twenty-four vicars. In the mid-sixteenth century many benefices in the smaller chapters were left vacant, allowing the remaining canons to collect larger incomes. In 1573 only four canons out of twelve were in residence at St. Guido.[88]

86. Stamer III/1, pp. 26–30.
87. Peter Hersche, *Die deutschen Domkapitel im 17. und 18. Jahrhundert*, 3 vols. (Bern: Selbstverlag, 1984), vol. 1, p. 165. Each quartering represents one greatgrandparent. The chapters wanted canons with noble grandparents.
88. Stamer II, p. 55, Stamer III/1, p. 37.

As a group the chapters dominated Catholic religious life in the city of Speyer as well as in the town of Bruchsal and also exercised considerable influence in the countryside. In the late Middle Ages, the bishopric had been divided into four archdeaconates, with the provosts of the four chapters in Speyer serving as archdeacons. The archdeacons had power to discipline the rural clergy and adjudicate marriage disputes. These powers declined when the Protestant Reformation fragmented Church organization, but the provost of the Cathedral Chapter nonetheless continued to claim authority parallel to that of the vicar general in the villages on the left bank of the Rhine.[89] The chapters were most important as patrons of rural parishes. Of the approximately eighty-five Catholic parishes in the bishopric (not including Baden-Baden), the Cathedral Chapter had patronage of thirty-one, and the other five chapters twenty.[90] The patronage system enabled the chapters to wield substantial influence over religious life in the villages, but this power was of secondary interest compared with the income derived from it.

The chapters all claimed extensive privileges, which in the city of Speyer included tax and legal exemptions. The chapters bypassed the bishop to negotiate directly with the city Council to specify these rights. The canons of the Cathedral Chapter were, of course, exempt from episcopal discipline, and appear to have been empowered to discipline the canons of the three other urban chapters (the *Nebenstifter*) as well. The Cathedral Chapter had built up formidable powers over the bishop in the preceding centuries. The clearest formulation of these powers, rights, and privileges can be found in the list of concessions known as the capitulations (*Wahlkapitulationen*) that the Cathedral Chapter made each bishop sign at the time of his election. In 1581, for example, Bishop Eberhard agreed to seek the consent of the chapter for any new taxes, pledged not to appoint an ecclesiastical judge without the chapter's consent, promised not to interfere with the internal affairs of the chapter, and agreed to consult the canons on all important decisions.[91] The Cathedral Chapter also maintained significant control of the purse strings of the

---

89. Ibid., pp. 38.
90. The power of patronage was even more fragmented than this. Although the Cathedral Chapter held the patronage of thirty-one parishes, only twenty-three were held by the chapter as a whole. The provost had patronage of three parishes, the cantor three, the custos one, and the Gregorian Vicars one. The patronage of the chapters was divided as follows: Weißenburg, seven parishes; St. German, seven parishes; *Ritterstift* Bruchsal, four parishes; St. Guido and Allerheiligen, one parish each.
91. Karl Kloe, *Die Wahlkapitulation der Bischöfe zu Speyer, 1272–1802* (Speyer: Verlag der Jaegerischen Buchhandlung, 1928), 74–91.

bishop.[92] Because of this influence and power all the chapters had a large stake in maintaining the status quo. For this reason, they felt little enthusiasm for the decrees of the Council of Trent, especially since—at least theoretically—it gave considerable new powers to the bishop.

The Ritterstift ("Knightly" Chapter) in Bruchsal was the most traditional and aristocratic of the chapters of the Bishopric of Speyer and exemplifies how these institutions operated. The Ritterstift was in many ways typical of the German Imperial Church (Reichskirche), but in the context of Tridentine Catholicism its canons were strikingly secular, neglectful of their religious duties, and traditional in their religiousity.

The chapter was originally a Benedictine abbey in the village of Odenheim in the Kraichgau. In 1494, probably in recognition of its long-standing tradition as a home for younger sons of the nobility, the monastery was transformed into a secular and aristocratic collegiate chapter. In 1507 the bishop allowed the chapter to move to Bruchsal, ostensibly for better protection in time of war, but probably also to allow the canons to enjoy the more varied life in town. Only two of the seventeen canons and vicars could be commoners; the others were all from families of free imperial knights of the region. The canons were required to participate in regular services, but the clerical nature of the chapter was limited. Even in the eighteenth century only the dean had to be an ordained priest.[93]

The canons of the Ritterstift considered their chapter an independent institution, and recognized only the authority of the emperor and the pope. As a result, the canons claimed exemption from episcopal authority, by virtue of the chapter's twelfth-century monastic origins and papal confirmation of its privileges. The canons resisted attempts by the bishops to interfere in the internal affairs of the chapter into the eighteenth century. Although by the late sixteenth century the bishop was the secular protector of the chapter (and the five villages under its lordship), the provost claimed the status of prince of the Empire and all the rights of low justice in the chapter's villages. The bishops never recognized all the privileges claimed by the chapter, but they always faced obstruction and resistance when

92. Duggan. See especially the introduction and conclusion.
93. Leopold Feigenbutz, *Kurzer Abriß der Geschichte von Odenheim und seiner Benediktinerabtei, dem nachmaligen Ritterstifte Odenheim im Kraichgau* (Bühl: Konkordia, 1886), 17: "die Abtei Odenheim in ein weltliches adeliges Chorherrenstift mit 5 Würdenträgern und 12 Kanoniker und Vikaren umgewandelt"; GLAK 65/11604 ("Ausfürlicher Bericht von dem Ritter-Stifft Bruchsal") [eighteenth century], p. 37r.

dealing with the canons or any of the clergy affiliated with the Ritterstift.[94]

The behavior of the Ritterstift canons was no different from that of other men of their background and class. Like typical noblemen, they demonstrated a total lack of interest in religious services, by neglecting their duties and the ornaments and relics of their church. In 1549 an episcopal visitation of the chapter found extensive abuses of office. "Most of the canons very rarely visit the choir, even fewer complete their canonical hours."[95] Few of them received communion regularly, and they violated the rules of residence with impunity. The decrees of the bishop's synods were neither read nor publicized in the chapter. Moreover, in violation of recent Church and imperial reforms, none of the canons had taken orders.

Even as religious, they maintained their aristocratic lifestyle. Several had concubines. They regularly appeared in town in lay clothing, sporting hats with feathers and carrying swords. They went hunting frequently, even on days it was forbidden, and were involved in military training without permission. Perhaps most serious, the canons treated the chapter's property as if they owned it and managed its finances for their personal benefit. At the Ritterstift, unlike at other chapters, the canons did not receive a fixed sum of money. Instead, they pooled all the income of the chapter (both money and kind) and then divided it among all the benefice holders. As a result, profits benefited not the chapter itself, but the individual canons. Because there was no money in reserve for chapter expenses, the chapter church and some of the residences were in terrible disrepair.[96] The individual canons, as temporary residents, had little incentive to maintain their houses or the church. There is no evidence that these conditions had changed significantly by the later sixteenth century.[97]

The Ritterstift had secular jurisdiction over five villages in the Kraichgau. The chapter possessed considerable property and various rights in these villages, including the patronage of three parishes. In the sixteenth century, the canons neglected conditions in the rural parishes. In 1557 the priest in the village of Odenheim complained that his income was very small and begged to be allowed to collect

---

94. GLAK 65/11604 ("Ausführlicher Bericht"), esp. pp. 30r–36r. In 1591, for example, the canons harassed the parish priest in Bruchsal for attempting to perform services according to new regulations published by Bishop Eberhard. The canons wanted services in the chapter church performed in the traditional way (GLAK 133/461).

95. GLAK 61/5341, p. 94r.

96. Ibid., pp. 94r–102v.

97. The canons also lived well, especially compared to the secular clergy of the bishopric. See the wills of canons and vicars of the *Ritterstift* (GLAK 94/33).

two small rents that were owed to the chapter. A year later, two representatives of the village appealed to the vicar general for a new priest. The parish had been vacant for quite a while, and the Ritterstift had neglected to name a new pfarrer. It was the opinion of both the villagers and the vicar general that the chapter had intentionally delayed the appointment so it could continue to collect the parish income without paying a priest. The vicar general, in an attempt to force the chapter to act, threatened a lawsuit.[98]

The Ritterstift also failed to resist the attempts by the Electoral Palatinate to install Protestant pastors in several of their villages. The elector held the patronage of the parish church in the chapter's village of Rohrbach, and in 1574 Palatine officials appointed a Protestant pastor. The chapter's response revealed an understanding of confessional politics very similar to that of Bishop Marquard. The dean of the chapter, Georg von Coppenstein, went in person to Rohrbach and made a short speech to the villagers, hoping to persuade them to boycott the Protestant services. He reminded the villagers how the Calvinists had come in and torn down the altar, ripped up the holy pictures, and knocked down the baptismal font. "We want you . . . to consider how dangerous and damaging it could be, in matters concerning the salvation of your souls, to agree to, or accept personally, quick and unfounded changes. Instead, [it would be] safer and surer to stay firmly within the old Catholic Church and its teachings, which your praiseworthy forefathers handed down to you and us."[99] This is clearly a traditionalist argument. Von Coppenstein hoped to keep the villagers loyal to the Church, not by convincing them of the superiority of Catholic doctrine or practices, but purely with an appeal to tradition. The effort seems to have failed and no Catholic services were held in Rohrbach for the next thirty years.[100]

The smaller collegiate chapters in Speyer (the nebenstifter) also neglected their duties in the countryside. Often slow to exercise their patronage rights, the chapters were frequently accused of grossly underpaying the parish priests. The Chapter of St. German seems to have been especially negligent. We have seen above how, in 1565, the village of Kirrlach complained about the insufficient income of their priest and, with the support of the bishop, forced the chapter to give him a raise. In Rheinsheim, the chapter habitually neglected to appoint a sacristan. In 1614, in response to complaints from the vil-

98. GLAK 229/79230/I (Odenheim), pp. 5r, 7r.
99. GLAK 42/no.4736.
100. See Chapter 5 on Protestantism in the *Ritterstift*'s villages.

lagers, an episcopal commission took the sole right of appointment away from the chapter and allowed the gemeinde to recommend a sacristan to the chapter for approval.[101] In all cases the chapters were most interested in safeguarding their economic rights in the villages. It was usually in the financial interest of the chapters to defer the appointment of a priest, the repair of a church or parsonage, and the purchase of ornaments and liturgical texts. This sort of neglect continued to cause complaints from the villagers into the eighteenth century.

Conditions inside the chapters in Speyer and Weißenburg were similar to those in Bruchsal. Concubinage was widespread, and canons and vicars disregarded their religious duties. Even the conservative mid-sixteenth-century bishops expressed concern about this situation. There were episcopal visitations of the Allerheiligen and the St. Guido chapters in 1555 and 1573. The visitations found the usual conditions: several benefices permanently vacant, no income set aside for repairs and upkeep of facilities, none of the canons ordained, and few masses said. The visitor in Allerheiligen in 1573 commented that the canons had found the money to hire someone to collect the wine tithe but not the money to pay a priest to say the required masses in their church. The dean of St. Guido was known to drink to excess and brawl in the city.[102] The visitors' admonitions had apparently little effect, at least before the 1580s.[103]

The lower collegiate clergy was more frequently guilty of basic abuses than the aristocratic canons. During the episcopate of Bishop Marquard (1560–81) forty-one vicars from the four chapters in Speyer were imprisoned for concubinage, brawling, and drunkenness. The episcopal authorities did not consider these serious crimes. Only five of these men were made to resign their benefices. Their crimes show that these clergymen mingled with the rest of the population and socialized in the same way everyone else did, and just like any other resident of Speyer, when they got out of hand they were punished. Such was the case, for example, of Nicolaus Schultheiss, a vicar at St. German. At Carnival (*Fastnacht*) in 1581, Schultheiss became drunk, vandalized some property, and made unseemly comments to a burgher's wife. Later the same year he went to a wedding and after once

101. GLAK 229/86586 (Rheinsheim).
102. GLAK 78/1552; Stamer III/1, p. 37.
103. Bishop Marquard promulgated new ordinances for several chapters in the 1570s, but had little success in improving conditions in the chapters. Also see Stamer III/1 pp. 37–38; concerning Allerheilgen, see GLAK 78/1552; concerning St. Guido, see GLAK 78/1773 and GLAK 78/1814; concerning Weißenburg, see GLAK 67/425, pp. 1751–1771, and ADBR 12 J 1656, esp. p. 130b; concerning Landau, see GLAK 67/425, pp. 111–1141.

again drinking too much, was seen dancing. This pattern of behavior earned him a reprimand from the vicar general and a couple of nights in prison.[104] In the 1580s, concubinage was as widespread among the lower urban clergy as it was among the rural priests.

The chapters, with the exception of the Cathedral Chapter, were as unenthusiastic about reform as Bishop Marquard. Like Marquard they had no interest in bringing the Jesuits into Speyer. In 1566 the Cathedral Chapter put forward an ambitious plan for financing the Jesuit College. The plan called for contributions from all the chapters, including those in Bruchsal and Weißenburg. The canons of the other chapters stalled for several years before rejecting the plan altogether in 1568, excusing themselves by claiming that they had heavy debts and taxes to pay including a new levy for the Turkish wars. Although they left open the possibility of contributing to the Jesuits later, it never happened.[105]

The monasteries were also strongholds of traditional Catholicism, but unlike the chapters, they exercised little influence. Of the eleven large rural monasteries of the late Middle Ages, only one, the Convent of Frauenalb, survived the Reformation. In the city of Speyer, the Franciscan, Dominican, and Carmelite monasteries continued to function, as did four convents. Few monks and nuns, however, lived in the urban monasteries after the Reformation, and they contributed little to Church reform in Speyer.[106] The regular clergy had been an important part of urban religious life in the late Middle Ages, but after the Reformation their monasteries and convents were only shadowy institutions of little importance.

The firm hold of traditionalist churchmen on the institutions of the Catholic Church in the Bishopric of Speyer weakened in the 1560s. The Cathedral Chapter took the lead in encouraging reform within the Church. Even at mid-century the Cathedral Chapter in Speyer was exceptional in the Empire for having remained completely Catholic and became one of the few Cathedral Chapters to push for reform.[107] It should be remembered, however, that this

104. GLAK 67/423, pp. 124v–126r.
105. For the plan, probably by the dean of the Cathedral Chapter, Andreas von Oberstein, see LASp. D2/905, p. 6r, and GLAK 61/10941, p. 92. For the reaction of the chapters see GLAK 61/10941, pp. 101, 825.
106. Alter, "Von der konradinischen Rachtung bis zum letzten Reichstag in Speyer"; Norbert Ohler "Alltag in einer Zeit des Friedens (1570–1620)," in Geschichte der Stadt Speyer, pp. 555, 635. The Franciscan monastery was put under the bishop's jurisdiction in the 1570s (GLAK 61/10942, pp. 379–80; LASp. D25/287; Remling UB, pp. 636–43).
107. The cathedral chapter in Breslau also pushed for reforms against the opposition of the bishops (Joachim Köhler, Das Ringen um die tridentinische Erneuerung im Bistum

group within the Cathedral Chapter was really only interested in limited reform. For these men reform meant a renewal and strengthening of Catholicism but not a major overhaul of Church organization. They clearly understood that the preservation of the political and religious status quo in the middle Rhine valley and of their influential position within that status quo would only be possible if the Church were to accept internal reform. To this end they brought the Society of Jesus to Speyer. Yet these same reformers were subsequently quite disturbed by the intense religiosity of the Jesuits, their enthusiasm for confessional conflict, and their techniques of popular religious instruction.

When the Tridentine Church came to the Bishopric of Speyer in the last forty years of the sixteenth century, the pre-Tridentine Church did not disappear. Younger sons of the nobility continued to pursue careers in the Church and the "traditionalist" institutions maintained much of their power, privileges, and influence.[108] Reforming churchmen were forced to deal with these conditions at every turn. The Catholic Church that emerged in the Bishopric of Speyer in the early eighteenth century reflected the traditions of the pre-Tridentine Church, both at the village level and in the Church hierarchy. Furthermore, the Counter-Reformation was clearly not a policy of a unified clerical "elite." The reformers had to compromise with a skeptical elite as well as with a reluctant population.

Breslau, *Vom Abschluß des Konzils bis zur Schlacht am Weißen Berg* [Cologne: Böhlau Verlag, 1973], esp. pp. 37–38).

108. Louis Châtellier emphasizes that authority was never really exercised at the level of the diocese in Strasbourg; this was true in Speyer too (*Tradition chrétienne et renouveau catholique*, pp. 53–54).

2

The Reform of the Clergy

The most consistent goal of Catholic reformers in the Bishopric of Speyer was to improve the performance and behavior of the clergy. With this aim in mind, they instituted a variety of reforms beginning in the 1560s. To raise the educational level of the clergy, the reformers moved to found an episcopal seminary to train priests and brought the Jesuits to Speyer to provide teachers for both the seminary and a Catholic secondary school. To tighten clerical discipline, they attempted to enforce clerical celibacy, eliminate absenteeism, and compel the rural clergy to attend to their pastoral duties more carefully. Reformers also tried to force the chapter clergy to perform their duties in the Cathedral and the chapter churches more diligently, and sought to improve the financial condition of the parishes and chapters.

This clerical reform constituted the first phase of the Tridentine program and was an aspect of the Counter-Reformation carried out more or less uniformly across Catholic Europe.[1] German churchmen, however, did not view the reform of the clergy as a major new development but rather as a response to the Protestant critique of the clergy and a culmination of reform measures dating back to the fifteenth century.[2] As Hsia has pointed out, Catholic reform of the

1. Molitor, *Kirchliche Reformversuche*, esp. part 3, chaps. 4 and 5; Köhler, *Das Ringen um die tridentinische Erneuerung im Bistum Breslau*, esp. pp. 9–14.
2. Reinhard, "Gegenreformation als Modernisierung," pp. 226–31. Many historians of the Counter-Reformation insist on the continuity between pre-Reformation and Tridentine

clergy was often "reactive."[3] This was the case in the Bishopric of Speyer, where local Catholics considered reform a conservative strategy.

In the view of most churchmen in Speyer, the suppression of clerical abuses was essential if popular dissatisfaction with the clergy was to end. An improved clergy, a population happy with the services provided by the Church, and a reorganized bishopric could better resist the political pressure from Protestant states and allow Catholicism to survive in the region. These men envisaged a moral regeneration of the local Church without organizational or institutional changes.

Despite this limited program, the reformers achieved many of their goals. By the 1620s most of the rural priests had met the minimum standards set by the Council of Trent. They were celibate, somewhat educated, resided in their parishes, and performed their pastoral duties diligently. For a variety of reasons, however, this was not as dramatic a transformation of the parish clergy as some have argued.[4] As we have seen, parish priests had generally fulfilled their pastoral duties in the pre-Tridentine era as they did after reform. Furthermore, support for extensive reform within the Church hierarchy remained lukewarm, and much of its success depended on the efforts of a few dedicated individuals supported by outside forces such as the papacy and the Jesuits. Few of the institutions necessary for more extensive reform were in place before the Thirty Years' War. There was, for example, no episcopal seminary, no ecclesiastical council (*geistlicher Rat*), and no regular system of inspecting the rural clergy.[5] The impact of clerical reform has to be seen, as all of the Counter-Reformation, in the context of a limited program and a lack of local support.

Perhaps most significant, however, was the shift in the social position of the parish priest. Here too the change was not sudden or dramatic. The peasant-priest of the mid-sixteenth century only slowly evolved into the educated professional of the eighteenth century. By 1620 almost all the priests were celibate, an important symbolic characteristic, but many were still farmers, and some were

---

reforms. For Speyer see the efforts of Bishop Philipp von Flersheim (1529–52) to reform the Church and reorganize the bishopric in Press, "Das Hochstift Speyer," pp. 260–61; Duggan, pp. 156–57.

3. Hsia, *Social Discipline in the Reformation* p. 39.

4. Hubert Jedin has called this a "Copernican revolution in favor of pastoral duties" (quoted in Albrecht, "Gegenreformation und katholische Reform," p. 717). See also Köhler, *Das Ringen um die tridentinische Erneuerung im Bistum Breslau*, esp. pp. 9–14.

5. Bavaria, for example, had all these institutions by the early seventeenth century. See Albrecht "Gegenreformation und katholische Reform," pp. 717–18, 726–30.

only poorly educated. The slow pace of change allowed for the gradual adjustment of priest-parishioner relations in the villages, an adjustment that was not without conflicts but did not cause a major disruption of local religious life.

The Early Reformers (1560–1582)

The decades after 1560 were a transition period for German Catholicism. As Heinz Schilling has pointed out, "On the one hand, the theology, Church politics, and especially the mentality of the clergy remained strongly traditional and pre-Tridentine in structure and form, while on the other hand the reforming impulse of the Tridentine system was gaining ground step by step."[6] As we have seen, pre-Tridentine mentalities and ecclesiastical structures were especially strong in the Bishopric of Speyer. Beginning in the 1560s, however, a group of canons and Church officials began to promote and institute a series of Church reforms.

Their achievements and failures tell us much about the nature of the Counter-Reformation in Speyer. Catholic reform before the 1580s was haphazard and limited. Faced with a lack of enthusiasm for Tridentine measures within the local Church, these reformers turned to outside support for help. Local resistance and external intervention would remain permanent features of the Counter-Reformation in this part of Germany.

Most of the reformers in Speyer were in the Cathedral Chapter. The undisputed leader of this group was Andreas von Oberstein, canon from 1556 and dean from 1568 to 1603. Oberstein had international connections and had spent time in Rome. In 1577 the papal nuncio, who had just visited Speyer, praised Oberstein highly. As dean, Oberstein led the fight to bring the Jesuits to Speyer, and they recognized him as their special protector.[7]

Other reformers in the Cathedral Chapter included the von Dienheim brothers, Eberhard and Hans Heinrich. Eberhard, who was to be elected bishop in 1581, actively supported Oberstein in the 1570s. Hans Heinrich was a canon in Mainz as well as Speyer.[8] Some of the lower cathedral clergy also backed reforms, including Heinrich Fabritius, who came to Speyer as a preacher, possibly on the recommendation of the leading German Jesuit, Peter Canisius.[9] Of great

6. Schilling, "Die Konfessionalisierung im Reich," p. 16.
7. Stamer III/1, pp. 29–30.
8. Remling II, pp. 298–99.
9. Stamer III/1, p. 31.

importance to the reform was Beatus Moses, sexprebendary and vicar general from 1571 to 1602. We know little about Moses' background except that he was a lawyer.

Oberstein's successor as dean of the Cathedral Chapter, Adolf Wolff von Metternich, was a classic example of the reforming cleric. Metternich had studied in Rome at the Collegium Germanicum and had committed himself to an ecclesiastical career when he joined the chapter in 1585. Metternich maintained very close ties to the Jesuits. He frequently expressed the wish to join the order, and his brother, Wilhelm, was for years the rector of the Jesuit College in Speyer. Metternich had a close relationship with the Wittelsbach dukes of Bavaria, the leading Catholic princes of the Empire. In the 1590s he served as tutor to two sons of Duke Wilhelm and did much diplomatic work for the Bavarians. Metternich's strict enforcement of discipline in the Cathedral Chapter caused conflict between the reformers and the "canons of the old style" in the early seventeenth century.[10]

Oberstein, Metternich, and their supporters were all well-educated men with contacts throughout the rest of Catholic Germany. Most significant, they all had long-standing connections with the Jesuits. These men were the first products of the Jesuit program to create a new clerical cadre. Louis Châtellier has emphasized the role of Jesuit congregations in building a Catholic elite, and the reformers in Speyer probably had ties to these groups in Mainz, Cologne, and Rome, even before the Jesuits came to Speyer.[11]

Pressure from both the papacy and from elsewhere in Catholic Germany provided vital support for the reformers. Peter Canisius, the leading German Jesuit, passed through Speyer in 1565–66, as did the papal nuncio in 1576.[12] These men exhorted the reluctant Bishop Marquard to institute reforms. The emperor backed their effort with several letters urging Marquard to conduct a visitation and encouraging him to reform local monasteries.[13] The bishop of Augsburg wrote to Speyer in support of reform, explaining that he himself was in the middle of an "ongoing reform" and had removed many priests with concubines from their parishes. He suggested that the Speyer officials be on the lookout for these renegade priests.[14] These sporadic

10. Ibid., pp. 132–35.
11. Châtellier, *Europe of the Devout*, esp. chap. 5.
12. Stamer III/1, pp. 18, 59.
13. GLAK 78/703; Remling *UB*, pp. 636–43.
14. GLAK 61/11494b, p. 11v; Georg Schreiber, "Tridentinische Reformdekrete in Deutschen Bistümern," in Remigius Bäumer, ed., *Concilium Tridentinum* (Darmstadt: Wissenschaftliche Buchgesellschaft, 1979). Other bishops shared Marquard's reluctance to

contacts with the rest of the Church helped reduce the isolation of the Bishopric of Speyer and weakened Marquard's policy of passive resistance to the mandates of the Council of Trent.

Before challenging the bishop, however, the reformers began an internal reform of the Cathedral Chapter itself. The dean of the chapter opened each general meeting by admonishing both the canons and the lower cathedral clergy to attend services diligently and to behave with proper decorum both in and outside the cathedral. Such exhortations were routine in the 1560s and 1570s, so that it is hard to determine whether the behavior of the urban clergy improved.[15] Disciplinary problems among the lower urban clergy certainly continued through the period.

The Cathedral Chapter moved more quickly than Bishop Marquard to put the decrees of the Council of Trent into effect in its areas of jurisdiction. In 1567 the canons wrote a *Confessio Fidei* (Confession of Faith) and required each new canon to swear to it. As Stamer points out, "Since all three authors belonged to the [group of] zealous reformers, one can assume that the oath closely followed [the precepts of] Trent." Bishop Marquard insisted that the content of the confession be kept secret. He probably hoped to avoid offending the bishopric's Protestant neighbors by publicizing the strongly worded oath.[16] In 1572 the canons ordered a second important reform of the Cathedral Chapter: nonresident canons were no longer allowed to collect the lucrative *Oblegiengelder* (money that came from the general income of the chapter and was not part of the individual canons' incomes). This measure, designed to enforce the residence of the canons, was a direct response to the requirements of the Council of Trent.[17]

The canons of the Cathedral Chapter did not feel that their role in the bishopric was limited to the internal workings of the cathedral and its clergy. The canons also intended to participate in the government of the bishopric, as they had throughout the Middle Ages. In the 1560s and 1570s, a major goal of the chapter was to have the rural parishes visited. Since the Council of Trent had given the power to order a visitation exclusively to the bishop, the canons could do no more than bombard Bishop Marquard with demands to direct a visitation.

---

begin reforms. The archbishop of Mainz, for example, never held a provincial synod, although even Marquard expected one (GLAK 61/11494, p. 135r).

15. GLAK 61/10943, pp. 3, 60–61, 101; GLAK 61/10945, pp. 61–62, 119–20, 163. There are many more examples of exhortations to the clergy besides these cited.

16. Stamer III/1, p. 60; GLAK 61/10941, pp. 772–73.

17. Stamer III/1, p. 60.

Marquard's interest in the rural parishes, like his interest in Church reform in general, was very limited. He was concerned with the financial problems of the clergy to the exclusion, apparently, of issues of clerical discipline, clerical education, and even loyalty of the rural clergy to the Catholic Church. Marquard appears to have found any reform of the rural clergy unnecessary, impractical, and politically inexpedient and issued few ordinances relating to them. On one rare occasion, in 1564, he ordered the priests in two districts of the bishopric to hold services each Sunday and holiday and required them to choose two members of the parish to record attendance and inform the civil authorities so that fines could be assessed against absentees.[18] It is interesting that this ordinance focused on the behavior of the villagers rather than the priests. Like most princes of his day, Marquard assumed that a forceful application of princely authority would improve the religious behavior of his subjects.

The reform-minded canons, by contrast, argued that the clergy, not the laity, was the problem. "The pfarrer in the countryside . . . are very disorderly and are a bad example to the common man and could lead him easily to apostasy. In addition, some [priests] are suspected of [being members of] the new sects, [some] order singing of psalms and give communion [as Protestants did] in both kinds, and otherwise behave generally badly."[19] Their solution was an episcopal visitation, which would give the bishop and his officials a more accurate picture of what the canons assumed was a terrible situation in the countryside.

The different viewpoints of Marquard and the Cathedral Chapter are made clear in an exchange from 1568. The bishop reported to the chapter that the incomes of the priests had declined and as a result the priests could not do their duties. The canons agreed and reminded Marquard that they had already suggested a visitation as a way of dealing with the problems in the countryside. They also pointed out that according to the decrees of the Council of Trent, it was no longer the duty of the archdeacons (that is, the deans of the four chapters in Speyer) to conduct a visitation, but rather the bishop's responsibility to order (and presumably finance) one. On this occasion Marquard asked the Cathedral Chapter to check its records to see how previous visitations had been organized. The chapter's officials found no records of previous visitations, and the canons insisted that their rights would not be violated if the bishop visited

18. GLAK 61/11494, p. 86v.
19. GLAK 61/10941, p. 438.

his diocese.[20] Was Marquard really afraid that a visitation would violate the traditional rights of the archdeacons? More likely he was stalling, hoping to avoid political problems with the Palatinate. If the archdeacons handled a visitation, Marquard would be shielded from the wrath of the neighboring princes.

In the end, no visitation took place during the Marquard's episcopate, and in 1570 the Cathedral Chapter complained again that incompetent priests had led the rural population astray. The canons continued to insist that this problem could be solved by a visitation and by the establishment of a seminary for the training of young priests.[21] Following the lead of the Council of Trent, the reformers in the Cathedral Chapter felt confident that a well-educated clergy would be able to mold the rural population into good Catholics. For this reason, the Catholic reform in Speyer emphasized the reform of the clergy and played down the reform of popular religion.

Second only to the visitation in importance for the development of an educated and reform-minded parish clergy was the seminary. The Council of Trent required that each bishopric found a seminary (or similar institution) for the training of priests. Here again, the Cathedral Chapter was forced to take the initiative. In 1561 the chapter reorganized the *Alumnat*, the cathedral school, to improve discipline among the students and to establish a more rigorous program of study.[22] In the 1560s the Cathedral Chapter hired new teachers (including several Jesuits) for the Alumnat and converted the cathedral school from a place to educate young cathedral clergy to a training school for parish priests,[23] The chapter even gave stipends to the students. Between about 1570 and 1636 the Alumnat provided the canons with a small but constant number of educated priests for the rural parishes in their patronage.

Yet the Alumnat never became a full-fledged seminary. In 1572 Bishop Marquard sent his chancellor to the Cathedral Chapter to discuss financing a seminary. The chapter was enthusiastic and proposed that all the various chapters in the bishopric should contribute to its support.[24] The bishop, however, favored using any new re-

---

20. GLAK 61/10942, pp. 36–37.
21. Ibid., p. 399.
22. Franz Mone, "Schulwesen vom 13. bis 16. Jahrhundert," *Zeitschrift für Geschichte des Oberrheins* 1 (1850): 281–96.
23. Ludwig Stamer, "Die ersten tridentinischen Priesterseminare des Bistums Speyer im 16. und 17. Jahrhundert," in *St.German in Stadt und Bistum Speyer* (Speyer: Verlag des Priesterseminars, 1957), 106; Ammerich, "Formen und Wege der katholischen Reform," pp. 303.
24. GLAK 61/10942, pp. 787–88.

sources to send promising students to universities outside the bishopric, which had been a traditional way of educating the upper clergy.
The Cathedral Chapter held a completely different view on the education of priests.

> It is not necessary to place highly educated people in all the parishes.
> Instead, if the young [priests] are brought up piously here [in Speyer]
> and receive a reasonable foundation in the humanities, law, grammar,
> dialectic, and rhetoric, and learn the rudiments of theology, especially
> the catechism, they will know how to give fine sermons and will be
> very useful in the parishes.[25]

Their statement reflects the Tridentine emphasis on the pastoral
duties of the priest. The canons admitted that a few university-
educated priests could be used for the "highest parishes" in the city of
Speyer, in Udenheim, and in the towns of Bruchsal and Deidesheim.
Otherwise, the bishopric needed a large number of priests with a
basic education. In any case, they added, university graduates would
probably refuse to serve in most villages.

The canons were understandably skeptical of Marquard's interest
in a seminary. Although it would be possible to start a seminary with
the funds of the Alumnat, augmented by the incomes of several
vicariates and chapels, the chapter doubted that either the bishop or
any of the other chapters would participate. In the end, the canons
realized that the Cathedral Chapter would have to train its own
priests.[26] Unfortunately the Alumnat had limited resources, and its
students were chronically short of money. In 1580 the canons considered reducing the number of students from twelve to six.[27] There
were also disciplinary problems in the Alumnat. In 1582 several of
the students (*Bursanten*) were punished for spending an evening
drinking in one of the villages outside Speyer. They compounded
their breach of discipline by verbally abusing their teacher when they
returned. The bishop's officials imprisoned the young men for several
days, prompting the Cathedral Chapter to protest that the bishop had
no authority over the students of the cathedral school. The canons
were not willing to concede any of their privileges, even in the cause
of Church reform. Because of the disciplinary problems in the Alumnat, the canons took another look at living conditions there. In their
opinion the students enjoyed an overly comfortable situation and as a

25. Ibid., p. 792.
26. Ibid., pp. 392–93; Stamer, "Die ersten tridentinischen Priesterseminare," p. 106.
27. GLAK 61/10945, pp. 674–75.

result had become "willful." The canons appointed the Jesuits to manage the Alumnat and ordered them to enforce rules with severity.[28]

The Cathedral Chapter was able to promote certain reform measures during Marquard's episcopate, but a full-fledged Tridentine reform was possible only with the financial and political support of the bishop, which Marquard was generally unwilling to provide. He did not, however, openly oppose the reformers. Although a pre-Tridentine bishop in his personal life, Marquard realized that the reformers shared his goal of preserving the political independence of the bishopric. Indeed, he went as far as to appoint Beatus Moses, the lawyer and reform-minded member of the cathedral clergy, vicar general in 1571. In the 1570s Moses worked with the reformers in the Cathedral Chapter to set the goals and emphasis of the reform program that would gain momentum after the election of Eberhard von Dienheim as bishop in December 1581. The reform would focus on placing a Tridentine clergy in the countryside. But the reformers' most impressive achievement was the establishment, against great resistance, of a Jesuit college in the city of Speyer itself.

The Jesuits

The history of the Jesuits in Speyer is a microcosm of the problems and possibilities that faced Catholic reformers in this part of Germany. Founded to improve Catholic ministry and education, the Society of Jesus was the great reforming order of the sixteenth century. Surrounded by Protestants, the Bishopric of Speyer was a perfect setting for the Jesuits, and the founding of a Jesuit residence and college in Speyer in the 1560s was a great victory for the reformers in the bishopric. The Jesuits did not disappoint them. The fathers were very active, teaching, preaching, converting Protestants, performing exorcisms, and conducting missions into the countryside and to neighboring cities. Yet ultimately the Jesuits had only a limited impact in the bishopric. The problems they faced—including opposition from within the Church and from the Protestants, as well as ongoing financial difficulties—were the same as those that limited the whole Counter-Reformation in Speyer. Furthermore, the Jesuit college was an independent institution. Church reform in Speyer was for the Jesuits just part of "a universal struggle between orthodoxy

28. Ibid., pp. 579–84, 916–17, 951–52.

and heresy."[29] For this reason, they pursued their own goals (in particular the conversion of Protestants), which often contrasted with the policies of local Catholic reformers.

The Founding of the College (1566–1568)

Beginning in 1564, P. Lambert Auer, a Jesuit based in Mainz, preached regularly in Speyer. The Cathedral Chapter, and especially Andreas von Oberstein, at the time scholaster, was impressed with the quality and popularity of Auer's sermons and tried to hire him permanently as preacher in the Cathedral.[30] Here the Chapter ran into the opposition of the archbishop of Mainz, who had funded the Jesuit college in Mainz, and was unwilling to lose one of the fathers. The Jesuits themselves were not interested in holding a single benefice in Speyer and wanted to establish an independent college. Auer remained in Speyer for much of 1565 and 1566 to facilitate the difficult negotiations between the Jesuits and the Church authorities over the funding of a college and the duties that would be required of the Jesuits.[31]

Conflicts quickly broke out within the Speyer Church between the supporters and opponents of the Jesuits. The initial reason for asking the Jesuits to Speyer was to fill two vacant positions in the Cathedral, both of which involved regular preaching. Prodded by the archbishop of Mainz, who suggested that a Jesuit college would improve the quality of the clergy in the bishopric, and by the Jesuits themselves, the reformers in the Cathedral Chapter quickly hatched a variety of plans for the establishment of a large Jesuit college.[32] Andreas von Oberstein probably submitted the most ambitious of these plans. Oberstein suggested that the Jesuits take over not only the preachership and the Cathedral school but also three parishes in the city. Furthermore, they should be given the income of several vacant chaplaincies. Finally, Oberstein confidently expected the three smaller chapters in Speyer and the chapters in Bruchsal and Weißenburg to provide financial support to the Cathedral Chapter in the project.[33] Bishop Marquard was also asked to contribute three hundred gulden and considerable quantities of grain and wine.[34]

29. Hsia, *Social Discipline in the Reformation*, p. 46.
30. Duhr I, p. 115; St.A.MZ 15/402; GLAK 61/10941, pp. 38–39.
31. Duhr I, p. 115–16; GLAK 61/10941, pp. 53–55, 72, 78, 81–82.
32. GLAK 61/10941, pp. 54, 78.
33. LASp. D2/905, p. 61.
34. GLAK 61/10941, pp. 106, 107, 109, 111.

Marquard was very reluctant to help the Jesuits. Like everyone, he recognized that the Jesuits represented the most militant wing of the Catholic Church and would cause serious conflicts with the Protestants. He also worried about the financial strain the new order would put on the bishopric.[35] The bishop delayed for over a year, repeating his "hesitations" (*Bedenken*) at every chance. When the Chapter finally prevailed, Marquard refused to attach his seal to the endowment (*Fundation*) of the college.[36] While Marquard did contribute some money to the Jesuits (200 gulden a year), the smaller chapters refused to support the new order in any way.[37] The traditionalist centers of the Church could not prevent the creation of a Jesuit establishment in Speyer, but they could refuse to support it.

The reform party in the Cathedral Chapter, however, considered the Jesuits essential to a reform of the Church. They rejected Marquard's various objections to the Jesuits and questioned the actual extent of his financial problems. Furthermore, in order to implement the decrees of the Council of Trent, they were adamant that the bishopric needed good teachers and preachers. The "learned people" (*gelehrte Leute*) necessary for these activities, said the canons, were not available in Speyer. To push the bishop further, the chapter commented several times how the archbishops of Trier and Mainz and the bishops of Würzburg and Augsburg had supported the Jesuits.[38] In an implied criticism of Bishop Marquard, the canons asserted:

> Because the almighty God has now shown us this way [i.e., the establishment of a Jesuit college], through which not only the pulpit but also the schools would be served properly, the Christian religion built up, restored, and spread, [and religious] services preserved. . . . My lords [the canons] do not consider [the founding of a Jesuit college] a little thing to be passed over lightly, but instead they want to put spiritual [concerns] before temporal ones.[39]

This statement also demonstrates the importance the reformers attached to the Jesuits and the results they expected of them. Through example, teaching, and preaching, the Jesuits were to strengthen and broaden the reform impulse in the Bishopric of Speyer.

Yet the Cathedral Chapter moved cautiously: "We feel it [the Jesuit

35. LASp. D2/905.
36. GLAK 61/10941, pp. 434, 436, 465.
37. Ibid., pp. 101, 825. The Cathedral Chapter seemed surprised at the refusal of the other chapters to help support the Jesuits and suggested, rather angrily, that the chapters might not have understood the request.
38. LASp. D2/905, pp. 26r–30v, esp. pp. 27v and 28v.
39. GLAK 61/10941, p. 131.

college] is a good Christian work, which should contribute to the preservation of religion and worship, if it can be brought about without more problems for the Church."[40] The canons also suggested that the Jesuits come to Speyer one at a time, so as not to attract too much attention. They were startled and dismayed when the Jesuits arrived en masse in Speyer at Easter 1567.[41] The Jesuits also surprised the canons with their insistence on a clear understanding of the reciprocal obligations of the chapter and the college and with their consistent effort to keep their own legal commitments to a minimum. From the minutes of the Cathedral Chapter one gleans that the canons had failed to grasp the goals and the mentality of the new order.[42]

The Activities of the Jesuits

The Jesuits had their own ideas of their role in the Bishopric of Speyer. Although the reformers in Speyer wanted the Jesuits to focus their efforts on the reform of the clergy, the Jesuits, especially the German Jesuits, were more interested in converting Protestants. The leaders of the Society immediately recognized Speyer's strategic role in the conflict with the Protestants. The provincial of the Rhine Province wrote to Rome in 1568: "In my opinion we must especially support this college [in Speyer], not only because of the importance of the city, but also because of [the college's] . . . good reputation with the Protestants in and outside the city . . . [which] increases the esteem of the Society itself. If [the college] collapses, the Protestants would celebrate [the event] as a special victory."[43] One of the reasons for the establishment of the college was its position in a city "surrounded by princes of the opposing religion."[44]

This focus on confessional conflict is nowhere more obvious than in the reports sent from the college to Rome. The rector always reported in great detail the successful conversions of Protestants. In 1595, for example, the fathers converted a noble girl as well as several prisoners and an Anabaptist.[45] Often the rector proudly described the successful methods used to convert Protestants. By giving alms in

40. Ibid., p. 475. Note that the canons recognized that projects that were good for religion and religious services could harm the Church as an institution. This opinion might well have been that of the more conservative canons in the Cathedral Chapter.

41. GLAK 61/10941, pp. 492, 577–78; Duhr I, p. 116.

42. GLAK 61/10941, pp. 405–8, 473–75, 489, 492, 841–44; Duhr I, p. 117; Remling *UB*, pp. 630–31.

43. Duhr I, p. 117.

44. St.A.MZ 15/402 (1566).

45. ARSJ Rh.Inf.48, p. 42r.

the city of Speyer the Jesuits won converts among the poor, and by pointing out family tombs in the cathedral they converted a young noblewoman.[46] The Jesuits claimed a large number of conversions in Speyer, rising from fewer than ten a year in the 1570s to more than one hundred annually from 1597 to 1616.[47]

The Jesuits enjoyed their greatest success as teachers. The fathers took over the cathedral school in 1567, and by 1568 it had expanded to five classes with about two hundred students. Although the city council forbade citizens from taking in the students as boarders, the school survived and even included some Protestants.[48] Here too the Jesuits wanted above all to impress Protestants, in this case with the quality of their instruction. In addition, the students presented religious plays on holidays, especially on Corpus Christi, in front of the Jesuit church. The plays not only reinforced the faith of Catholics, but also attracted Protestants to Catholic services.[49]

The Jesuits were enthusiastic preachers and preferred to deliver sermons where they would have the opportunity to reach the Lutheran citizens of Speyer. For this reason they were happy to preach in the cathedral, where many people went out of curiosity, and only reluctantly agreed to give theological lectures to the cathedral clergy. Despite the father general's disapproval of the practice, some sermons were cast in the form of disputations with the city's Lutheran preachers, in all likelihood a contributing factor to the large audiences that Jesuit services drew.[50] There is no doubt that the Jesuits increased the quantity and quality of Catholic sermons in Speyer.

As they did everywhere in Europe, the Jesuits tried in Speyer to revive existing Catholic practices and institutions.[51] By tying Catholic belief to traditional popular practices such as processions, and labeling Protestant doctrine "new," they hoped to draw people back to the Church. In 1568 they began to encourage and participate in processions in the city which the Catholic clergy had neglected during the years after the Reformation. In an effort to stress the differences between Catholic and Protestant (especially Calvinist) doctrine, the Jesuits vigorously promoted the Corpus Christi proces-

46. Ibid., pp. 135v, 136r (1605).
47. St.A.MZ 15/402; ARSJ Rh.Inf.48. The peak was in 1604, when the Jesuits reported 213 converts.
48. Duhr I, pp. 116, 119; St.A.MZ 15/402, 1568; St.A.MZ 15/401, p. 59v; ARSJ Rh.Inf.48, p. 42r.
49. ARSJ Rh.Inf.48, p. 42r; St.A.MZ 15/402. 1575, 1579, 1583.
50. GLAK 61/10941, pp. 841–44; Duhr I, p. 117; ARSJ Rh.Inf.48, p. 32v; ARSJ Rh.Inf.4, p. 235r.
51. Hsia, Society and Religion in Münster, chap. 3.

sion and frequently discussed the sacrament of the Eucharist in their sermons and teaching.[52] By the 1590s, the fathers were claiming success. Over one thousand people participated in the Corpus Christi procession of 1595, and in 1597 the procession included high ecclesiastics, members of the bishop's bureaucracy, noblemen, judges and lawyers of the Imperial Chamber Court (Reichskammergericht), and a large contingent of peasants from neighboring Catholic villages. The rector, in his report to Rome, emphasized that the "heretics" were impressed and surprised by this "rare show of piety."[53]

With a similar goal in mind, the Jesuits undertook the establishment of several confraternities. The first of these was a Marian sodality, founded in 1578 for the students.[54] By 1615, this confraternity had been expanded to include ecclesiastics and erudite laymen. Here again, the Catholic members of the Reichskammergericht were prominent, giving the confraternity a certain social status as well as a critical mass of members. The members attended daily masses and monthly meetings, all of which was "good for the Church and the propagation of the faith."[55] The Jesuits also revived several moribund confraternities, including those dedicated to the Nativity of Christ, St. Sebastian, and St. Marcello.[56] Again the Jesuits combined the new Counter-Reformation piety (Marian cult, Cult of the Eucharist) with a revival of confraternities of local interest.

Jesuit efforts were focused primarily within the city of Speyer and contributed little to the reform of the rural Church, a situation that reflected their strategy of working with the educated and the influential. There is no doubt that they were successful in doing just that. Especially in the period 1594–1610, however, the fathers became a fairly familiar sight in the countryside around Speyer. Most often they went to the villages to assist the parish priest at Easter or to give catechism classes,[57] as in 1604, when twelve Jesuit father spent Christmas outside the city helping the overworked parish priests.[58] Although the Jesuits always claimed great success for these "missions," we know that the Jesuit who taught catechism classes in Otterstadt was not popular. Certainly the villagers and the parish priests viewed the Jesuits as outsiders and as agents of the bishop

52. St.A.MZ 15/402, 1568.
53. ARSJ Rh.Inf.48, pp. 42r, 58v.
54. Ibid., p. 4r; St.A.MZ 15/402, 1578.
55. ARSJ Rh.Inf.48, pp. 168r–168v; Duhr, II/1, p. 171.
56. ARSJ Rh.Inf.48, pp. 115v, 137v; Rh.Sup. 29, p. 55r.
57. St.A.MZ, 15/402, 1587. The Jesuits taught catechism classes in Dudenhofen, Otterstadt, Waltzheim, and Rheinhausen (ARSJ Rh.Inf.48, p. 32v [1594]).
58. ARSJ Rh.Inf.48, pp. 115v, 116r.

(and, indeed, in 1600, for example, the father general of the Society, Aquaviva, told the Jesuits in Speyer to pass on complaints about, and praise of, the parish priests to the proper officials).[59] The villagers treated the Jesuits as temporary visitors, and the Jesuits saw themselves the same way, since they were not a constant or even frequent presence in the rural parishes.[60]

The Jesuits more willingly took on missions involving direct confrontation with the Protestants than those entailing reform of the Catholic villages. They participated in the attempted recatholicization of the village of Landshausen (1600) and of the region around Dahn (1610).[61] They also undertook regular missions from Speyer to the Lutheran city of Worms and to the Catholic city of Weil der Stadt, where the Catholic city council faced Protestant threats from within the city and from Lutheran Württemberg.[62] The reformers may have hoped to use the Jesuits to further Catholic reform, but the Jesuits considered the college in Speyer above all an ideal base for converting Protestants.

The city of Speyer's reaction to the Jesuits is clear evidence of the high level of activity of the new order. In 1575 the city government tried to drive out the Jesuits, claiming that the Society was a new sect and hence not protected under the Peace of Augsburg, but they were thwarted by the intervention of the emperor.[63] Nevertheless, the Protestants in Speyer never accepted the presence of the Jesuits. In a 1581 letter to the city council, a group of Lutheran citizens and clergymen expressed the fear that several citizens, including some councilmen, had been converted to Catholicism by the Jesuits.[64] They argued that the presence of Catholics in important positions threatened the political independence and religious peace in the imperial city. Indeed, the Jesuits' presence caused difficulties and conflicts with Protestants throughout the region.

The Jesuits and the Reform of the Church

The Jesuits were never integrated into the Bishopric of Speyer or into the reforms led by Bishop Eberhard and his vicar general, Beatus

59. ARSJ Rh.Inf.4, pp. 10–11. For Otterstadt see Chapter 3. Aquaviva's comments were in response to questions from Speyer on how to handle complaints from villagers about their parish priests.

60. Between 1573 and 1621 the Jesuits conducted approximately fourteen missions to villages of the Bishopric of Speyer. In addition they went six times to the city of Weil der Stadt, at least twice to Worms, and once to Landau.

61. ARSJ Rh.Inf.48, pp. 104v, 160v. See Chapter 5.

62. For Weil der Stadt, see Chapter 4.

63. Duhr I, pp. 118–19. See Chapter 4.

64. St.A.Sp. 1A 450/11. See Chapter 4.

Moses. This is no surprise, since the Society of Jesus always carefully maintained its independence and its own agenda. Their emphasis on the conversion of Protestants contrasted with the local Church's interest in maintaining peaceful relations with their powerful Protestant neighbors.

Yet the Jesuits did much to bring new "reformed" ideas to Speyer. Their personal asceticism and irreproachable morality must have contrasted sharply with the traditional behavior of the clergy in Speyer. The Jesuits self-consciously acted as an elite model for good Catholics. Furthermore, they gave theological lectures to the clergy in the cathedral, beginning in 1570 with an explanation of the new Tridentine catechism.[65] After 1583 they taught in the Alumnat, helping to train new parish priests. They also gave sermons at the diocesan synods, an excellent opportunity to influence much of the clergy.[66] Both Bishop Eberhard and his successor, Philipp Christoph von Sötern, had Jesuit confessors. Despite their high profile, however, the Jesuits' influence remained limited, as demonstrated by the fate of their small establishment in Bruchsal.

Founded in 1615 by Bishop Sötern, the mission in Bruchsal survived for less than twenty years. The Jesuits downplayed its importance from the start, because they found the town too small for a permanent house and felt that occasional visits from Speyer would be sufficient to fill the pastoral needs of the locals. The food and housing were unsatisfactory, mostly because of the hostility of the bishop's officials. Finally, the canons of the Ritterstift in Bruchsal were no friends of the Jesuits and resented the bishops' giving the fathers the task of preaching in their church. After the Jesuits were driven out of Bruchsal in 1631 by the Swedes, they refused to return.[67]

Although the Jesuits were the embodiment of the Counter-Reformation, the resistance they encountered from the established Church prevented them from dominating the Catholic Reformation in the Bishopric of Speyer. The Society of Jesus never exercised the broad influence Louis Châtellier credits it with in other parts of the "Rheno-Flemish world." Perhaps the absence of a large Catholic urban population limited the importance of the Marian sodalities like the ones the Jesuits organized in Cologne and Antwerp.[68] The Jesuits never succeeded in creating a lay Catholic elite and trained only a small, although influential, clerical elite. By insisting on their inde-

65. Duhr I, p. 117.
66. St.A.MZ 15/402, 1583 and later.
67. Duhr II/1, pp. 172–73; Anton Wetterer, "Die Jesuiten in Bruchsal, 1616–1632," *Freiburger Diözesan-Archiv* 65 (1937): 218–25.
68. Châtellier, *Europe of the Devout*, p. 27.

pendence from the local Church and by viewing the Speyer college primarily as an outpost in Protestant territory, the Jesuits missed a chance to effect lasting reforms in local Catholicism.

Episcopal Reform from 1582 to 1621

In 1588, in his seventh year as bishop of Speyer, Eberhard von Dienheim sent the pope his *Designatio status ecclesiae Spirensis ad limina apostolorum,* a report on conditions in the bishopric. The picture he painted was bleak.[69]

After a brief review of the history of this bishopric, Eberhard described its clergy, with a fittingly hierarchical framework, detailing first the Cathedral Chapter and then the five smaller chapters. He mentioned the rural clergy last, emphasizing their obedience to episcopal ordinances and synod statutes.[70] Eberhard's description of the clergy was traditional, but he also wanted to make it clear that he was conscious of the Tridentine emphasis on pastoral work and had regular contact with the rural priests.

Eberhard devoted much of the report to lamenting the hold the Protestants had on the region and explaining how it curtailed his freedom of action. The bishop was virtually impotent in the city of Speyer, could do little against the power of the Electoral Palatinate in the gemeinschaften villages, and had difficulty even enforcing the marriage edict among Palatine serfs in Catholic villages. Eberhard delineated a political and religious situation that he feared was poorly understood in Rome. Like Marquard, he had a solid grasp of the political realities of the middle Rhine valley, but unlike his predecessor, he did not restrict himself to carrying out traditional policies within his bishopric.

In his report, Eberhard reviewed his program of reform in some detail. The recently completed visitation had revealed that a large number of priests were living with concubines or were guilty of other abuses. As a result, Eberhard had directed the vicar general to punish all offenders severely. Furthermore, he had ordered that all priests in the diocese confess at least seven times a year. He had selected the Jesuits, along with several other specially designated clerics, as confessors and had instructed them to impress the importance of proper priestly behavior upon the clergy.[71] Eberhard emphasized that a more

---

69. GLAK 78/1052, pp. 671–71v.
70. Ibid., p. 67v. Eberhard's report claimed that the deans of the rural chapters attended four synods a year.
71. Ibid., p. 69v.

moral clergy would "prevent the ills that have plagued the Church in Speyer for many years and return her to her pristine tranquillity."[72] This reform of the clergy was, for Eberhard, the essence of the program, not a first step to be followed by a more general reform of the population. In his opinion, a better behaved clergy would improve the reputation of the Catholic Church and help prevent further gains by the Protestants. This rather defensive viewpoint was the basis of reform in the Bishopric of Speyer.

Eberhard, in conclusion, asked the pope for help. He pointed out how vital it was that students from Speyer continue to train at the Collegium Germanicum in Rome. The bishop also appealed to the pope to give him total control of benefices in Speyer. Apparently the Curia had appointed several unqualified priests to benefices vacated during designated "papal months." Eberhard pointed out respectfully that the pope was unable to judge whether or not these men were qualified and asked for an end to the practice of filling benefices vacated in papal months.[73] Control of all benefices by the bishop (or at least by local authorities) was vital to the effective reform of the clergy.

Historians of the Counter-Reformation in Germany have often focused on the role of bishops in promoting Tridentine reforms.[74] This focus is to some degree justified by the decisive role given the episcopate by the Council of Trent and by the secular authority held by most German bishops. Following this historiographical tradition, historians of Speyer have considered Eberhard the driving force behind Catholic reform in the bishopric.[75] As his report to the Pope makes clear, Eberhard supported reforms; however, we must remember that Eberhard differed little from Marquard in personal style, family background, and political policy. Continuity in the recruitment of bishops, indeed of the whole upper clergy, existed across all of Germany through the Counter-Reformation and served to prevent radical reform of the Church.

Eberhard's family, like Marquard's, was Rhenish nobility, and its members served in both the Catholic Church and the administration of the Protestant electors of the Palatinate.[76] Eberhard was well

72. Ibid., p. 70r.
73. Ibid.
74. Some examples include Molitor, *Kirchliche Reformversuche;* Köhler, *Das Ringen um die tridentinische Erneuerung im Bistum Breslau;* Johannes Meier, "Die katholische Erneuerung des Würzburger Landkapitels Karlstadt im Spiegel der Landkapitels Versammlungen und Pfarreivisitationen, 1549 bis 1624," *Würzburger Diözesangeschichtsblätter* 33 (1971): 51–125.
75. Especially Stamer III/1 and Ammerich, "Formen und Wege der katholischen Reform."
76. Remling II, p. 398; Stamer III/1, p. 88.

educated and had served twenty years in the Cathedral Chapter before his election as bishop. By electing Eberhard, the cathedral canons showed, as much as their interest in reform, their determination to keep the bishopric in familiar hands.

For all his devotion to reform, Eberhard's inability to manage the finances of the bishopric hindered his policies and damaged his relationship with the Cathedral Chapter.[77] Eberhard's personal lifestyle was in part responsible for these financial problems. Like his predecessors, he insisted on a proper princely court. Debts brought the Bishopric of Speyer to the verge of bankruptcy in the 1590s, largely because of several costly building projects, "many expenses for silks, silverware, and fine linens," and a huge account at a goldsmith's in Frankfurt.[78] Bishop Eberhard was, then, hardly the devout, pious, austere reforming bishop on the model of St. Charles Borromeo. Instead, he remained first and foremost a prince of the Empire, determined to live in a style appropriate to his status.

Nor did Eberhard dramatically change the political stance of the bishopric. As the level of confessional conflict rose in the late sixteenth century, Eberhard could not (and likely did not want to) maintain the close personal ties Marquard had kept with neighboring Protestant princes. At the same time, however, Eberhard was politically very cautious. In 1582, probably under duress, Eberhard gave three thousand gulden to the elector of the Palatinate, Johann Casimir, who was fighting on the Protestant side in the Cologne War. Later he did nothing to protest the Protestant occupation of the Catholic Margravate of Baden-Baden.[79] Eberhard accepted the political realities of the middle Rhine region. Despite his earlier differences with Marquard over the measures of the Council of Trent, he worked hard to avoid serious conflicts with his Protestant neighbors. To this extent he continued Marquard's political policies.

Although Eberhard was in many ways a traditional prince-bishop, he did undertake a major reform of the clergy, according to the model set by the Council of Trent. The Cathedral Chapter, which had advocated such a reform for almost twenty years, continued its efforts in this direction during Eberhard's episcopate. The electoral capitulation signed by Eberhard at the time of his election contained few, but important, changes from the capitulation signed by Marquard in 1560. The most significant was the second clause, in which

---

77. GLAK 61/10947, pp. 205r–205v.
78. Remling II, p. 421; GLAK 61/10947, pp. 205v–208r.
79. Stamer III/1, pp. 88–89.

Eberhard promised "diligently [to] visit and reform our chapters and parishes in the countryside and in the city of Speyer."[80] The visitation ordered by Eberhard and undertaken by his vicar general, Beatus Moses, between 1583 and 1588 was a turning point in the history of the Catholic Church in the Bishopric of Speyer.

The Visitation as Reform

The long conflict between Bishop Marquard and the reformers in the Cathedral Chapter over the visitation demonstrates the symbolic and practical importance of this measure. Symbolically, a bishop proclaimed his willingness to undertake Tridentine reforms by launching a visitation. Practically, of course, the visitation was a way to gather information about conditions in the parishes and to promulgate reform as well. The episcopal visitation of 1583–88 in Speyer was intended to serve both these purposes.

Bishop Eberhard, Beatus Moses, and the reformers in the Cathedral Chapter were all keenly aware of the connection between the visitation and reform: it was the visitation that revealed the problems to be addressed. In 1587 the canons wrote to the bishop, encouraging him to "execute [the visitation] in the already visited parishes and correct the problems discovered."[81] On some occasions the canons specifically referred to the relationship between the visitation and "reformation": "There is obviously a great lack of diligence in the parishes, [therefore] it seems necessary respectfully to suggest to his Grace [the bishop] that . . . the ongoing visitation should not only shed light [on conditions], but that he should also enforce it and bring about a reformation."[82]

The canons also knew—in fact, at times argued explicitly—that the very process of visiting a parish could lead to immediate changes. There was considerable fear that Protestantism was making inroads in the Bruhrein region; therefore "a visitation is all the more to be encouraged." The visitors were instructed to reform conditions on the spot if possible: "During the visitation not only a reformation should take place, but the bishop's officials . . . should be ordered to help the priests in the execution of their pastoral duties."[83]

One can assume that the personal participation of Beatus Moses, the vicar general, made the visitation an impressive occasion. At the

---

80. Kloe, *Die Wahlkapitulation der Bischöfe zu Speyer*, pp. 74–91, esp. p. 75.
81. GLAK 61/10947, p. 354r.
82. Ibid., p. 311v.
83. Ibid., pp. 15r–15v, 171v.

same time, it was conducted in a businesslike way. Although the Council of Trent had described the visitation as an opportunity "to animate the people by exhortations and admonitions," there is no evidence that Moses or his assistants preached or heard confessions in the villages.[84] Instead, the visitors focused primarily on two issues: the lifestyle and professional qualifications of the clergy and the condition of ecclesiastical property.[85] The religious life and behavior of the laity was secondary.

Moses, accompanied by several assistants, began his work in May 1583. By October he had visited fourteen villages on the left bank of the Rhine, most of them wine-growing villages along the Palatine Weinstraße. The following spring and summer he investigated ten more parishes on the southwestern edge of the diocese, between Lauterburg and Weißenburg. It seems likely that Moses went to all the villages on the left bank of the Rhine within the bishop's territory (at this time there were about thirty-eight Catholic parishes in this area), but the only extant minutes are those of the visits to these twenty-four.[86] Moses, or his assistants, also visited at least some of the villages on the other side of the Rhine in the years between 1583 and 1588.[87] They worked methodically, asking the same questions at each stop. Questions to the parish priest focused on his education and experience, his duties in the parish, the obedience of his parishioners, the practice of the sacraments, the affairs of the rural chapter, and the priest's personal morality. The visitors also asked a series of questions pertaining to the financial and material condition of the parish.[88] They interviewed the sacristan and church wardens about the same matters, although in somewhat less detail.

The visitation was more than a fact-finding mission. The visitors had a program of reform in mind as they traveled through the par-

---

84. Rev. H. J. Schroeder, ed., *Canons and Decrees of the Council of Trent* (Rockford, Ill.: Tan Books, 1978), 194. The Jesuit fathers who conducted the visitation of 1683 in Speyer, for example, preached, held services, heard confessions, and converted Protestants in the villages. See Chapter 6.

85. GLAK 78/703.

86. Stamer III/1, pp. 90–14; Remling II, p. 412; Ammerich, "Formen und Wege der katholischen Reform," pp. 297–301.

87. Stamer III/1, p. 90; GLAK 61/11140, pp. 46v, 48r. These are indirect references to a visitation in the right bank villages. It is not clear from these records (of the *Fiscus*, the ecclesiastical court) what sort of visitation took place in these villages, or if it was as extensive as the visitation on the left bank.

88. The parish priest was the only resident priest in most villages, although there were endowments for assistant priests (chaplains or primissaries) in most parishes. These benefices were mostly held by nonresidents. The original functional distinction between the chaplain (*Kaplan*), who had no pastoral duties, and the primissary (*Frühmesser*) who was to assist the priest of a large parish, was no longer important in the late sixteenth century.

ishes. The visitors' commitment to reform meant that they commented to the villagers on the things they considered abuses. The
focus of the visitation on concubinage, on clerical dress, and on the
behavior of the priests in general surely led to some immediate
changes in clerical lifestyle. The visitors also sought to do more than
discourage abuses of the clergy. The visitors' interest in the sacraments (and to some extent processions) may have encouraged priests
to promote them and villagers to practice them.

Beatus Moses was a well-organized man, and he moved quickly to
follow up the visitation with the necessary disciplinary measures.
Evidence of his actions survives in a fragment of the minutes of the
Fiscus, the ecclesiastical court. These rough notes, from the years
1585 and 1586, all in Moses' own hand, are mostly lists of questions
to be asked of accused clergymen.[89] Because these records are frag-
mentary, it is difficult to determine if the number of clergymen
punished in the 1580s was greater than in previous years, or if the
punishments became more severe. It is possible, however, to say
something about the kind of cases the vicar general prosecuted.

A record of the cases before the *Fiscus* in the early 1560s (that is, in
the pre-Tridentine era) reveals that the court dealt almost exclusively
with disputes among the clergy or between the clergy and the laity
over inheritances and other financial matters. There were a few cases
of disciplinary action against priests, but most of these involved the
collegiate clergy in Speyer.[90] The episcopal authorities did, however,
discipline the rural clergy as well. During Marquard's episcopacy
sixteen parish priests were imprisoned for various crimes.[91] In the
1580s, however, there was an important change in tone as Moses
made a self-conscious effort to impose Tridentine codes of behavior.
Because of the visitation, Moses had much more information on
conditions in the villages than had been available to his predecessors.
One result was that more priests were imprisoned during Eberhard's
episcopacy (thirty-two in thirty years) than under Marquard (sixteen
in twenty years).[92] Finally, the cases before the *Fiscus* in the 1580s all

89. GLAK 61/11140.
90. GLAK 61/11139, pp. 408r.
91. GLAK 67/423.
92. GLAK 67/423, 67/424. It is impossible to know how many priests served in the
parishes of the bishopric. There were over eighty parishes under the bishop's jurisdiction.
Estimating (very roughly) an average tenure of five years, over two hundred parish priests
served under Marquard and close to four hundred under Eberhard. These numbers are
probably too high, because they do not take into account priests who served several parishes
simultaneously or consecutively, as well as delays in replacing priests who died or left the
bishopric.

concern the abuses of the clergy, for this was the primary interest of the Catholic reformers in the Bishopric of Speyer.

The extensive case against the pfarrer from Wiesental is perhaps the best example of the variety of clerical abuses Moses attempted to eliminate.[93] Specifically mentioning that the case had been brought as a result of a recent visitation of the parish, he began his indictment with a charge of concubinage. Correcting what was perhaps a common misconception in the countryside, Moses insisted that the synodal statutes against clerical concubinage applied to the parish priests as well as to the collegiate clergy. Moses also accused the pfarrer of promising to marry his concubine. Although the charge of concubinage would easily have been sufficient for the court to remove the priest from his parish and punish him severely, Moses clearly wanted to make an example of this man and therefore submitted a number of other charges as well.

The pfarrer in Wiesental did not perform his duties faithfully: he did not teach the catechism and he did not hear confessions correctly. The visitors had warned the priest to hear confessions of both men and women privately and to stop withholding absolution from those who had confessed properly. Yet he continued to hear group confessions "in the sacristy, as is the custom of the heretics."[94]

Like almost every other priest investigated by Moses, the pfarrer in Wiesental drank too much. Not only was he a bad example to the people and one who gave the Catholic clergy in general a bad name (always a primary concern for Moses), he also drank before Easter services, seriously mixing the sacred and the profane. Moreover, he got into disputes with his neighbors when drinking, accepted wine as payment for performing burials, and ate meat during Lent. To these accusations Moses added charges that the pfarrer had stolen some flour that had been set aside for a hospice and that he was guilty of perjury.

In this case and in all the others contained in these minutes, Moses made no effort to single out some abuses as more serious than the others. Perhaps he felt that concubinage, because it was so public and so obviously violated the rule of clerical celibacy, was the most dangerous deficiency. Yet he appears to have been just as concerned about the behavior of the pfarrer in Schifferstadt, Nicolaus Pistoris, whose sins did not include concubinage.

Pistoris had served several parishes in the bishopric, and unlike the

93. GLAK 61/11140, pp. 47r–48v.
94. Ibid., p. 48r.

pfarrer in Wiesental, he had never been accused of neglecting his duties or giving improper services. Nevertheless, in Moses' opinion, his conduct was unseemly. Pistoris was a pre-Tridentine priest who had been a vicar in the St. Guido Chapter and had worked his way up to the fairly wealthy parish of Schifferstadt.[95] His problem was his love of wine. He participated regularly in the traditional post-burial gatherings in the village, and on these occasions he drank wine, even on a holiday or during Lent. He also frequented various inns and drank and socialized with the peasants. During these drinking bouts Pistoris was heard to insult local episcopal officials and to boast about his prowess in brawls; at one point he even declared that he considered the parish property his personal possession. Furthermore, Pistoris had verbally insulted one of the villagers and his wife. As a result he earned a reputation, at least among episcopal officials, as "brash, combative, deceitful, shrewd, unruly, scandalous, [and] quarrelsome."[96] Moses and the Tridentine Church considered these characteristics inappropriate in a parish priest. Unfortunately, there is little evidence of the villagers' opinions of Pistoris. While he seems to have had enemies in Schifferstadt, there was no movement in the village to remove him.

There were several cases similar to that of Nicolaus Pistoris. The temporary priest in Waltzheim (Waldsee) was cited for drinking daily during Lent and as a result celebrating Easter Mass with "trembling hands."[97] The pfarrer in Großfischlingen, Conrad Planckh, drank, carried a sword, and, when drunk, may have impregnated a local woman. Planckh denied the last charge. Wilhelm Mosen, the priest in Untergrombach, was accused of only one abuse, gambling publicly in the inn.[98] These cases indicate that in the aftermath of the visitation of 1583–88, Moses tried to reform the daily behavior of the parish priests along the lines indicated by the Council of Trent. He began each court hearing with a short sermon on how a priest should behave. "Is it not true that all priests should live a sober and honest life and should live without scandal?"[99]

Episcopal officials scrutinized the rural priests more closely immediately after the visitation of 1583–88 than at any other time. They continued, however, to prosecute disobedient priests up until the Thirty Years' War. Concubinage or related sexual offenses were pun-

95. GLAK 61/11105, p. 104r.
96. GLAK 61/11140, pp. 13r–13v, 20r–21r, 14r, 20v; quotation from p. 21r.
97. Ibid., pp. 17r–17v.
98. Ibid., pp. 45r–46v.
99. Ibid., p. 6v.

ished most frequently. By the first decade of the seventeenth century, this policy had succeeded, and priests no longer openly kept concubines. Still, it remained necessary for the vicar general to punish priests for sexual crimes. In 1606 the pfarrer in Maikammer was removed for having impregnated his maid. This pregnancy, unlike most in the mid-sixteenth century, was not evidence of a long-term relationship.[100] In 1608 the vicar general fined the priest in Heiligenstein for fathering a child. Here the woman involved is referred to as a "suspicious pregnant woman" and is nowhere called a concubine.[101]

The parish priests continued to drink, gamble, and brawl. Because of the omnipresence of these abuses, the vicars general had a difficult time preventing them. As in the 1580s, almost every priest who was punished for concubinage was also convicted of excessive drinking. Here too the officials focused on public misbehavior. The chaplain in Hambach, Christian Hauler, was imprisoned for public drinking. While drunk Hauler started a fight with another priest at the diocesan synod and on other occasions had publicly insulted villagers in Hambach.[102] Hauler's crimes damaged the effort to improve the public image of the Catholic priest.

The vicars general punished disobedience to higher authorities with particular severity. Several priests in the 1580s and 1590s refused to appear before the *Fiscus*. Moses banished the pfarrer from Odenheim from the bishopric for failing to obey a summons to appear in court. In general, however, Moses and his successors had considerable success enforcing their authority over the parish priests.[103]

There were no visitations in the Bishopric of Speyer between 1588 and 1683. Although the Cathedral Chapter periodically lamented problems with the rural clergy and did suggest at least an "inspection" of the parishes in 1600, the interest in further visitations faded after 1588.[104] In 1606, Bishop Eberhard obtained the permission of the Cathedral Chapter to conduct a visitation, and his vicar general went as far as to present the chapter with the plan of the visitation. In the end, however, no visitation took place. No system of regular visitations, such as took place in the Bishopric of Würzburg, ever

---

100. GLAK 61/11496, pp. 135r–135v.
101. GLAK 61/10953, pp. 167v–168r.
102. GLAK 67/424a, pp. 6r–7v (1612, 22 December).
103. GLAK 67/424, pp. 35r–36r. The vicars general had much more trouble disciplining the chapter clergy. See GLAK 65/11604, pp. 31v–33r ("Ausführlicher Bericht von dem Ritter-Stifft Bruchsal") for problems in the Ritterstift in Bruchsal; and GLAK 61/10955, p. 25v for the nebenstifter in Speyer.
104. GLAK 61/10951, pp. 225–26.

existed in Speyer.[105] Without regular inspections, it was difficult for episcopal officials to control or even stay informed about conditions in the rural parishes.

There are several likely explanations for why visitations were never "institutionalized." Certainly after 1600 the reform party was no longer as powerful as it had been in the 1570s and 1580s. After Moses died in 1602 there may not have been anyone with the drive to conduct the visitation. In addition, the financial difficulties of the bishopric curtailed such ambitions. Moreover, most members of the clergy perceived the problems within the Church as relatively minor. A reform of what they considered the most serious abuses, such as concubinage and absenteeism, was sufficient.

The Improvement of the Clergy

The episcopal visitation, while central to the reform of the clergy, was only the beginning of the reform program. Of vital importance were institutions that kept the Church hierarchy and the parish priests of the Bishopric of Speyer in regular contact. Traditionally, these ties had been maintained by means of regular synods and through the work of the archdeacons and the rural chapters. The reformers understood that these institutions had to be revived and strengthened if the reforms of the Council of Trent were to be introduced and maintained in the parishes and collegiate chapters. Furthermore, the material conditions necessary for a reformed clergy had to be provided. These included a rationalization of the Church's property holdings, an adjustment of financial arrangements to the realities of post-Reformation conditions, the repair of churches and parsonages, and the purchase of liturgical books. All of these measures were common to Catholic reform across Europe.

Regular diocesan synods had been held throughout the sixteenth century, although it is not clear how well attended or widely publicized they were. Under Marquard the synod recesses consisted primarily of sermons that lamented the bad behavior of the clergy in fairly general, formulaic terms.[106] The synod recesses under Eberhard had much the same character.[107] Eberhard, however, also used

---

105. GLAK 61/10953, pp. 35v–36r, 63v, 70v. Meier, "Die katholische Erneuerung," pp. 58, 61.

106. *Collectio processuum synodalium* pp. 355–85. Marquard was quite specific in condemning concubinage.

107. For example, at the recess of the fall synod of 1584 Eberhard delivered a clear, well-organized, and rather superficial Latin sermon telling the clergy that a proper "fear of God" (*timor dei*) would cure the sins of the clergy (*Collectio processuum synodalium*, pp. 394–95).

the synods to publicize ordinances and to give the parish priests concrete suggestions on how to improve pastoral care. The marriage ordinance was publicized at a synod in 1583, and Eberhard ordered the teaching of the catechism at the fall synod of 1587. He specifically discussed clerical clothing, admonished the priests to stay out of inns, and offered advice on how to give effective sermons.[108] The effort he made to have the synod recesses publicized in the recalcitrant Ritterstift in Bruchsal suggests that he considered them very important.[109]

The synods would have little effect in the rural parishes if there was no mechanism to inform the priests of the decisions of the bishop. Such an intermediary function had once been carried out by the archdeaconates, but this structure had disintegrated in the Reformation; and Eberhard had no interest in restoring a system that gave considerable power to the collegiate chapters, whose deans had served as archdeacons. Instead, Eberhard and Moses set out to reform and revitalize the rural chapters.

The rural chapters had originally been founded as confraternities for rural priests. The regular meetings of the rural chapters became important social occasions for the pfarrer, and before the Reformation this institution also played an important role in disciplining the clergy.[110] But by the mid-sixteenth century the rural chapters met rarely and were not important in publicizing episcopal decrees and synod recesses. Some disputes also arose in connection with the election of the officers of the chapters and with the handling of the chapters' finances, matters that had caused resentment among those parish priests who were shut out of decision making.[111] Under these conditions the rural chapters functioned poorly.

In the late 1580s, no doubt as a result of information gathered during the visitation, Beatus Moses moved to reform and revive the rural chapters. Between 1588 and 1598 he wrote new statutes for the rural chapters of Herxheim, Weißenburg, Hambach, and Deidesheim. It seems likely that the other three chapters received new statutes in this period as well.[112] Moses clearly understood this effort as an important part of the reform of the Church. In the introduction to the statutes of the rural chapter of Deidesheim he stated that "a

---

108. Ibid., pp. 385, 395–96. Concerning clothing, see no. 10, no. 12 (p. 404); concerning inns, no. 15; concerning sermons, no. 17, no. 12 (p. 403).

109. GLAK 133/461. This conflict was in 1591.

110. Rapp, *Réformes et Réformation à Strasbourg*, pp. 195–200.

111. LASp. D2/306/10, p. 302v.

112. LASp. D2/35/1 (Herxheim); ADBR G5847(1) (Weißenburg); LASp. D2/313b (Hambach or Edesheim); LASp. D2/311a (Deidesheim).

visitation [conducted] without design and correction would be worthless . . . [and therefore] we reform and correct the ancient statutes of the chapter . . . [so] we can devote ourselves to the spirit of a general reform of the churches."[113] Moses used the opportunity to repeat the goals of the reform (and to write them permanently into the statutes.

The rural chapters, according to Moses' statutes, were to enforce the residence of parish priests. He reminded the priests that the Council of Trent had stated expressly that all priests with pastoral duties must reside near their churches. It was the duty of the rural chapters to ensure that this decree was followed. Furthermore, all priests had to be confirmed in their benefices by the rural chapters, giving the chapters an important role in checking the credentials and qualifications of new priests.[114]

The meetings of the rural chapters, which were to take place twice a year, became important occasions for the reinforcement of the Tridentine norms of clerical behavior. Moses wrote very specific instructions into the statutes concerning the conduct of the priests both during and after the meetings. He expected them to be attentive and orderly during the meetings and the accompanying religious services. They were to distribute alms to the poor. After the meetings, whether on the streets of the village or in the inn, the priests were to dress and behave "modestly, soberly, calmly, both in action and word" so as not to " offend the laity or denigrate the status of the clergy."[115] Apparently the behavior of the clergy at the meetings of the rural chapters had caused so much trouble in the past that it had become a main goal of the clerical reform movement to improve the reputation of the priests and their relations with the laity.

Although Moses gave the rural chapters a role in the reform of the clergy, his statutes make it clear that episcopal authorities were sovereign in this matter. He specifically told the priests that the dean of the rural chapter had no right to discipline his fellow priests.[116] The most significant business of the chapters was to read episcopal mandates and synod recesses, a passive function in which the chapters acted as organs of the bishop's administration. Moreover, all elections of the chapter officers (dean, *Camerarius*, and *Definitor*) had to be confirmed by the bishop or his vicar general.[117] Moses was

113. LASp. D2/311a.
114. Ibid., p. 17v; LASp. D2/311, p. 11r.
115. LASp. D2/311a, pp. 14r–14v.
116. Ibid., p. 3r.
117. Ibid., pp. 5r, 7r, 7v, 12r, 13v, 14r.

intent on creating an institution that would function as a conduit for the bishop's ordinances. He was careful to make sure that the rural chapters could not become independent institutions capable of uniting the priests and resisting Church authorities.

It appears from the documents that the rural chapters functioned as Moses had intended, at least in the years before the Thirty Years' War. An account book (*Rechnung*) of the rural chapter in Hambach from 1602 to 1603, for example, indicates that the chapter met twice a year during this period and was financially solvent.[118] In 1585 the pfarrer in Otterstadt tried to avoid going to the meeting of the rural chapter in Deidesheim. He claimed he had already heard a reading of the synod statutes at the St. Guido Chapter where he was a vicar. He was ordered to attend the meeting anyway.[119] Later, pfarrer in Otterstadt attended (or were invited to attend) rural chapters in Deidesheim in 1588, 1592, 1593, and 1616.[120] The structures were in place and regular meetings took place. However the parish priests responded to the efforts at reform, they certainly could no longer pretend to be unaware of the reformers' efforts and goals.

Bishop Eberhard also attempted to improve the quality and availability of liturgical books in the rural and urban churches, an improvement that was necessary if the priests were to do their pastoral duties correctly. The visitation had revealed that many of the rural pfarrer used outdated liturgical books, and in 1588 the bishop lamented that the lack of recent breviaries (which contained especially important lists of feast days) was a serious problem. Eberhard wanted assistance in producing and printing a new and revised breviary,[121] but although the Jesuits agreed to help, nothing came of this effort, perhaps because of the cost. It was not until 1607 that new liturgical books were distributed in the Bishopric of Speyer. This time it was the archbishop of Mainz who suggested that the Mainz agenda, missal, and breviary be used in all the bishoprics where he was metropolitan. The canons of the Cathedral Chapter in Speyer balked, arguing that the Mainz breviary would not work because of the specific religious traditions in the Bishopric of Speyer. They accepted the agenda, however, since the previous Mainz agenda was already in use in Speyer. This new agenda was strongly influenced by the Council of Trent and contained discussions of proper priestly behavior.[122] In

118. LASp. D2/313e.
119. GLAK 61/11105, pp. 316r, 318r.
120. GLAK 61/11106, 1588,27 May; GLAK 61/11107, pp. 30r, 61v; GLAK 61/11109, pp. 291v–92r.
121. GLAK 61/10947, p. 409v.
122. GLAK 61/10953, p. 134v; Lamott, *Das Speyerer Diözesanrituale*, pp. 60–62.

many ways the attempt to bring new liturgical books to the parishes is characteristic of the effort to bring Catholic reform to Speyer. Some important reform measures succeeded, but extensive changes (in this case the imposition of a complete series of revised liturgical books) failed because of the resistance of traditional-minded clergymen and the financial problems of the bishopric.

The reformers knew that they had to improve the financial condition of the benefices in order to be able to offer higher incomes for the parish priests and make the bishopric more attractive to well-qualified candidates. Reformed priests also demanded that churches and parsonages be kept in better repair. Rural parishes could be made solvent by improving the management of existing property and incomes and by combining scattered resources. The consolidation of resources sometimes involved selling property. In 1592, for example, the bishop sold over thirty-seven *Morgen* of property that belonged to the vacant primissary in Rheinsheim to the residents of the village. The money was then invested to return a yearly income.[123] Presumably cash investments were more dependable and easier to manage than property. Eberhard sold a whole group of chaplaincies and primissaries in the 1590s, in part to prevent neighboring Protestant princes from gaining control of the property.[124] Furthermore, in all these cases the benefices were vacant and the incomes no doubt difficult to collect. By 1597 the Church had sold property worth over eleven thousand gulden.[125] It is not clear, however, if the profits from the sales went to increase the income of the parish priests or if this money disappeared into the coffers of the bishop.

Eberhard also exchanged some properties with neighboring princes. In most cases these exchanges allowed each side to dispose of property, tithes, and assorted rights that were deep inside the other's territory. One result of this process of rationalization was that the bishop of Speyer acquired the right of patronage in three villages in his territory, ending the threat that Protestant patrons would appoint Protestant pastors for these parishes.[126]

Between about 1570 and 1600, Church officials conducted detailed renovations, or surveys, of Church property in the villages. The purpose of the surveys was, of course, to find lost or neglected sources of income. It is clear from the renovations that the Church was an

123. GLAK 229/86582 (Rheinsheim).
124. Remling II, p. 414.
125. GLAK 61/10949, pp. 866–68. In January 1597 the Cathedral Chapter refused to approve the sale of more property, this time in Bruchsal, saying that this violated the wishes of the original donators.
126. Remling II, pp. 413–14.

important landowner but that the fragmentation of the property was so extensive that the collection of rents and seigniorial dues must have been very difficult. In Neipsheim, for example, the parish owned forty morgen of land, all of which was rented in small plots, none larger than four morgen and most between one-quarter and one morgen. Twenty residents of four different villages owed yearly interest payments on small loans to the primissary in Rauenberg.[127] The economic ties between the Church and the villages were so extensive and complicated that systematizing them proved difficult.

In 1603 the bishop's officials conducted a survey of all the rural benefices of the bishopric for the purpose of taxing the clergy.[128] The survey listed all the various sources of income of the priests. Almost all the priests in the bishopric lived from fixed payments in cash and kind, from the income or products from Church property, and from fractions of the tithe. The survey indicates that the pfarrers had a fairly good grasp of their rights. Perhaps this was the result of the ongoing effort to organize the holdings of the parishes. Furthermore, rough calculations show that the priests were not impoverished. Of the forty-seven priests surveyed, only eight earned less than the equivalent of 100 gulden in a year. By comparison, a schoolteacher in Speyer earned 50 and a professor at the University of Heidelberg around 150 gulden.[129] Even if these calculations are skewed, the pfarrer did not complain about their financial situation in the period from 1580 to 1620 with the same frequency as before and especially later.[130] Possibly the financial reforms had some success. What is more likely is that the priests benefited financially from the rising prices and peaceful conditions of the late sixteenth century. Certainly income from tithes rose as population and productivity increased.

Within the limitations imposed by traditions within the Church and the political and institutional fragmentation of the bishopric, the Catholic reformers succeeded in implementing a series of changes designed to improve the quality of the parish priests. Did the Alum-

127. GLAK 229/72044 (Neipsheim); GLAK 229/84487 (Rauenberg).
128. LASp. D2/306/1, GLAK 78/615.
129. Ohler, "Alltag in einer Zeit des Friedens," p. 602.
130. The income lists from 1603 could be misleading in several ways. Because they were drawn up for the purposes of tax assessment, the bishop's officials may have overestimated the priests' incomes so as to justify higher taxes. The priests' income from grain and wine is estimated at market prices, which they may not actually have obtained. Income from land is very hard to estimate. What percentage of rents were uncollectible? The survey rarely indicates the quality of land, so it is difficult to tell how much rent (or how much produce) could be expected. It was also difficult to collect interest on loans, another important source of clerical income. Because few priests in Speyer received a significant proportion of their income in cash, they were protected from the effect of inflation in the late sixteenth and early seventeenth centuries.

nat, visitation, disciplinary measures, synods, rural chapters, and financial reorganization succeed in altering the character of the clergy, especially in the countryside? An examination of the education, professional conduct, and careers of the priests in the Bishopric of Speyer between 1560 and 1621 shows that the reformers were at least partially successful.

The Parish Priests

The parish priests of the 1620s were different from their predecessors in the 1560s. The disciplinary measures of the Church authorities forced them to be celibate, to avoid excessive public drinking, and to stay out of village disputes. Increasingly they studied for the priesthood in Speyer or even Rome and internalized the values taught by the Tridentine church. Even when they had little formal education, the parish priests often received on-the-job training in chaplaincies before taking on the responsibility of a parish. In the period between the 1580s and the Thirty Years' War priests also stayed longer in each parish. Perhaps this was a sign of greater dedication to their pastoral duties.[131]

Throughout much of the sixteenth century the education of the rural clergy had been rather haphazard. Some, like Philip Franckh of Stettfeld, had worked their way up to the priesthood. Franckh's parish priest had taken him under his wing and given him some education. Then, in 1561, the village council in Stettfeld gave Franckh the primissary benefice of the village. Although the income was small and irregular, it allowed him to continue his education.[132] A certain number of parishes were served by former vicars in the collegiate chapters or by former monks. This background qualified these men as priests, but it did not include training in pastoral duties. Furthermore, these sources never provided enough priests and the bishopric had to depend on priests from other dioceses.

The efforts of the Cathedral Chapter to educate priests for the

---

131. Most of the section that follows is based on prosopographical research done on a group of 303 parish priests who served in the Bishopric of Speyer between 1560 and 1621. I have divided them into two groups: the priests from the "pre-reformed" era (1560–83) and from the "reformed" (1583–1621). While these divisions are artificial and some priests served in both periods, the year 1583 was a major turning point. These 303 parish priests are not nearly all the priests who served in the bishopric in this period. The sources are Stamer II, III/1, III/2; Remling II; GLAK 61/10941 to 61/10955 (Cathedral Chapter minutes); GLAK 61/11494 to 61/11497 (Bishop's Council Minutes); GLAK 67/423 to 67/426 (*Urfehden, Libri Spiritualium*); GLAK 61/11104 to 61/11112 (Minutes, St. Guido Chapter), GLAK 229 (Local records), GLAK 61/11262; LASp. D2/306/8 (Visitation of 1583–88), LASp. D2 (Rural Parishes); ADBR 19 J (Riedseltz).

132. GLAK 61/11494, pp. 162v–163r.

parishes under its patronage began to bear fruit in the 1590s. Between 1593 and about 1620, at least twenty graduates of the Alumnat in Speyer served in the rural parishes. Of these twenty, nine had also studied at the Collegium Germanicum in Rome.[133] The canons of the Cathedral Chapter considered this group of students, who had all studied with the Jesuits, the solution to problems in the parishes. In 1593 they sent two of the alumni to the countryside to replace two pfarrer whose life-styles were unacceptable.[134] Generally the alumni did their duties well, although the Cathedral Chapter had occasional trouble keeping them in the parishes. One alumnus, for example, left the service of the chapter (a violation of an oath he swore when he took the *stipendium*) and went to Worms where he received a better benefice.

A number of Speyer priests also trained at the Collegium Germanicum in Rome. Between 1559 and 1619, thirty-three priests from Speyer studied in Rome, most of them between 1580 and 1600. It is not clear how many of them served in the bishopric, but like the alumni, they constituted an elite group of priests who had been immersed in the spirit of the Tridentine Church.[135]

The reformers also wanted to use the resources of the chaplaincies and primissaries for the training of priests. In 1593 a young priest received a chaplaincy in Deidesheim. The parish priest in the village was an "exemplary man" and had the duty of housing and training the young priest.[136] There were other examples of this sort of training. Many holders of these secondary benefices, however, continued the traditional practice of performing only the necessary services and avoiding all pastoral duties. The pfarrer in Diedesfeld complained in 1597 that the two chaplains in his village refused to help him.[137] As with all aspects of the reform, it was very difficult to change traditional modes of conduct. Furthermore, the shortage of priests continued, and in times of crisis the chapters still had to send vicars out from Speyer to serve vacant parishes.[138]

The reform did not drastically change the career paths of priests, except that the educated ones often served the "better" (that is, better paid) parishes soon after completing their education. Most priests,

133. Stamer III/1, pp. 80–84.
134. GLAK 61/10949, p. 360.
135. Peter Schmidt, *Das Collegium Germanicum im Rom und die Germaniker. Zur Funktion eines römischen Ausländerseminars (1552–1914)*, (Tübingen: Max Neumayer Verlag, 1984), esp. 191, 216–321.
136. GLAK 61/10949, pp. 376, 377.
137. Ibid., p. 862.
138. Ibid., pp. 693, 695, 717.

both before and after the reform, began their careers in poor parishes and moved up to the wealthier and more prestigious ones later. Thus Johan Fischer served over fifteen years in the small parishes of Büchig and Neipsheim before becoming dean of the rural chapter in the sought-after parish of Hambach.

Church authorities gave the best parishes (especially those of Udenheim and Deidesheim) as rewards for long or especially devoted service. Sometimes they punished priests with demotions. Johan Haltner was convicted of concubinage in 1602 and removed from the parish of Kirrlach. After convincing the vicar general that he had mended his ways, he was given the less desirable parish of Büchenau.

The Church had the greatest difficulty in dealing with elderly and retired priests. Traditionally they had been given chaplaincies, preferably in towns like Bruchsal, Deidesheim, or Lauterburg. Johan Merckell served in the Bishopric of Speyer from 1561 to 1585 before retiring to a chaplaincy in Bruchsal. As Church officials began to use the resources of the chaplaincies to train young priests, prospects for retired priests may have become more meager. Caspar Scheckhdorff was the pfarrer in Riedseltz for thirteen years before retiring in 1607 due to age and illness. In 1610 he complained that the tiny income he received from the patrons of the village was insufficient. The patrons, the canons in Weißenburg, commented that Scheckhdorff should be happy that he did not have to live on alms.[139] It seems that quite a number of aged priests suffered under this sort of callousness. One result was that, in order to keep an income, they continued as active priests as long as possible, sometimes to the detriment of their parishioners.[140]

The reform had some positive effects on the kinds of service the villagers received from their priests. The priests served longer in each parish after the 1580s than they had between 1560 and 1583. Of course there were exceptions, and some parishes had always been well served. Only two parish priests, for example, officiated in Lauterburg between 1574 and 1605; Johan Schelling, who served eight years, and Martin Liebrandt, who served twenty-three. Lauterburg, however, was a wealthy and well-equipped parish. Others, such as Otterstadt and Rauenberg, never kept priests longer than two or three years. In a whole series of parishes, however, the average length of tenure rose in the late sixteenth century. In Deidesheim the priests stayed an average of 2.5 years in the pre-reformed era and 5.6 years

139. ADBR 19 J 397.
140. The "problem of old age" continued through the eighteenth century in rural areas. See Tackett, *Priest and Parish in 18th Century France*, pp. 141–42.

after 1583. In Bauerbach the average tenure rose from 1.1 to 2.85 years, and in Geinsheim it went from 1.4 to 5.1 years. These figures are especially surprising since the records for the later period are more complete and include the turnover in priests following the visitation of 1583–88.[141]

The villagers had complained since the mid-sixteenth century that priests did not remain long enough in one parish, and the longer tenures must have pleased them. It certainly must have pleased the reformers, for any consistent effort to reform religious practice required a stable rural clergy. Yet from the point of view of the reformers, there was a trade-off here: priests who stayed in a village a long time tended to take the side of the villagers in disputes with outside authorities. To the extent that the Counter-Reformation was imposed from outside, long tenures did not always help the cause of reform. Conversely, priests who knew their parishioners and the traditions of the village often acted as intermediaries between the villagers and the Church and, in the long run, may have prevented a major split between the people of the Bishopric of Speyer and the Catholic Church.

The longer tenure of parish priests in the reforming era also indicates that the financial conditions of the parishes had improved noticeably. Does it also mean that the villagers were happier with their priests or that the priests were more dedicated to their pastoral duties? The sources shed little light on this question.

The reformers in the Bishopric of Speyer focused their efforts on the rural clergy partly because this was a group with few political or institutional defenses. Unlike the chapter clergy and the village communes, the parish priests were directly subject to episcopal authority. Furthermore, most of the decision makers in Speyer were attached to the status quo in the bishopric. They continued to perceive the reform as a defensive policy designed to restore the loyalty of the population to Catholicism and instinctively rejected all major institutional or organizational changes. They had no interest in reducing the influence of the aristocratic elites who ruled the bishopric and shared with the rest of the German Church the traditional suspicion of reforms ordered by Rome. This attitude did not change as the reform progressed. In fact, the influence of the reform party declined

---

141. Some other examples: Weyer unter Rietburg, 4.5 to 7.25 years; Schifferstadt, 5.5 to 10 years; Neipsheim, 1.3 to 1.6 years; Heiligenstein, 4.5 to 7.8 years; Obergrombach, 0.75 to 10.5 years.

after about 1610. Eberhard's successor's first report to the pope, written in 1616, emphasized the political problems of the bishopric but did not even mention reform of the clergy.[142] The upper clergy may have considered the reform complete.

The educated, celibate, and "reformed" priests who appeared in the rural parishes after about 1600 were not as easily integrated into the village communities as their predecessors. They were not tightly controlled from Speyer either. Church authorities remained concerned with obvious abuses such as concubinage, but because there were no regular inspections of the parishes, priests were often left to their own devices for years on end. As a result, the rural clergy functioned, not as "agents" of the Tridentine Church, but as intermediaries between the rural population and the Church authorities.

142. Josef Schmidlin, *Die kirchlichen Zustände in Deutschland vor dem dreißigjährigen Kriege nach den bischöflichen Diözesanberichten an den heiligen Stuhl*, vol. 3, *West und Norddeutschland* (Freiburg in Breisgau: Herdersche Verlag, 1910), 96–101.

3

The Reform in the Villages

The reformers attempted to go beyond improving the behavior and education of the clergy. Proponents of Tridentine reform also wanted to bring popular religious practice into harmony with established Church doctrine. To this end, the Church, generally with the support of secular authorities, instituted disciplinary measures designed to eliminate abuses of the sacraments as well as other popular "excesses" and "superstitions," such as the veneration of unofficial shrines, the appeal to cunning folk and "witches," and excessive drinking and feasting on religious holidays. In addition, reformers supported the institution of catechism classes and primary schools for the purpose of providing the people, especially the young, with a better understanding of Tridentine Catholicism.

These various measures reflect two related aspects of the interaction between Tridentine Catholicism and the people of Catholic Europe. First there was what Peter Burke has called the reform of popular culture.[1] Both Protestant and Catholic elites sought to end what they considered the immorality and license that prevailed in popular festivities, youth culture, and forms of sociability. Reforming popular culture also entailed "cleaning up" popular religion, which in the eyes of the educated had become a dangerous mixture of

1. Peter Burke, *Popular Culture in Early Modern Europe* (New York: Harper and Row, 1978), esp. chap. 8 and 9.

the sacred and profane with frequent recourse to superstition, magic, and a variety of other pagan practices. Modern historians of popular culture have often viewed this reform very critically, contrasting the spontaneity and innovation of popular culture and traditional religion with the rigidity and austerity of the elites.[2]

There was no aggressive reform of popular culture in the Bishopric of Speyer. Church authorities forbade popular "abuses" of religious holidays, such as dances on Sundays, usually in the name of order and respect for holy days. Ordinances also restricted more generally disorderly conduct, such as the wearing of masks and costumes at carnival time. Overall, however, these measures were quite limited. In fact, there was considerable sympathy within the local Church for popular religious practices, especially when they did not blatantly contradict Church teachings.[3] Furthermore, a moderate reform of popular practice contrasted favorably with the harsh policies of the Calvinists in the Palatinate.

The second aspect of the interaction between the Church and the people was the effort to confessionalize the population—to give the people a sense of the differences between Catholicism and Protestantism, and to inculcate them with specifically Catholic religious culture. Bishop Eberhard took some significant steps in this direction. He reinstated and encouraged catechism classes, the most direct method of popular religious instruction. The marriage ordinance of 1582 was designed not only to end popular "misunderstandings" of this sacrament but also to make interconfessional marriages more difficult.

The weaknesses of state institutions, however, restricted the development of confessional consciousness in the Bishopric of Speyer. German historians of confessionalism have generally focused on regions such as Lutheran Württemberg or Catholic Bavaria, where religious reform and state-building proceeded together. In these places, religious reformers worked with the princes and their officials to enforce unity, discipline, and order in the political and religious

---

2. These works include: Natalie Z. Davis, *Society and Culture in Early Modern France* (Stanford: Stanford University Press, 1975); Carlo Ginzburg, *The Cheese and the Worms. The Cosmos of a Sixteenth Century Miller* (Baltimore: Johns Hopkins University Press, 1980); Keith Thomas, *Religion and the Decline of Magic* (New York: Charles Scribner's Sons, 1971).

3. See Burke's discussion of this issue in *Popular Culture in Early Modern Europe* pp. 229–34; Bossy, "The Counter-Reformation and the People of Catholic Europe," pp. 62–63. Veit and Lenhart, *Kirche und Volksfrömmigkeit*, see a close tie between the needs and preferences of popular religion and the practices encouraged by the Church. See also Hsia, *Social Discipline in the Reformation*, chap. 6.

lives of their subjects.[4] This symbiotic relationship between state-building and religious reform did not exist in the Catholic villages around Speyer. Instead, Catholic reform proceeded independently, without either the benefit or the stigma of an association with an emerging state.

Reformers understood these limitations and recognized that a reform of popular religion could not be effected by episcopal edicts alone. They expected educated and reformed parish priests to enforce the ordinances and discourage popular abuses through teaching, preaching, and personal example. Although the priests, unlike the authorities, had daily contact with the population, they found it very difficult to change religious practice in the villages. The people had a strong tradition of local autonomy and resisted disciplinary measures and outside interference in local religious life. Few priests were able, or even willing, to force changes on their parishioners. It is an important indication of the weakness of the Counter-Reformation in the Bishopric of Speyer that parish priests rarely implemented regulations which their parishioners opposed.

The Reform of Popular Religion

The relative tolerance of popular practices shown by the Catholic Church was in part a reaction to the intolerant policies of the Protestant territories. Catholic officials hoped to gain popular support by espousing a policy that seemed moderate compared to the determined efforts of the neighboring Protestant authorities to wipe out a variety of so-called superstitions. The officials in the Calvinist territories of the Electoral Palatinate and Pfalz-Zweibrücken were making a concerted effort to end various popular festivities that in their opinion led to intemperance. The most significant of these were carnival (*Fastnacht*), the festival of St. John, and the parish festival (*Kermesse*), all of which involved drinking and eating to excess and included traditions that reformers of all confessions considered "pagan." In the Electoral Palatinate, the Calvinist authors of the Heidelberg Catechism also attacked all belief in healers and magicians as "idolatry," and Palatine officials persecuted suspected healers and cunning folk.

The Protestants also worked more aggressively to confessionalize

---

4. Schilling, "Die Konfessionalisierung im Reich," pp. 1–45; Zeeden, *Die Entstehung der Konfessionen*.

their territories. They fostered a Protestant consciousness by attacking in sermons and pamphlets Catholic practices such as the Mass, the cult of the saints, pilgrimages, and processions, as well as by emphasizing specifically Protestant forms of piety. In Lutheran territories, for instance, the use of song in Church services was important, as was domestic piety, including the family reading of the Bible; Calvinists emphasized the *Bettag*, or day of prayer. All confessions taught a catechism, and the Protestants claimed some success in teaching the population the rudiments of their faith.[5]

Protestant confessionalization, of course, had the effect of increasing religious tensions and promoting confessional polarization on all sides. Furthermore, the political fragmentation of the region meant that villagers had regular contact with neighbors of other confessions. As Bernard Vogler points out, this familiarity had two somewhat contradictory results: there was a relative tolerance of other religions and, at the same time, a consciousness of religious differences that could lead to hatred.[6]

Some of the reforms that came with the Counter-Reformation also widened the divisions between Protestant and Catholic. One of these was the imposition, in 1585, of the Gregorian calendar. The pope had ordered this innovation in 1583, but Bishop Eberhard hesitated for two years, fearing the opposition of the Protestant princes.[7] There was resistance to the new calendar in the countryside. In Deidesheim, the schultheiß and many of the villagers refused to obey the parish priest when he publicized the papal order from the pulpit and ordered the St. John's Fire lit according to the new calendar.[8] Since the Protestants continued to follow the old reckoning until the eighteenth century, the new calendar both complicated relations between villages and distinguished Catholics from Protestants.

The regular processions in Catholic villages led to conflicts with Protestant authorities, who regularly disrupted them.[9] Nevertheless, Catholic reformers encouraged these rituals because they fostered communal and parish unity and actively involved the laity in religious services. In 1591, Eberhard directed the canons of the Ritterstift in Bruchsal to participate in and lead the special processions

5. Bernard Vogler, *La vie religieuse en pays rhénan,* esp. part 2, chaps. 2 and 4, and part 3; idem, "Die Entstehung der protestantischen Volksfrömmigkeit in der rheinischen Pfalz zwischen 1555 und 1619," *Archiv für Reformationsgeschichte* 72 (1981): 158–96; idem, "Die Ausbildung des Konfessionsbewußtseins."
6. Vogler, *La vie religieuse en pays rhénan,* p. 1118.
7. Stamer III/1, p. 115.
8. GLAK 61/10947, pp. 227–227v, 229v–230r.
9. GLAK 61/11496, pp. 168r–168v.

he had ordered.[10] During the visitation of 1583–88, Beatus Moses took a special interest in this matter.

The Catholic reformers thus tried to revive traditional practices like processions, especially in regions like the Palatinate, in order to contrast the Catholic defense of religious tradition with the Calvinist "innovations." In the same vein, the Jesuits and other reformers worked to revive old confraternities and institute new ones in the city of Speyer.[11] There was an attempt do the same in the countryside. In 1602 in Deidesheim, the village council renewed the regulations of the Brotherhood of Saint Ann.[12] In Jöhlingen the canons of the Cathedral Chapter made an interesting attempt to bring a newly formed Confraternity of the Eucharist into the village. The canons founded this confraternity in 1612 partly in memory of the recently deceased Bishop Eberhard. In January 1613, they invited the citizens of Jöhlingen to join and to benefit from the special papal indulgence that it had been accorded.[13] There is no evidence that any villagers accepted the offer.

The marriage edict of 1582 caused important changes in popular practice. Designed to bring marriage practice in the Bishopric of Speyer into line with the decrees of the Council of Trent, this edict was generally obeyed. The visitation records make it clear that the pfarrer publicized it as they were supposed to. The bishop's council (the Hofrat) regularly handled cases of adultery and other sexual offenses that resulted from the stricter regulations.[14] In most cases the guilty parties were punished with fines and required to do penance by standing through regular church services holding a lit candle, though by the 1620s offenders could avoid this public disgrace by paying an additional fee.[15] Once again, the Catholic authorities avoided confrontation with the population by moderating the most severe punishments.

By encouraging processions, using the new calendar, promoting confraternities, and regulating marriage, Catholic reformers made a modest attempt to build a sense of Catholic consciousness in the population. To a great extent this policy, like other aspects of the

---

10. Remling UB, pp. 643–44.
11. Stamer III/1, pp. 129–30.
12. LASp. D2/340 (Deidesheim).
13. GLAK 61/15536, p. 297.
14. GLAK 61/11494/a, nine cases between 1582 and 1596; GLAK 61/11495/b, fifteen cases between 1597 and 1603; GLAK 61/10496, thirty-five cases between 1604 and 1615; GLAK 61/11497/I, eight cases between 1616 and 1618.
15. Ibid.

Counter-Reformation, was in reaction to the Protestant confession-alization in the Palatinate. But the overall impact of these measures was limited by the sympathetic attitude of Catholic authorities to-ward popular culture and by the villagers' resistance toward reforms imposed from above.

The moderation of Catholic policy can be seen in Bishop Sötern's carnival *(Fastnacht)* ordinance of 1616. The ordinance banned the use of masks and the participation of actors in carnival.[16] The bishop deplored the excesses that went with this festival, but ended his decree by showing sympathy for the "normal" behavior of his sub-jects and perhaps implying that the ordinance would not be strictly enforced. "Notwithstanding [these new regulations] we want neither to prevent nor to forbid honorable meetings and moderate drinking against thirst."[17] Finally, this decree was late and fairly mild com-pared to the policy of neighboring Protestants, who had outlawed *Fastnacht* entirely fifty years before.

Some Tridentine reforms were directly aimed at traditional re-ligious practices. In 1604, for example, the villagers of Odenheim protested against the first reformed Catholic priest in the village: "The pfarrer has now begun a great many innovations *(Neuerungen)*, namely, he does not want to marry newly joined couples, be they young or old, he allows no one to lift children out of the baptismal font (i.e. act as godparents), nor does he want to bury people who are not Catholics in the cemetery."[18] The new priest was apparently a stickler for all the regulations of the Council of Trent. The villagers objected to his handling of the three most important ceremonies in community life: baptism, marriage, and funeral.

The opposition in Odenheim to changes in religious practice was typical, although perhaps stronger than elsewhere in the Bishopric of Speyer. There was a large Protestant minority in the village and reform measures threatened the delicate religious balance there. In 1601 some of the villagers protested a new ordinance, claiming that they had no objections to attending church, but found the fines somewhat excessive.[19] The Odenheimer also disobeyed rules against dancing on Sundays and neglected catechism classes.[20] The peasants were especially disobedient; an armed group of them besieged several

16. *Collectio processuum synodalium*, pp. 424–26.
17. Veit and Lenhart, *Kirche und Volksfrömmigkeit*, p. 52.
18. GLAK 229/79260 (Odenheim).
19. GLAK 61/5431, pp. 777–78.
20. GLAK 61/5431, p. 938.

canons of the Ritterstift in the *Amthaus* of the village in 1595 in a
dispute over a case of witchcraft.[21] The gemeinde also engaged their
lords, the canons in Bruchsal, in a long lawsuit that was only resolved
in 1616.

Burials often caused conflict. It was the view of the villagers that
any member of the community had a right to be buried in the cemetery. The Tridentine Church, of course, only allowed burial of good
Catholics in sacred ground. In 1583 the parish priest in Zeutern
refused to bury an Anabaptist in the cemetery. The gemeinde responded by refusing the priest access to water and pasture (a measure
that symbolized ostracization from the community), then removed
him from his parish.[22] In Schifferstadt, Church authorities compromised with the villagers on this very issue—under pressure from the
Palatinate. Non-Catholic members of the commune could be buried
in the cemetery and the church bells could be rung (another essential
part of a burial), but the priest was not to participate in the service.[23]
In both these cases, it is apparent that the commune continued to
have an important role in local church affairs, even as the reformers
sought to change traditional behavior.

Finally, the parish priests themselves were not always enthusiastic
about reform and indeed were often reluctant to force changes on the
villagers. In 1588 the new pfarrer in Schifferstadt reported that the
previous priest had held only group confessions. The villagers, he
said, were not used to individual confessions and would not change
their habits easily. Furthermore, it was a large village, and the pfarrer
complained that it would be a lot of work to hear all the confessions
individually.[24] Here again one sees the problems the reformers faced
in trying to bring Tridentine Catholicism to the people of the Bishopric of Speyer.

Ultimately, the Counter-Reformation was forced to compromise
with the structures of traditional Christianity and village life, as well
as with the institutional weight of the traditional Church. The forms
of local Catholic religious life and the nature of confessional consciousness in the villages developed out of this compromise. This
development, beginning in the 1560s and continuing into the eighteenth century, must be understood as a dynamic process, not as the

21. GLAK 61/5431, pp. 41–46, 56–59, 60–61, 94, 111–12.
22. GLAK 61/10947, p. 61r.
23. GLAK 61/11495a, pp. 89r–89v.
24. GLAK 61/10947, p. 427v.

simple imposition of Tridentine Catholicism on a reluctant population.

Catholic Reformation in the Villages: Jöhlingen

How did the process of reform affect religious and social life in the villages? To trace the process of resistance and accommodation that formed Catholicism in Speyer, it is necessary to examine the Counter-Reformation at both the village and regional levels. The new ordinances and regulations directed at the religious life of the population were the same across sixteenth-century Germany wherever church and state worked to educate and reform popular religious life.[25] The people were to attend services, send their children to catechism classes, behave appropriately in church, and respect the sanctity of Sundays and holidays.

In addition, the authorities also tried to force the villagers to grant membership in their communes only to Catholics and to avoid contact with neighboring Protestant villages. This attempt to compel the villagers to respect the (essentially political) confessional divisions of the region was unsuccessful. Until the 1620s, servants and journeymen from Protestant areas were welcomed in Catholic villages, and economic and social ties between villages changed little.

Popular resistance forced Catholic reformers to abandon large parts of this program. Historians have documented the ability of rural populations across Europe to resist changes imposed from outside, and German peasants were no more obedient than other rural people.[26] After the 1580s, however, the Counter-Reformation came to the villages with the priests as well as through Church ordinances. The day-to-day presence of these new priests, so different from the peasant priests of the mid-sixteenth century, brought a new element into village society. Their more austere ways placed new strains on the relationship between the rural clergy and the villagers. Old disputes over property and tithes continued, but new problems arose. Villagers sometimes complained about the "arrogant" behavior of the priests, and the priests often lamented their parishioners' neglect

---

25. See especially Strauss, *Luther's House of Learning.*
26. See especially David Sabean, *Power in the Blood: Popular Culture and Village Discourse in Early Modern Germany* (Cambridge: Cambridge University Press, 1984).

of their religious duties. The story of the priests in Jöhlingen in the half century before the Thirty Years' War illustrates the changing and ambiguous role of the new clergymen.

Jöhlingen: Experiment in Reform

Jöhlingen, one of the larger villages in the Bishopric of Speyer, is on the edge of the Kraichgau just off the main highway from Durlach to Bretten. The village extends along a road in a small valley. In the sixteenth century the steeper hillsides were no doubt covered with vineyards, while the fields were planted in grain. To the south of the village was a large forest (much of which survives to this day) that belonged to the Cathedral Chapter. Although there are no exact figures on Jöhlingen's population in the sixteenth century, it is possible to compare it with similar-sized villages elsewhere in the region.[27] The population was probably around five hundred in 1530 and certainly more than that by the 1560s.

The Protestant Reformation had left Jöhlingen surrounded by Protestant villages but far from isolated economically and socially. The villagers had close ties to the Palatine town of Bretten and to Durlach, the residence city of the Lutheran margraves of Baden-Durlach. Several Jewish families lived in Jöhlingen, and with their close ties to the large Jewish communities in Frankfurt, Speyer, and Worms, as well as to smaller communities in the region, they provided the villagers with an important link to the outside world. The villagers were also in constant contact with their secular and religious overlords, the canons of the Cathedral Chapter in Speyer.

In the sixteenth century the canons held regular court sessions in Jöhlingen. These sessions, called Vogtsgerichte, served a double purpose: the representatives of the chapter, usually a canon and a secretary, adjudicated a wide variety of legal cases, and they also publicized ordinances of all kinds. Upon arrival in the village, the representatives of the chapter addressed a gathering of all the citizens. They read aloud edicts and ordinances, swore in new citizens, and admonished the villagers to obey existing statutes.[28]

The Cathedral Chapter was also in regular contact with the village

27. Meinrad Schaab and Kurt Anderman, "Leibeigenschaft der Einwohner des Hochstifts Speyer, 1530," Erläuterung zu *Historischer Atlas von Baden-Württemberg*, map IX,4; p. 9. In Jöhlingen in 1701 there were 125 Catholic families and 3 Jewish families (GLAK 61/11267, p. 21v). In 1816 Jöhlingen had 234 houses, 377 families, 1748 "souls," and "several" Jews (J. V. Kolb, *Historisch-Statistisch-Topographisches Lexicon von dem Großherzogsthum Baden* [Karlsruhe, 1816]).
28. GLAK 61/15535, 61/6981, 61/15536.

through its representative in the village, the *Keller* (or *Amtmann*). While the keller's main duty was collecting taxes and tithes for the chapter, he was also expected to keep the canons informed on conditions in Jöhlingen. In addition, the villagers did not hesitate to appeal to the Cathedral Chapter for assistance in resolving disputes or for help in conflicts with other princes. The minutes of the Cathedral Chapter indicate that the canons dealt regularly with affairs in Jöhlingen.

As the reform party came to dominate the Cathedral Chapter in the 1560s and 1570s, Jöhlingen became a testing ground for the Tridentine reforms. Between 1565 and 1581, the canons bypassed the reluctant Bishop Marquard and enacted in Jöhlingen several ordinances that foreshadowed Bishop Eberhard's reforms in the 1580s. This is not surprising since Eberhard, as cantor, and Beatus Moses, as sexprebendary, both enthusiastic supporters of reform, frequently represented the Cathedral Chapter at the Vogtsgericht in Jöhlingen in the 1570s.[29]

In the 1560s the efforts of the reformers were somewhat haphazard. In April 1566 a fine of five *Batzen* was set for those who went fishing or hunted birds on Sunday mornings. Apparently some of the villagers did not consider these activities forbidden work.[30] In August of the same year the canons ordered that the inn (*Wirtshaus*) be closed during church services and that dancing be restricted to Saturday afternoons. This ordinance had to be renewed a year later. The canons complained that there were more people in the inn than in the church during vespers in the late afternoon. Anyone found in the inn at this time was now to be fined ten batzen.[31]

In 1569 the chapter announced a stricter regulation. Complaining that "attendance at Church [has been] neglected on Sundays and holidays and they [the villagers] are out and around during the Mass and the sermon, in the inn or wherever their desires take them," the chapter levied a new fine of one gulden (fifteen batzen) on anyone found in the inn or on the street during services.[32] While the canons were obviously making a major effort to encourage church attendance, it is clear that the villagers had not changed their habits over the previous three years. Furthermore, it is hard to tell how these regulations were enforced. Perhaps the reform-minded canons were

29. GLAK 61/6981, pp. 257, 263, 273, 291, 311, 391.
30. GLAK 61/15535. 22 April 1566, no page numbers.
31. Ibid., 21 August 1566 and 14 May 1567, no page numbers.
32. Ibid., 22 November 1569.

finally becoming aware of the difficulty of forcing people to attend church services.

In 1575 the chapter began a more directed reform of the Church in Jöhlingen. Beginning in that year, Eberhard von Dienheim regularly presided over the Vogtsgericht in Jöhlingen, a sign that the reform party in the Cathedral Chapter was extending its influence. Eberhard promulgated a series of extensive church ordinances for Jöhlingen. He ordered the peasants to go to church on Sundays and Church holidays, to confess and take communion on Easter, and to pay the required fees for funerals. The punishments for disobedience were much harsher than the fines that had been levied in the 1560s: "My lords have ordered the disobedient not to be tolerated in [their villages] . . . , but rather to be banished."[33]

The Cathedral Chapter also enacted a marriage ordinance for Jöhlingen in 1580, two years before Bishop Eberhard's marriage decree. The concern of the chapter in 1580 was that young people were getting married without parental permission. Although the text of the Jöhlingen marriage ordinance has not survived, it is likely that the new regulations read by the priest from the pulpit were similar to those of 1582.[34] In June 1583 the bishop's marriage edict was read at the Vogtsgericht. The presiding canon was the dean of the Cathedral Chapter himself, Andreas von Oberstein. Oberstein emphasized that marriages were only possible with the permission of the parents and that the pfarrer had to be present for a promise of marriage to be legitimate. He also went out of his way to explain the new edict to the priest, whose duty it was to enforce it. In January 1584 some of the poorer members of the community complained that the ordinance required everyone to have a ceremony, and this was too costly for the poor. "Not everyone [they said] can afford [the costs] of the bishop's . . . edict." We do not know how the chapter responded to this difficulty. The villagers had no other objections to the marriage ordinance, except to complain about the cost of sending offenders to the bishop's court in Obergrombach, about ten kilometers away.[35]

In 1588 the canons moved to enforce the bishop's catechism ordinances. The parish priest had indeed been holding classes on Sunday afternoons, but few parishioners attended. The chapter ordered the village council to force everyone, young and old, to attend.[36] But the adults in the village never did go to catechism classes, and in 1601

33. GLAK 61/6981, pp. 273–74, 291–92.
34. GLAK 61/10945, pp. 423–24.
35. GLAK 61/6981, pp. 455–56, 458, 509.
36. Ibid., p. 588.

one of the canons lamented the failure of classes for the youth as well: "[If] the youth are allowed to grow up without the right knowledge of God and Christ and as a result [they] live such a crude life, then the consequence, unfortunately, is [the situation] before our eyes here [in Jöhlingen]."[37] For enforcement purposes, the schoolmaster was ordered to keep a register of all children in the village over the age of seven. Parents of children who missed the classes were to be fined. This measure was not completely successful, since in 1602 the canons had to warn the parents again to send their children to catechism class.[38]

In 1612 catechism took on a new significance. The Cathedral Chapter decided to require all candidates for citizenship (*Bürgerschaft* or *Bürgerrecht*) in Jöhlingen to pass an examination on the catechism. This new requirement had a double purpose. Not only did it force youths who wanted to become full citizens to study their catechism, it also prevented Protestants and sectarians from neighboring villages from gaining citizenship. The catechism requirement was part of an ongoing effort to enforce confessional uniformity in Jöhlingen. In 1576 all servants, journeymen, and maids, even if their parents were not Catholic, had been ordered to attend Mass and take communion, "since the authorities will not allow another and new religion [in Jöhlingen]."[39] Protestant journeymen and servants were common in Jöhlingen in the late sixteenth century. Most of them came from nearby villages in Protestant territories and seem to have caused no unusual problems in the village. They generally did not stay in Jöhlingen after their service was over. The new requirements of 1612 primarily affected sons of Jöhlingen residents.

The parish priest examined candidates for citizenship on the catechism and quickly realized that the village youths were unable to pass even a simple examination.[40] In May 1612 he approved only one of three candidates, and even the one who succeeded had answered only some questions correctly and was ordered to study more. In 1613 eight people received citizenship, even though none of them knew the catechism. The priest reported that most of them were over twenty, and some were already married. It was not possible for him to hold up their applications for full citizenship in the village any longer. By refusing citizenship to grown men the canons risked se-

---

37. GLAK 61/15536, p. 90.
38. Ibid., pp. 90, 107.
39. GLAK 61/6981, p. 273.
40. The candidates for citizenship were all young men. Widows could obtain considerable rights in the village, but they were exempt from the test.

rious social disruption in Jöhlingen. The parish priest recognized this fact and refused to enforce the ordinance strictly. Thus after only four years the experiment was dropped entirely; the last mention of cate-chism tests occurs in 1616. Between 1618 and 1623 thirty-five new citizens were sworn in without having to take this test.[41]

It is difficult to assess the impact of church ordinances in other areas. The canons regularly reminded the villagers of their duty to attend weekly church services. In September 1597 twenty-eight peo-ple were fined for coming late or completely missing Sunday or holiday services. This was not a large group, since it included all offenders during a period of at least several months. In 1602 "several" villagers failed to take communion at Easter and faced serious fines. The youths of the village continued to hold festivals with drinking and dancing on religious holidays. The effort to enforce religious uniformity was even less successful. Not only did Protestant ser-vants and journeymen continue to come to Jöhlingen, villagers also intermarried with Protestants from neighboring villages.[42]

The Cathedral Chapter made a concerted effort between the 1560s and 1621 to reform religious life in Jöhlingen, but with limited suc-cess. The authorities were unable (or unwilling) to take harsh mea-sures. Between 1595 and 1603, for example, the Vogtsgericht, al-though an organ of the ecclesiastical lords of the village, confined itself to resolving disputes within the village. Only three people were fined for working on Sundays, while forty-four were fined for brawl-ing.[43] Between this reluctance to force changes on the village from above and the villagers' resistance, the Counter-Reformation had only a small impact in Jöhlingen before the Thirty Years' War.

Jöhlingen: The Villagers and Their Priests

The reformers had more success imposing Tridentine ideals on the rural clergy than on the rural population. After the 1580s parish priests became better educated, were publicly celibate, and partici-pated in village life less as members of the community and more as part of an outside elite. The villagers of Jöhlingen came more often into conflict with their parish priests as the latter became representa-tives of the Counter-Reformation. The gulf between the parish priest

41. GLAK 61/15536, pp. 290, 307–8, 334, 340, 347, 356, 389, 402, 422.
42. Ibid., pp. 52, 107, 178–79.
43. Ibid., pp. 178–79.

and his community in the period before the Thirty Years' War, however, should not be exaggerated. The priest in Jöhlingen remained a participant in local economic and social life and often became involved in village conflicts. Often caught between the demands of the authorities in Speyer and those of his neighbors, the pfarrer was forced to compromise, usually to the benefit of the villagers.

Jöhlingen was a sought-after parish. Although it is difficult to compare parish incomes since the priests were paid both in kind and in money, the parish priest in Jöhlingen received an income of over two hundred gulden in 1603. This made it one of the five richest rural benefices in the Bishopric of Speyer.[44] As a result, priests were willing to stay in Jöhlingen for extended periods and often came to the village with considerable experience. It is perhaps fair to say that the priests in Jöhlingen were the elite of the rural clergy.

One of these priests, Johann Merckell, has already been mentioned. His will, written in 1592, makes it clear that he was the last of the pre-Tridentine priests in Jöhlingen. A proud father of two and grandfather of nine, Merckell had been part of the village community.[45] His daughter married a Jöhlingen *Bürger*, and in 1582 his son was given special permission to become a citizen. The Cathedral Chapter made an exception to the rule denying citizenship to illegitimate children because of Merckell's long tenure.[46] He served in Jöhlingen for at least twenty years and retired honorably to a chaplaincy in Bruchsal. Yet he was certainly no ideal priest. He obviously had had a concubine and apparently frequented the inn. In 1571 he was reprimanded (and perhaps fined) for a dispute in the inn during which, under the influence of wine, he verbally abused one of his neighbors.[47] Merckell also neglected some of the church property in the village: "The pfarrer has let the parish property go to ruin and instead has bought property for himself which [he keeps] in better condition [than the church property]." Although he had regular disputes with the Cathedral Chapter, Merckell had few problems with his parishioners. The only conflict that came to the attention of the canons was over the right of the priest to collect fees for funerals.[48]

44. This figure is based on lists of income of all the parishes in the bishopric (GLAK 78/615 and LASp. D2/306/1). It is a very general estimate. The primmissary in Jöhlingen, who handled services in the small neighboring village of Wöschbach, earned about one hundred gulden. At various times this benefice was vacant and the pfarrer in Jöhlingen was paid this money as well, to compensate him for the added duties.
45. GLAK 42/2491.
46. GLAK 61/10945, p. 850.
47. GLAK 61/15535, 11 December 1571, no page numbers.
48. GLAK 61/6981, pp. 366, 231–32, 298.

Merckell retired in the early 1580s, just as the reformers took control of the bishopric. Between 1585 and 1635 five parish priests served in Jöhlingen. None had a concubine, and all made some effort to bring Tridentine Catholicism to Jöhlingen. There was certainly more tension in the relationship between these priests and the villagers than there had been when Merckell held the post.

We know little about Merckell's immediate successor, Steffan Breunlung, pfarrer from about 1585 to 1590. Soon after his arrival in the village Breunlung protested bitterly about the condition in which Merckell had left the parish property. He also had trouble with the villagers, who complained that he was putting pressure on people to make deathbed contributions to the Church. He in turn criticized the villagers for neglecting church services.[49]

Breunlung was succeeded by Johan Reuter, whose six years in the parish (1590–96) were filled with conflict. Reuter's biggest problem was a long running feud with the keller. It is not clear what caused this feud, but the dispute exploded in September 1590. After church on a Sunday the keller verbally assaulted Reuter, accusing him of sending false reports to the Cathedral Chapter, reports that put the keller in a bad light with his superiors. He also criticized the priest for putting on airs because he was a clergyman.[50]

This latter accusation suggests that Reuter was behaving in new ways that offended the villagers. At the same time, it may have reflected an older anticlerical tradition. During that same summer of 1590 the primissary in Jöhlingen, Hans Weber, was badly beaten on a lonely road near the village. Weber accused the miller in Jöhlingen of the attack and reported that his attacker told some passing shepherds, "It does not matter much if one beats a priest [*Pfaffen*] to death, there are always more."[51] This remark sounds more like traditional popular anticlericalism than any new opposition to "arrogant, over-educated" priests that appear in the post-Tridentine period. The timeless *Pfaffenhaß*, grounded in the economic exploitation of the peasants by the clergy, was still alive in Jöhlingen in the 1590s.[52]

The Cathedral Chapter tried to adjudicate the dispute between its two representatives in Jöhlingen, the keller and the priest. Although the canons initially sympathized with Reuter and fined the keller for his outburst in the church, by 1592 they were threatening to remove

49. Ibid., pp. 541–42, 601.
50. Ibid., pp. 613–14, 619–20, 61/10949, pp. 146–47.
51. Ibid., pp. 611–12.
52. For anticlericalism and *Pfaffenhaß* see Rapp, *Réformes et Réformation à Strasbourg.*

the priest, apparently having finally been persuaded of his incompetence by the keller. The villagers, however, interceded on behalf of Reuter, apparently without great enthusiasm, but effectively enough that he stayed in the parish until 1596.[53] In fact, the canons fired the keller in November 1592, when a deputation from the Cathedral Chapter found that he was living with another man's wife. In addition, he "not only neglected religious services, but also at times mocked all that goes with them."[54] This episode reflects several problems that faced the canons in their effort to govern Jöhlingen. There was no unity between the officials they had in the village itself. It was not easy to remove a priest if the villagers liked him. And, finally, priests like Reuter quickly settled into the village and supported the villagers in their conflicts with the central government in Speyer.

It was the issue of witchcraft that brought the latter difficulty to a head. At least four times between 1574 and 1595 local authorities in Jöhlingen arrested women for witchcraft and turned them over to the bishop's officials for questioning. In almost every case the judges questioned the women and released them, causing the villagers to protest vehemently.[55] In 1595 the villagers (against the wishes of the village council) refused to be assessed for a new imperial tax unless an accused woman was convicted of witchcraft. Although the Cathedral Chapter responded very negatively to this sort of "tax strike," one woman was, in fact, burned for witchcraft.[56]

Reuter was one of the ringleaders in the 1595 tax strike. He had preached frequently and violently about the dangers of witchcraft and had attacked the village council (gericht) for failing to pressure the Cathedral Chapter into proceeding against the "evil women." It was Reuter who called the assembly where the villagers decided to withhold tax payments.[57] Reuter, who had also made important enemies in the village, especially among the members of the village council, was severely reprimanded by his superiors in Speyer:

> He should study his sermons . . . and admonish the people to do penance, and not bring up the terrible evil [i.e. witchcraft]. If he wishes to stay in Jöhlingen, he should stop doing this and take care of his job. He should not stir up the community and get involved in . . . affairs that are the responsibility of others . . . and, except during confession, he

53. GLAK 61/10949, pp. 251, 275, 283–84.
54. Ibid., p. 315.
55. For one example in 1578 see GLAK 61/10945, pp. 110–11.
56. GLAK 61/10949, pp. 553–57, 680.
57. GLAK 61/15536, pp. 27–31.

should not spread, discuss, or speak publicly about the bothersome witchcraft issue, least of all from the pulpit.[58]

The Cathedral Chapter was as upset that Reuter had become involved in internal village disputes as it was with his support of the villagers against the chapter. Reuter clearly shared the villagers' fear of witches, rather than the skepticism of the canons and judges.[59] He was still far from being an ideal representative of the Tridentine Church in the village. Within a year of the 1595 dispute the chapter removed him from Jöhlingen.

The next pfarrer, Heinrich Benerungst, also had difficulties in Jöhlingen. Benerungst resolutely enforced the ordinances of the chapter, which brought him into conflict with the villagers. He complained about the attendance at catechism classes and at Mass, and he even attempted to enforce deathbed contributions to the Church over the objections of the surviving family members. The village council protested to the Cathedral Chapter that Benerungst had refused to hear the confession of dying villagers unless they had prepaid for the masses to be said for their souls. He also refused to marry a couple (for unknown reasons), and lectured the villagers on blasphemy from the pulpit. He quickly developed a reputation as a "combative person."[60]

Benerungst was, however, more concerned with the management of the parish property than with his pastoral duties. His letters and petitions to the Cathedral Chapter are full of complaints about his neighbors. They cut his wood, he said, took pieces of his fields, failed to pay all tithes and fees, and so on. In 1603 Benerungst was called before the vicar general and removed. Although the reasons for his removal are unknown, it took place soon after the villagers had complained about his behavior.[61]

The last two parish priests in Jöhlingen before the Thirty Years' War were also the first true "reformed" priests in the village. Julius Bossart (1603–5) and Friderich Klein (1605–35) had both studied in the chapter's Alumnat in Speyer, and both had had on-the-job train-

58. Ibid., p. 35.
59. Since the records of the witchcraft trials have been lost, it is impossible to tell why the authorities refused to punish most of the accused witches sent to them from Jöhlingen. Perhaps the judges found the evidence inconclusive. Their distance from Jöhlingen, I suspect, allowed them some freedom from pressure for conviction. See H. C. Erik Midelfort, Witchhunting in Southwestern Germany, 1562–1684: The Social and Intellectual Foundations (Stanford: Stanford University Press, 1972).
60. GLAK 61/10951, p. 517; GLAK 61/15536, pp. 65–66, 83–84, 92, 100.
61. GLAK 61/15536, pp. 65, 83–84, 108–10, 116, 123; GLAK 61/10951, p. 517, 561–62.

ing as chaplains in Deidesheim before coming to Jöhlingen. The Jesuit teachers in Speyer had singled out Klein for special praise.[62] Neither of these men had the problems of their predecessors. Klein's handling of the catechism dispute of 1612–16 probably explains why. As mentioned earlier, it was he who refused to enforce the chapter's ordinance that made proficiency in the catechism a prerequisite for village citizenship.

Bossart and Klein served the people of Jöhlingen without a hint of controversy, possibly because of their training. Louis Châtellier has argued that in training priests, French Jesuits emphasized "the isolation of the priest in the parish," while German priests were taught to be less aloof.[63] Perhaps, then, because Klein and Bossert had learned to be more in tune with their parishioners than their French colleagues, and were better educated than their predecessors, they handled their parishioners with more finesse.

The uneventful thirty-year tenure of Klein indicates that a tacit compromise had been reached between the villagers and the church reformers. Changes in religious life in Jöhlingen had indeed taken place between the 1560s and 1621. The villagers attended services with some regularity, respected the sanctity of holidays, and accepted an educated and celibate priest. They generally obeyed the marriage ordinance. On the other hand, the Church gave up efforts to test candidates for citizenship on the catechism and failed to prevent the villagers from continuing their contacts with their Protestant neighbors. In fact, there is no indication that the Counter-Reformation brought a major change in lay behavior in Jöhlingen. On the eve of the Thirty Years' War, adultery and brawling continued to provide the bulk of the work of the Vogtsgericht, dances still took place on Sundays, and the inn continued to do a brisk business.

The Catholic Reformation in the Villages: Otterstadt

The village of Otterstadt is only a few kilometers outside the city of Speyer. In the second half of the sixteenth century it probably had a population of over four hundred. Located on low ground near the Rhine, the village was always threatened by floods. Most of the villagers were grain farmers, but a sizable group were fishermen. The

---

62. GLAK 61/10951, p. 917.
63. Châtellier, *The Europe of the Devout* p. 83.

people of Otterstadt had frequent contact with the Lutheran city of Speyer, and by the 1560s a number of Protestants lived in the village.

Like Jöhlingen, Otterstadt had a peculiar juridical status. The secular overlords of the village were the canons of the Chapter of St. Guido in Speyer who, like their more powerful neighbors in the Cathedral Chapter, took a special interest in religious affairs of their village. Unlike the other smaller chapters, St. Guido was fairly cosmopolitan and had an influential reform party, led by Dionysius Burckhart (canon 1564–1605, dean 1578–1605).[64] This group attempted, with considerable diligence, to enforce the decrees of the Council of Trent in Otterstadt. As early as 1565 the chapter published a major reform ordinance for Otterstadt.[65] Between 1575 and 1621 the canons discussed conditions in Otterstadt at every general meeting of the chapter, heard reports by the priest on the behavior of his parishioners, and passed new ordinances regulating religious life in the village.

The reform-minded canons emphasized attendance at church services and catechism classes. They especially wanted the Otterstadter to participate in all the Catholic sacraments correctly, and so they introduced the sacrament of Extreme Unction in the village, encouraged more frequent confession, and enforced the new marriage regulations. The chapter promulgated a series of ordinances covering all these issues in the 1580s. The proximity of Otterstadt to Speyer allowed the canons in Speyer to keep a close eye on the progress of what they recognized themselves as the "reform" in the village. This reform effort peaked in the 1590s. After 1605 the canons ceased to promulgate new ordinances and demonstrated less interest in conditions in Otterstadt. Just as in the rest of the bishopric, the reform impulse had run its course.

The effect of the reform was limited, as it was in Jöhlingen. By the 1620s the villagers certainly attended church services with more regularity than they had done in the 1560s, and they generally obeyed the new marriage ordinance. Catechism classes, however, were poorly attended, and, to the dismay of the authorities, the annual Church festival continued to be an excuse for a major celebration to which inhabitants of neighboring villages, including Protestants, were invited. Attempts to end other popular traditions and practices also failed. The villagers' resistance to extensive changes in their

64. Stamer III/1, p. 134.
65. LASp. F1/77b, pp. 73v–78v.

religious lives had a lot to do with the slowed pace of reform after 1605.

Because Otterstadt was so close to Speyer, the canons at St. Guido were able to interfere easily in village affairs. This proximity also allowed them to save money on a priest for the village. Instead of having a resident priest, Otterstadt was served by a vicar who came from St. Guido on Sundays and holidays. The vicars considered this a difficult and poorly paid job, and as a result they rarely kept the position for long. Between 1573 and 1605 fifteen different clergymen served Otterstadt. No priest served longer than five years and most resigned after one or two years in order to take better positions. This arrangement certainly benefited St. Guido financially. In 1592 the vicar who performed services in Otterstadt was paid sixty-two gulden for his pastoral duties. This amount would not have been enough to support a resident priest, but it was sufficient for a vicar who lived in the city and was paid for his duties in the chapter as well. In the same period the chapter collected a tithe in the village of around two hundred malter of grain a year, at an approximate value of four hundred gulden.[66]

In the absence of a resident priest, the reform in Otterstadt had a peculiar nature. There were none of the conflicts between the villagers and the priests that occurred in Jöhlingen. Nor was there any mutual affection or loyalty between priest and parishioners. The priests did not operate as buffers between the villagers and the Church authorities, nor did they help to bring about an accommodation between the villagers and the Catholic reformers. As a result, the reform in Otterstadt was imposed from outside to a greater extent than in Jöhlingen. It should be kept in mind that the most significant effect of the Counter-Reformation in the Bishopric of Speyer was the appearance of a new kind of clergyman in the villages. But no such change occurred in Otterstadt or in several other villages around Speyer, which were served by priests from the city. What did occur was a consistent and thorough reform program imposed from "above."

In 1576 the canons of St. Guido declared that "the reformation of some deficiencies and errors found among the subjects (*Under-thanen*) in Otterstadt must be continued" and that punishments should be announced in the village.[67] The most important "deficien-

---

66. GLAK 61/11107, p. 22v (for income); GLAK 61/11106, 6 July 1591. (for tithe).
67. GLAK 61/11105, p. 28v.

cies and errors" were in the practice of the sacraments. The villagers practiced neither Extreme Unction nor Confirmation, and the canons were intent on instituting these sacraments. The priest explained them in his sermons and asked the village council to inform him of ill people who were in need of last rites.[68]

In the 1580s the emphasis was on the catechism. The canons, rather optimistically, gave the pfarrer extensive instructions:

> Pfarrer Bettenhöfer should, every Sunday and holiday after the sermon in Otterstadt, explain, teach, and inspire . . . the children and adults about the Our Father, the Hail Mary, the Apostle's Creed, the Ten Commandments, and the general confession. . . . [He should do this] without fail in distinct and understandable German. In this way the adults will learn from him, their minister, what their elders had neglected and the children will be brought up in respect and fear of God's power.[69]

The reformers confidently assumed the effectiveness of catechism classes. At the same time, they recognized that some priests were ineffective teachers and hoped to avoid these problems in Bettenhöfer's case; for one thing, some priests apparently spoke dialects the villagers did not understand. Several of the priests assigned to Otterstadt did neglect the catechism classes, and, in an attempt to improve the situation, the canons of St. Guido asked the Jesuits to handle the classes. This idea was a complete failure. In September 1587, the canons expressed concern that the Jesuit who was teaching in Otterstadt only spoke Low German, a dialect totally incomprehensible to the villagers. A month later the Jesuit father was attacked in the church by several peasants and beaten.[70] There is, unfortunately, no evidence of the objections the villagers had to the Jesuit. Was it his manner, his dialect, or the fact that he pressured people to attend catechism classes that brought the beating upon him? It was perhaps a combination of these factors, since catechism classes continued in Otterstadt and, while there was passive resistance to them, no other priest was physically attacked.

Faced with a lack of enthusiasm on the part of both the priests and the villagers of Otterstadt, the canons reduced their goals. Only children were required to attend the classes. Furthermore, by 1600, the canons no longer expected the children to learn a series of prayers

68. GLAK 61/11104, 20 July 1573.
69. GLAK 61/11105, pp. 288v–289r.
70. Ibid., pp. 386v–387r; GLAK 61/11106, 1587 (Fall General Chapter).

and instead required only that they all learn the Our Father.[71] The pfarrer again and again blamed the parents for failing to send their children to the classes, while the canons found that the priests themselves neglected them, especially on holidays.[72] It is important to note, however, that despite the resistance of the villagers and the priests, catechism classes were regularly given in Otterstadt from the 1580s until the 1620s.

Although the villagers came to Church services consistently, their behavior was far from perfect. In 1592 a pfarrer reported, "When he is just reading the Mass, before the sermon, they [the villagers] do not come in for the Mass, instead they stand outside in front of the church and peer inside like dogs [peering] into the kitchen . . . [and they disrupt] the sermon with their turmoil." This report differs little from those of Protestant pastors in neighboring areas.[73] By 1600, the priest reported, the villagers were no longer coming to only "half the Mass," although they still sometimes came "somewhat late."[74]

A long-standing difficulty was that the women in the village came to services less often than the men. In the early 1590s the priests reported that the women neglected the services. In 1600 they came on Sundays, but stayed home on holidays.[75] Perhaps the women considered housework, as opposed to field work, acceptable on Church holidays and stayed away from Church to attend to these duties. By about 1610, however, this problem was solved, at least to the satisfaction of the priests. A report from 1614 is typical of the priests' responses to the canons' questions about Otterstadt in the years after about 1605: "[Everyone] is obedient enough, . . . except the youths are a bit neglectful of the catechism."[76]

The canons of St. Guido, like the cathedral canons in Jöhlingen, made a concerted effort to reform the parish of Otterstadt. As in Jöhlingen, however, the villagers did not change their traditional behavior. They continued to hold dances on Sundays and church festivals that included drinking and gaming. They neglected catechism classes and went to a healer to save their sick cows.[77] After 1605 the canons recognized that only limited reforms were possible

71. GLAK 61/11108, p. 233r.
72. Ibid., pp. 389v, 390r, June 1606; GLAK 61/11109, p. 3v, October 1606.
73. GLAK 61/11107, p. 25r. For the Protestants, see Vogler, *La vie religieuse en pays rhénan*, esp. part 2, chap. 2, sect. 1.
74. GLAK 61/11108, pp. 233r–233v, 1600; and pp. 323v–324r, 1603.
75. GLAK 61/11108, p. 247v.
76. GLAK 61/11109, p. 225v.
77. Concerning the "healer" see GLAK 61/11107, 108v, 111r. He was in charge of the village cows (the *Kuhehirt*) and used both incantations and herbs to help sick cows.

and concentrated on making the villagers attend services. The interest and involvement of the St. Guido Chapter in conditions in Otterstadt waned in the second and third decades of the seventeenth
century. Here again the reformers compromised with the villagers
rather than attempting to enforce a comprehensive Tridentine reform.

Extensive Tridentine reform did not occur in the Bishopric of
Speyer because the Church was neither willing nor able to undertake
such a task, especially where popular religious practice was concerned. In an attempt to gain the high ground of tradition against the
Protestants, Catholic authorities hesitated to attack popular religion. Catholic reformers also followed a moderate policy because
they sympathized with, and participated, in many elements of popular religion. This moderation, combined with the resistance of village communes to changes in traditional religion, meant that Tridentine Catholicism reached the countryside in a very diluted form.

Finally, it was left to the parish priests to bring reformed Catholicism to the parishes. These were mostly practical men who understood their role in the villages. Backed up only by a weak episcopal
bureaucracy, the priests were careful to accommodate the desires and
interests of their parishioners. They rarely attempted to impose unpopular reforms and mostly endeavored to maintain good relations
with the villagers. It is therefore misleading to view the Counter-
Reformation as a process of reform imposed from above. The ecclesiastical elite in Speyer was itself divided, and the members of this
elite who were in regular contact with the people, the parish clergy,
were unwilling to push reform. In the long run, a tacit compromise
involving the villagers, the priests, and the Church authorities determined the contours of post-Tridentine religious practice in the Bishopric of Speyer.

4

Confessional Conflict and the Limits of Episcopal Authority

In much of Germany the combination of three competing religions and multiple territorial states intensified confessional conflict. This problem was most apparent in imperial politics. Beginning in the 1590s, religious issues, exacerbated by the ambitions of territorial princes, increasingly threatened the pragmatic peace of 1555. The differences that led to the Thirty Years' War became irreconcilable with the growing intransigence of the political and religious power blocs.[1]

How were religious conflicts played out at the regional and local level? Were confessional lines, as Heinz Schilling has argued, "drawn in the society of the empire down to the level of the cities and villages, even individual houses and families"?[2] Recent research has established that rising confessional tensions after about 1570 had serious consequences in German cities. R. Po-chia Hsia's study of Münster shows that Tridentine reforms, pushed by the Jesuits, ended the long-standing coexistence there of traditionalist Catholics and Protestants. Such measures had a similar effect in the territories of the bishop of Würzburg in the 1570s.[3] "Confessionalization" as practiced

---

1. Martin Heckel, *Deutschland im konfessionellen Zeitalter* (Göttingen: Vandenhoeck und Ruprecht, 1983), esp. part 1, chap. 1, and part 3; Schilling, "Die Konfessionalisierung im Reich," p. 28.
2. Schilling, "Die Konfessionalisierung im Reich," p. 28.
3. Hsia, *Society and Religion in Münster*; Rublack, *Gescheiterte Reformation*.

in Münster and Würzburg was not just Catholic policy. Protestant princes, especially those who governed well-organized territories, evicted Catholics and sectarians, often ending a de facto toleration of religious minorities. Confessionalization thus brought political and religious conflicts that threatened the stability of the empire.

Religious conflicts in the Bishopric of Speyer, however, did not follow the path described by Hsia and Schilling. Although the level of confessional tension there increased with the arrival of the Jesuits, especially in cities and towns, Protestant and Catholic officials and the Church successfully defused religious conflict in the 1590s. Political tensions between the bishopric and the neighboring Protestant states also increased, but these conflicts had little impact on the Catholic or Protestant population. A hard-nosed understanding of the realities of economic and social interdependence, not an insistence on religious differences, characterized relations between villagers of different religions. Within the cities and towns of the region, people of different religions generally coexisted peacefully. It was only after 1650 that the people of the bishopric began to develop a strong confessional consciousness.

The city of Speyer, with its large Catholic clerical establishment and Lutheran population, was threatened by the same divisive trends as Münster and other German cities. The arrival of the Jesuits and the Protestant reaction to them caused an increase in confessional conflict and violence in the city in the 1570s and 1580s. Most Catholics in Speyer, however, were not militant and worked hard to minimize the friction caused by the Jesuits and their supporters. The Lutheran magistrates, who also feared the consequences of unbridled religious conflict, supported this effort. By 1590 these groups had calmed the religious situation in Speyer and most disputes between the clergy and the city remained traditional, involving the economic and judicial privileges of the clergy.

Religious conflicts in the middle Rhine region as a whole escalated at the end of the sixteenth century. The Electoral Palatinate pursued an aggressive anti-Catholic policy, which greatly affected the policies of the bishops of Speyer, even within their own territory. Officials in the Palatine court even proposed plans for the secularization of the bishopric.[4] Yet these conflicts remained political and did not penetrate to the people of the Catholic villages. Catholic authorities refused to use Protestant attacks as a political resource to strengthen the Church in the countryside. This nonmilitant policy meant that

4. Press, "Das Hochstift Speyer," p. 264.

Catholic villagers developed only a limited confessional conscious-ness.[5] Furthermore, the social, economic, and geographical realities of this divided region made confessional conflict impractical.

The political dominance of the Electoral Palatinate also reduced the militancy of the Church. Before the Thirty Years' War, it was generally the Protestants who increased political and religious tensions. The bishops of Speyer and most of the Catholic clergy recognized the dangers of open confessional conflict for their small bishopric and followed a conciliatory policy toward the Protestants.

Yet according to the Council of Trent, the bishops were to lead the revitalized Church. A goal of the Counter-Reformation was to strengthen the authority of the bishops and centralize Church organization. This policy, formulated by Italian and Spanish bishops, had little impact on the German situation. The bishops of Speyer, confronted by powerful Protestant princes and independent-minded Catholic magistrates, could not enforce their spiritual authority beyond the bounds of their secular principality. In this region the political situation and particularist traditions helped preserve the local character of Catholicism against Tridentine innovation.

The Catholic Imperial City of Weil der Stadt provides an example of this locally focused Catholicism. The city magistrates did not allow the bishops to exercise their ecclesiastical authority in the city. Weil der Stadt maintained a traditionalist Catholic Church and re-sisted interference from both Lutheran Württemberg, whose territory surrounded the city, and reforming churchmen. The city fathers had little interest in admitting Tridentine reform measures that gave the bishop of Speyer authority over the city's clergy and that threatened to drive the town's Protestant minority into open revolt. In Weil the bishops of Speyer were exclusively spiritual overlords with few financial or political rights.

One might expect Church officials across the bishopric to embrace Tridentine reform with enthusiasm, hoping to increase episcopal authority within their diocese. But this was not the case. Local authorities generally did not want episcopal interference and when it was requested, the bishops responded apathetically. Clearly, in the Bishopric of Speyer, episcopal centralization as advocated by the Council of Trent was not the unquestioned model of Catholic reform. An important result was that the Counter-Reformation did not lead to a unified form of Catholicism in this region. Without strong

5. Wolfgang Reinhard, "Konfession und Konfessionalisierung in Europa," in Wolfgang Reinhard et al., eds., *Bekenntnis und Geschichte. Die Confessio Augustana in historischem Zusammenhang* (Munich: Verlag Ernst Vogel, 1981), 179.

episcopal leadership, each territory, city, and even village maintained its own traditions and practices. Nor did the Counter-Reformation cause confessional conflict or create Catholic militancy. The Catholics could not expect to convert the Protestants of the region and chose to avoid trouble with their neighbors. In confessional politics, as in internal religious reform, the Catholic Church in the Bishopric of Speyer followed a policy that was both moderate and practical.

The Imperial City of Speyer

In the city of Speyer, Protestantism and Catholicism, the Reformation and the Counter-Reformation, were in direct contact. Conflict between the clergy and the citizens of Speyer was not new, however. Since at least the thirteenth century the city had attempted to restrict the privileges of the clergy and to reduce the power of the bishops. In the fifteenth century the townsmen drove the bishops from the city, and Speyer gained full political independence. In the sixteenth century, relations between the Lutheran-governed city and the Catholic clergy were dominated by the interaction of the city council and the urban chapters, with little involvement of the bishop.

Protestant control of the city government changed this situation very little. The Rachtung, a treaty negotiated every fifteen years between the chapter clergy and the city council, continued to regulate their relationship. This treaty specified the legal and economic privileges of the clergy. It was these privileges that caused most of the disputes between clergy and city in the sixteenth century.

The beginnings of a Catholic reform movement, and especially the arrival of the Jesuits in Speyer, caused an increase in confessional tensions and threatened to destroy the urban peace. The 1570s and 1580s were difficult decades in Speyer. Religious conflicts, stirred up by the Jesuits, some Lutheran preachers, and the small Calvinist community, combined with economic difficulties, threatened the control of the city council and caused a considerable amount of violence.

Before the Thirty Years' War, however, there was a tacit alliance between the traditionalist and moderate Catholic clergy and the Lutheran ruling class. Although divided by religious belief, these groups were united by economic and personal ties, by loyalty to the empire, and by a fear of extremism. The Counter-Reformation and the Protestant reaction to it threatened the comfortable particularist status quo in Speyer. Both the magistrates and the urban clergy also feared that a successful Counter-Reformation might give the bishop increased power in the city. To prevent this, Catholic and Lutheran authorities worked together to defuse tensions and restore balance. Although conflicts between Catholics and Protestants continued through the seventeenth century, these were traditional and negotiable disputes over the privileges and rights of the clergy.

The Historical Legacy and the Effect of the Reformation

The city of Speyer was an important regional center in the sixteenth century, and the first half of the century was in many ways the high point in Speyer's history. A prosperous textile industry and the popularity of the Rhenish wines produced in the region made the city a major trading center. The population rose steadily to about eight thousand in 1565.[6] Speyer stagnated economically in the second half of the sixteenth century, however. In 1600 its population was still around eight thousand and by 1670 it had declined to less than five thousand.[7] The city also declined in importance. Between 1529 and 1570, five imperial diets were held in Speyer, and the last, in 1570, put a tremendous strain on the city. There was a shortage of beds, and some of the representatives were forced to stay in neighboring villages. Many delegates complained of the scarcity of food and drink and the poor quality of the inns.[8] The diet demonstrated that Speyer was no longer one of the leading cities in Germany.

Politically, Speyer gained its independence from the bishop in the thirteenth century and later forced him to reside outside the city walls. As a free imperial city it maintained an independent foreign policy in the sixteenth century, although it was under the domination of the powerful Electoral Palatinate. Internal political developments in Speyer paralleled those in other German cities. In the late fifteenth and early sixteenth centuries the city council became smaller, more autocratic, and more oligarchical. Popular resistance to this trend may have been accompanied by increased social and economic polarization. In 1512–13 and again in 1525 (at the time of the Peasants' War) there was serious popular unrest in Speyer. Both

---

6. Alter, "Von der konradinischen Rachtung bis zum letzten Reichstag in Speyer," p. 554; Ohler, "Alltag in einer Zeit des Friedens," pp. 580–82.

7. Keyser, ed., *Städtebuch Rheinland-Pfalz und Saarland*, pp. 384–416.

8. Alter, "Von der konradinischen Rachtung bis zum letzten Reichstag in Speyer," pp. 535–36.

revolts were suppressed by the Rat, with the support of the emperor and the Palatinate, but the tensions that caused them continued to smolder throughout the early modern period.[9] The fear of popular revolt caused by political, economic, or religious conflict dominated the thinking of the city council.

The relationship between the city and the clergy in Speyer had always been problematical. In 1420 the first Rachtung (or treaty) was signed. As Willi Alter has pointed out, this agreement "consolidated the traditional special status of the clergy and with it the legal distinction between the citizen (*bürgerliche*) and the clerical (*geistliche*) residents of the city."[10] The Rachtung remained the basis of the clergy-city relationship for the next 250 years. The most important of these treaties was the *Große Rachtung* of 1514, which was signed and approved by both the emperor and the pope. The Große Rachtung was divided into four parts. The first regulated the import and export of wine and grain by clerics and restricted their right to sell wine in the city. Essentially, the clergy could bring goods into the city toll-free only if they were for personal use. The second part of the treaty established what kinds of clerical income and property were exempt from taxes. Property purchased by the clergy from nonclerics was taxable, as was property donated to the Church. The third section dealt with the legal status of the clergy, and the fourth limited the number of lay servants of the clergy who could receive special status. In exchange for these privileges the four chapters in Speyer agreed to pay the city four hundred gulden a year each.[11]

The Rachtung, then, dealt above all with the economic and legal problems caused by a large clerical establishment. It limited the ability of the clergy to engage in the wine and grain trade in competition with Speyer merchants. At the same time the treaty gave the clergy extensive tax exemptions and legal privileges. Both sides resented the restrictions the Rachtung placed on them. Throughout the sixteenth and seventeenth centuries clergymen tried to circumvent the treaty and engage in the profitable wine and grain trades, while the Rat tried to assess new taxes on the clergy and bring it under their legal control. Room for conflict remained even within the agreements they had worked out.

The Protestant Reformation changed the religious life of the population but not the relationship between the clergy and the city. After the 1520s many of the bürger were Lutherans (or Lutheran sym-

9. Ibid., pp. 455–58, 461–72, 487–95.
10. Ibid., p. 373.
11. Ibid., pp. 473–74.

pathizers), and in 1540 the city appointed its first evangelical preacher, Michael Diller.[12] To the extent that the residents of Speyer no longer attended Catholic services, the clergy lost contact with the Lutheran population and became even more of a "foreign body" than it had been before the Reformation. The legal status of the clergy did not change, however, and relations between the city council and the chapters remained cordial.

The confessional situation in Speyer in the second half of the sixteenth century was quite complicated.[13] Most residents (over 80 percent) were Lutherans, but there were a large number of Catholics in the city, including the clergy and the judges and lawyers of the Imperial Chamber Court (Reichskammergericht). Because almost all Catholics in Speyer belonged to these two legally defined groups, Catholic-Protestant relations tended to remain political. There was also an important Jewish community of about 120 persons and a small but militant Calvinist group.

Confessional divisions did not end social contact between the clergy and the citizens of Speyer, especially within the upper class. As one Lutheran citizen commented at mid-century, "the Catholics eat meat with us, so we socialize (feiern) with them."[14] Furthermore, economic ties between the urban clergy and the city were close. In times of food shortages, the city council often purchased grain from the chapters.[15] In 1575 the Cathedral Chapter successfully appealed to Bishop Marquard to withdraw an ordinance that restricted the economic activity of the townsmen in the bishop's territory. The interdependence of the clergy and the city meant that the ordinance hurt the clergy as well as the city.[16] This traditional coexistence, even cooperation, was imperiled in the 1570s. Within both the Protestant and Catholic communities new, more radical groups, bent on discipline and unity within their respective churches, and on competition with other confessions, threatened to tear the city apart.

12. Ibid., p. 542.
13. Ibid., pp. 555; Ohler, "Alltag in einer Zeit des Friedens, pp. 629–35. See also Keyser, ed., *Städtebuch Rheinland-Pfalz und Saarland*, p. 391, who gives the following breakdown of the confessional divisions in the city around 1560: 1. Full citizens with families—c. 5000 individuals (about 50 were Catholic, a similar number were Calvinist, the rest Lutheran). 2. Non-citizen residents—c. 800+ (mostly Lutheran, some Catholics). 3. Jews—c. 120. 4. Imperial Supreme Court and families—c. 420 (mostly Catholic). 5. Episcopal officials—c. 20 (Catholic). 6. Clergy in chapters and parishes—c. 450 (Catholic). 7. Monks and nuns—c. 160 (mostly Catholic).
14. Alter, "Von der konradinischen Rachtung bis zum letzten Reichstag in Speyer," p. 562.
15. GLAK 61/10942, pp. 526–28, 531–33. This was in 1571. The Cathedral Chapter was more willing to help the city than the smaller chapters.
16. GLAK 61/10943, pp. 324–28, 329–35.

Confessional Conflict in Speyer

As they did in many German cities, the Jesuits disrupted the peaceful coexistence of Protestants and Catholics in Speyer. The reformers in the Cathedral Chapter, who had let in the Jesuits, did not anticipate the extent to which they would focus their efforts on converting Protestants.[17] In 1573 the canons said to the city council that the Jesuits were "[the chapter's] servants just like the secular priests and clergy of the old religion [who served as preachers and teachers] were."[18] The canons wanted the Jesuits to help with the internal reform of the Church, not to attack Protestants.

The establishment of a Jesuit college in Speyer in the early 1570s happened to coincide with the St. Bartholomew's Day massacre in France. This massacre of thousands of Huguenots had a profound impact on German Protestants. Coming at a time of Catholic revival, the massacre raised the fear of secret Jesuit plots and radicalized the Protestant population. All Catholics became suspect, even those who had never demonstrated anti-Protestant tendencies in the past. These factors were all present in Speyer in 1573 as the city council and the clergy began to discuss the new Rachtung for 1575.

In November 1573, the Cathedral Chapter protested to the city council that rumors were circulating in Speyer that the clergy was planning a "bloodbath" of Protestants.[19] The chapter was upset that the council took the rumors seriously and had reinforced the watch on the city walls. Hoping to calm the situation, the clergy offered to allow the city to search the houses of clerics for weapons. The canons' willingness to forfeit the immunity of their houses, a possibly dangerous precedent, attests to the gravity of the situation.

The city council did not seriously suspect a clerical plot. Instead, the magistrates hoped to use the overheated situation in the city to force the removal of the Jesuits. The council argued that the Jesuits were a "new sect and not included under the status of clergy" and therefore were not included in the Rachtung.[20] The council, more quickly than the chapters, recognized the innovative and threatening nature of the Society of Jesus. When the Cathedral Chapter pointed out that the Jesuits were Catholic and not a new sect, and that they were employed by the chapter as preachers and teachers, and therefore were indeed part of the clergy, the magistrates took a different tack and argued that "this order is new and the Rachtung is old and

17. See Chapter 2.
18. GLAK 61/10942, pp. 962.
19. Ibid., pp. 958–60.
20. Ibid., p. 954.

therefore they do not belong under it."[21] The Rat advanced many arguments to prove that it was defending tradition against Catholic innovations.

The careful legalistic arguments of the city council masked a serious conflict within the city. Strongly anti-Catholic elements, led by the Lutheran pastors, were pressuring the city council to act against the Jesuits. The magistrates communicated this threat to the clergy. Having the Jesuits in the city, they said, could cause "not a little disorder" among the common people.[22] The chapter, somewhat disingenuously, pointed out that the common people had always protested about the "immoral" behavior of the clergy; yet now that they had brought in the Jesuits, whose personal morality was above reproach, there were still problems.[23] The Rat continued the attack on the Jesuits, formally protesting their inclusion in the Rachtung. Legally, the city was in a weak position, and in July 1575 Emperor Maximilian ordered the city to include the Jesuits in the Rachtung and to protect them as they protected all other members of the clergy.[24]

Although the city council accepted the imperial order, conflicts between the Jesuits and some of the population of Speyer continued. Both Protestants and Catholics were responsible. In July 1576 a Lutheran preacher suggested in a sermon that various members of the clergy "should have their heads cut off in the marketplace."[25] The Jesuits were far from defenseless. Their sermons regularly denounced the Lutherans as heretics and, according to their enemies, fostered divisions within the city.[26] The city council was often caught in the middle of these conflicts. The Cathedral Chapter protested to the magistrates that anti-Catholic sermons violated the Rachtung as well as the religious peace of 1555, while the Lutheran pastors denounced the Jesuits' sermons.

Confessional conflict spread to the city streets. A Protestant journeyman hurled invectives at a Jesuit father outside one of the Catholic parish churches in Speyer.[27] In 1578 a townsman beat a student from the Jesuit school bloody in the cloister of the cathedral.[28] Lu-

---

21. Ibid., p. 974.
22. Ibid., p. 974.
23. Ibid., p. 993.
24. Duhr I, pp. 118–19.
25. GLAK 61/10943, p. 485r.
26. Duhr I, p. 118; St.A.Sp. 1A/450/11, p. 3.
27. GLAK 61/10947, p. 281.
28. GLAK 61/10945, p. 148. The assailant may have been the brother of the student. There were Lutheran students in the school and perhaps the assailant objected to his brother attending the Jesuit school.

theran Bürger frequently confronted the young men studying under the Jesuits on the streets.[29] Here again, however, the Jesuits and their students were not always the victims. In 1607, in a rather pitiful appeal to the city council for protection, a Lutheran minister named Christopher Algyer complained of the abuse he had suffered at the hands of the Catholic students. The students mocked the minister, who was lame, for his walk, insulted him and his religion, and even threatened him physically. Algyer reported that these students were abusive in public to other ministers as well, and that the problem was long-standing. Interestingly, Algyer not only appealed to the Rat for help but also spoke to a friend of his in the cathedral clergy, the Catholic parish priest in the church of St. Johan in Speyer. The priest said he would try to help and lamented the behavior of the students.[30] Such attacks on neighbors of the other religion were not supported by all, or even most, members of the Catholic clergy in Speyer.

These kinds of encounters, along with the public processions and plays organized by the Jesuits, imperiled urban peace and unity.[31] Confessional conflict threatened everyone in the delicately balanced urban society of Speyer. The Catholics, with the exception of the Jesuits, did not want to antagonize the Lutheran majority, while the political weight of the emperor, the presence of the Catholic-dominated Reichskammergericht, the economic interdependence of the clergy and the city, and the prescriptions of the Peace of Augsburg made it impossible for the Protestants to drive the Catholics from Speyer. The conflicts of the decades after 1570 drove conservatives of both religions to defuse these conflicts. Yet the Jesuits and the more radical Protestants remained in Speyer and continued to push their religious viewpoints. The continuous low-level confessional conflict, which lasted into the eighteenth century, and the fact that no violent civil war erupted in Speyer, attest to the ability of an early modern city to survive division.[32]

The Restoration of Traditional Relations

Protestants and Catholics continued to coexist in Speyer because the city council and the Cathedral Chapter recognized the danger of

29. GLAK 61/10943, p. 289.
30. St.A.Sp. 1A/450/4, pp. 9r–11v.
31. The city, like the Palatinate, recognized the restoration of processions by the Jesuits as part of a reform of Catholicism and tried to prevent them from taking place in Speyer (St.A.Sp. 1A/347/1, pp. 2r–11v, 1600, 1610, 1611).
32. Warmbrunn, *Zwei Konfessionen in einer Stadt*, esp. chap. 1.

confessional enmity and restricted their conflicts to traditional areas of dispute. The higher clergy and the magistrates, following the lead of the Peace of Augsburg, tacitly agreed not to bring differences in religious belief and practice into disputes between the clergy and city. The two parties resolved conflicts as they had done for centuries, by legal and political means and, above all, by compromise.

In 1590, when it came time to discuss a new Rachtung, the two parties did not repeat the difficult and dangerous dispute over the Jesuits that had marred the negotiations in 1575. The Cathedral Chapter wanted to avoid a "disputation" and hoped that a "neighborly" agreement could be reached. The only area of conflict concerned the legal status of widows of clerical employees, an issue trivial enough to be left unresolved when the treaty was signed.[33]

The secretary of the Cathedral Chapter carefully recorded the ceremony that surrounded the swearing of the Rachtung of 1590.[34] These rituals confirmed the legalistic and essentially secular nature of this treaty and reflect its pre-Reformation origin. First, the clergy swore to uphold the Rachtung in a ceremony held in the cathedral. The clergy assembled in careful order of precedence and welcomed the representatives of the city as guests and equals. The cathedral, which in this period was never full for services, was packed with citizens of Speyer eager to witness this important event. Then representatives of the clergy went to the Rathaus to attend the oath taking of the members of the city council. This ceremony took place in the courtyard of the city hall, once again highlighting the public nature of the event. The magistrates greeted the representatives of chapters with great friendliness. After the ceremony everyone shook hands and "took friendly leave." The ceremonies emphasized peace, cooperation, and the cordial nature of the relationship. Not once were religious differences apparent.

In 1605 a variety of disputes had to be resolved before the treaty could be signed, but once again only traditional problems were at issue. The Rat complained above all that the clergy was involved in the wine trade. The clergy mentioned several minor complaints, but called them "misunderstandings" and did not doubt that they could be easily resolved.[35] In fact, the Rachtung was put into effect with these issues still unsettled, an indication of how unimportant they were compared to the value of the treaty as a whole.

In 1608 the city and the clergy negotiated a major treaty, dealing

33. GLAK 61/10949, pp. 125–33.
34. Ibid., pp. 134–38.
35. GLAK 61/10951, pp. 885–88.

with sixteen complaints (*gravamina*) of the clergy and sixteen of the city. The issues were almost all economic and ranged from the fairly important effort of the city to restrict the right of the clergy to buy property in the city, to the regulation of the fish trade. The magistrates were especially intent on preventing the clergy from competing economically with the townspeople. Both sides compromised and resolved all disputes. The only issue that might be said to have been caused by the Counter-Reformation involved the popular cathedral school, now run by the Jesuits. The city council asked that the students' behavior be controlled and especially that they be stopped from practicing shooting in the city. The Cathedral Chapter agreed to discipline the students more strictly.[36]

These agreements show the willingness of the chapter clergy and the city magistrates to restrain their conflicts and compromise when necessary. The clergy and the council continued to cooperate in times of economic crisis and worked together to keep the bishops out of the city. They also had common enemies. Lutherans and Catholics agreed that the Calvinists were a great danger. Not only was the Electoral Palatinate Calvinist, but there was a Calvinist community in the city of Speyer. In 1576 the city council feared a Calvinist uprising in the city and asked the Catholic canons to keep them apprised of any information they received concerning this group. The clergy agreed to help and pointed out that the Rat had made a mistake giving the Calvinists a church in the city. The same clerics, however, reassured the city council that they considered the Calvinist danger to be very small.[37]

The city council and the Catholic clergy were much more concerned with the danger of general popular unrest. In trying to get the Jesuits out of Speyer, the city fathers peppered their discussions with the Cathedral Chapter with references to the threat of popular violence against the Catholics. The council clearly used this threat to pressure the clergy, but this does not mean that the danger did not exist.[38] The magistrates also referred to the possibility of mob violence in 1605, when clergy-city relations were good.[39] In fact, flashes of popular anti-Catholic violence occurred throughout the period. In 1584 a Catholic clergyman was pelted with rock-laden snowballs and

36. GLAK 65/626a, pp. 45r–51v.
37. GLAK 61/10943, pp. 549–53. The city council had been forced to allow the Calvinists to take over the parish church of St.Aegidius. The patron of this church was the Palatine elector. The council had to deal carefully with the Calvinists because of this powerful protector.
38. Ohler "Alltag in einer Zeit des Friedens," pp. 605–6.
39. GLAK 61/10951, p. 885.

left for dead.[40] Over twenty years later, a group of Protestant journey-men destroyed a picture of the Virgin Mary from the cathedral.[41] Yet these cases, while spectacular, were exceptional. Furthermore, city authorities neither condoned nor tolerated such violence. When caught, the guilty parties were punished, as were Catholic clergymen who abused their privileges or fought with Protestants.

Relations between the Lutheran population and the large Catholic clerical establishment of Speyer were not always good. There was a constant level of conflict and tension. It is important to realize, however, that this was not a new problem caused by either the Reformation or the Counter-Reformation. As we have seen, since the fifteenth century the special position of the clergy within the city had been regulated by a periodically renegotiated treaty, the Rach-tung. This system continued after the Reformation. The Jesuits threatened the peaceful coexistence of several confessions in Speyer when they openly attacked the Protestants in their effort to win converts for Catholicism. In the 1570s and 1580s this policy threat-ened to give rise to a Protestant backlash that might have divided the city into two warring camps. Such a division occurred at times in other cities, such as Münster and Augsburg. In Speyer, however, the dominant powers in both camps, the city council and the upper clergy, struggled successfully to restrain confessional conflict. They continued to base the city-clergy relationship on the Rachtung and agreed to respect one another's religious rights. Even with the pres-ence of the Jesuits, the impact of the Counter-Reformation in the city of Speyer was limited.

The Electoral Palatinate and the Counter-Reformation

The Electoral Palatinate (*Kurpfalz*) was an important power in Germany and by the late sixteenth century one of the leaders of militant Protestantism. In imperial politics, the Palatinate led the organization of the Protestant Union; and it was the Bohemian ad-venture of Elector Frederick V (the "Winter King") that triggered the Thirty Years' War. Palatine rulers and their officials followed an ag-gressive anti-Catholic policy in regional politics as well. From the

40. GLAK 61/10947, p. 238r.
41. GLAK 61/10955, p. 160r.

1550s on the Palatinate increased political pressure on the Bishopric of Speyer.[42]

The rising level of conflict between the bishops and the Calvinist Palatinate could have been used by Catholic officials to reinforce the villagers' loyalty to Catholicism. But this did not happen. In fact, Palatine policy succeeded in weakening the Counter-Reformation. Palatine officials were especially interested in disrupting the efforts of Church reformers; they supported Protestants who resisted eviction from Catholic villages, broke up processions, and held back financial resources earmarked for the Catholic clergy. For the Catholic Church, these practical problems caused by the Palatinate far outweighed the increased Catholic militancy caused by politico-religious conflict.

The disputes between the Palatinate and the Bishopric of Speyer were, in fact, more political than religious. To be sure, Palatine officials protected Protestants in the bishop's villages and disrupted some Catholic services, but the main focus of Palatine policy was to bring the Hochstift under the political control of the Palatinate. This was a traditional strategy. From the late fourteenth to the middle of the sixteenth centuries the Bishopric of Speyer had been under the (more or less formal) protectorate of the Palatinate. The Reformation in the Palatinate ended this relationship, but the Palatine electors sought to restore it, if necessary by military pressure.[43]

If Palatine policy toward the bishopric was aggressive and often hostile, its policy toward the Catholic inhabitants of the Electorate was surprisingly moderate. Although they could not worship in public, Catholics could reside in Palatine territory. The close proximity of Catholic and Protestant villages also promoted a practical tolerance at the popular level, a tolerance that frustrated the attempts of the Protestant clergy and some of the Palatine elite to create a "Protestant consciousness" in the countryside.[44] The Catholic population of the region did not have to deal with self-consciously Protestant neighbors on a daily basis. Protestant attacks did not force Catholics in the countryside to develop strong religious loyalties.

Relations between the Palatinate and the bishopric deteriorated after the election of Eberhard in 1582. The Palatinate had hoped to

---

42. I use the term "Palatinate" to refer to the principality of the Electors Palatine (the *Kurpfalz* or Electoral Palatinate). Strictly speaking, the Palatinate (*Pfalz*) is the geographical region on the west bank of the Rhine, which included the city of Speyer. The *Kurpfalz* extended into other regions. There were also other "Palatinate" principalities, the most important being Pfalz-Zweibrücken.

43. Duggan, chap. 4 and esp. pp. 152–54; Press, "Das Hochstift Speyer," esp. p. 262.

44. Vogler, *La vie religieuse en pays rhénan*, part 3, esp. pp. 1264–70.

organize the election of a Protestant prince and was unhappy with the election of the reform-minded bishop.[45] In addition, the ardently Calvinist *Pfalzgraf* Johan Casimir became administrator of the Palatinate in 1583, after the death of his more moderate brother, Ludwig V. Johan Casimir had fought beside the Huguenots in the French Wars of Religion and lent a decidedly anti-Catholic stamp to Palatine policy. The Calvinist party in the central administration in Heidelberg, which had close ties to the university, increased its influence in these years as well. Volker Press has argued that it was these men who promoted the foreign policy that led to the Bohemian adventure. Not surprisingly, this group in Heidelberg also favored an aggressive policy against the Palatinate's Catholic neighbors. By the 1580s, university-trained Calvinists also dominated the local administration of the Palatinate, filling many positions as Amtmänner (bailiffs). The Catholics dealt most often with these local officials and their subordinates.[46]

The militant Protestant policy of the Palatinate notwithstanding, Eberhard did not radically change the bishopric's political course.[47] Respect for the strength of the Palatinate remained central to the bishop's program. His local officials usually cooperated closely with Palatine officials, especially in the jointly governed gemeinschaft villages. In the 1570s, for example, the bishop and the elector jointly published an alms and police ordinance for these villages. The bishop's council expressed reservations because the ordinances spoke of "the preaching and illumination of the Word of God," a reference to the Protestant services held in these villages, but commented further that it was too late to change the confessional situation.[48] Nothing could be gained by challenging the Protestants.

Palatine and Speyer governments cooperated in evicting the Anabaptists from the region. During Marquard's episcopate the Anabaptists apparently had been tolerated in the Hochstift, at least until 1575, when the bishop ordered their property confiscated.[49] The numbers of Anabaptists may have even grown as they fled from

---

45. Press, "Das Hochstift Speyer," p. 264.
46. Press, *Calvinismus und Territorialstaat*. On the Palatinate see also Ludwig Häusser, *Geschichte der rheinischen Pfalz* (1856; reprint, Pirmasens: Buchhandlung Johann Richter, 1970); Paul Münch, *Zucht und Ordnung. Reformierte Kirchenverfassungen in 16. und 17. Jahrhundert (Nassau-Dillenberg, Kurpfalz, Hessen-Kassel)* (Stuttgart: Klett-Cotta, 1978), esp. sec. 2.3; Ernst W. Zeeden, *Kleine Reformationsgeschichte von Baden-Durlach und Kurpfalz* (Karlsruhe: Badenia, 1956).
47. See Chapter 1 for traditional episcopal policy toward the Palatinate, and Chapter 2 for Eberhard's policies.
48. GLAK 61/11494b, pp. 3v, 4r, 53v, 54r.
49. Ibid., p. 131r.

Palatine villages to the relative safety of Catholic villages. Bishop Eberhard's regime was much stricter, confiscating Anabaptist property and forcing them to emigrate to Moravia.[50] His policy dovetailed with that of the better-organized Palatine church officials, who drove out most of the Anabaptists by 1600.[51]

Relations between the confessions were not always amicable. The officials of the *Kurpfalz* attempted at times to spread Calvinism into Catholic areas. One such attempt took place in the bishop's village of Maikammer in 1582. The elector held the patronage of this parish and attempted to install a Protestant pastor at the death of the Catholic priest. The Cathedral Chapter, which held most of the tithe, and the bishop, as prince, were able to prevent the designated Calvinist preacher from residing in Maikammer, but they could not force the elector to appoint a Catholic priest. After a year without a clergyman, the village council (gericht) protested that they wanted a resident priest to administer the sacraments and give sermons. Without a resident priest (the council specifically asked for a Catholic), the village elders feared a collapse of order in the village.[52] After much delay, however, a Catholic priest was appointed for Maikammer.

The Palatine effort to install a Protestant pastor in Maikammer failed. The Catholics, however, were thrown into a panic. The Cathedral Chapter discussed at length the possibility that the Palatinate might try to impose Protestant clergy in other villages in the Hochstift.[53] These fears were exaggerated, however; the principle of *cuius regio, eius religio* enshrined in the Peace of Augsburg prevented the Palatinate from installing Protestant practice within the bishop's territory.[54]

The political domination of the Palatinate did allow Protestant authorities to protect Protestants within Catholic villages. Such protection was especially effective in villages where there were large numbers of Palatine serfs. Catholic authorities tolerated a significant Protestant minority in the villages of Maikammer, Dudenhofen, Heiligenstein, and Schifferstadt because these villagers often appealed to nearby Palatine authorities if threatened. In 1599, for example, several Palatine serfs from Heiligenstein claimed they could not be cited

50. Stamer III/1, pp. 135–36; GLAK 61/11495a, 11495b. There are a number of property confiscations in these minutes from 1582 to 1604.

51. For Protestant policy see Vogler, *La vie religieuse en pays rhénan*, part 3, chap. 3, sec. 1.

52. GLAK 61/10947, pp. 80r–80v.

53. GLAK 61/11495a, pp. 193r–193v; GLAK 61/10947, pp. 6v–7v; Stamer III/1, p. 144.

54. GLAK 61/11495b, pp. 120r–121r. In 1601, in exchange for appointing a Catholic priest for Maikammer, Palatine officials tried to extract a written guarantee that Protestants in the village would continue to be allowed to travel to neighboring villages for services. The bishop's council was only willing to renew the verbal agreement.

before the Catholic ecclesiastical court.[55] It was impossible for the bishop's officials to "confessionalize" their villages, that is, evict all non-Catholics, without causing a major conflict with the Palatinate, something they had to avoid at all cost. At the same time, Speyer officials were incapable of enforcing any rights over the bishop's serfs who resided in the Palatinate. When a local Catholic official reported to the bishop's council that Speyer serfs were sending their children to schools in Protestant areas, the council informed him that "unfortunately this is not the time . . . for the *Stift* to move against its neighbors on such matters."[56] Caution and accommodation dominated the policy of the Church.

Palatine officials considered all manifestations of the Counter-Reformation threatening. In 1583 the central government in Heidelberg protested against the new "Church ordinance" in the bishop's villages, which required that the villagers attend Mass and bring their children to baptism in the Catholic Church. The Protestants referred to these measures as "innovations" since Marquard's time. "The [Palatine] elector cannot in good conscience allow his serfs to be burdened in this way, and such things did not happen under Bishop Marquard."[57] Here again, the bishop wrote a conciliatory letter to the elector.

In the 1590s, the Jesuits encouraged the Catholic villagers to set up crosses on the side of the highway at the boundaries of the villages. The Palatinate responded forcefully: local Palatine officials, apparently acting on orders from the capital city of Heidelberg, tore the crosses down. In all cases, however, it was local officials who destroyed the crosses. Neither Catholic nor Protestant villagers were involved in either destroying or protecting the crosses.[58]

Processions also caused conflict. The visitation records of 1583–88 make it clear that Protestant officials forbade Catholic processions through their territory. Catholic reformers, especially the Jesuits, encouraged processions in the countryside as well as in the city. In 1608, Palatine officials attacked a group of Catholic peasants in a procession returning to their villages from Speyer. The Protestants verbally insulted the peasants and destroyed their flags and crosses, the emblems of the religious purpose of their journey.[59]

---

55. GLAK 61/10951, p. 111.
56. GLAK 61/11495a, p. 170r.
57. GLAK 61/495a, pp. 9r–9v.
58. GLAK 61/11495b, pp. 52v–53r, 78v–79r; GLAK 61/11497/II, pp. 158r–158v, 166r–166v.
59. GLAK 61/11496, pp. 168r–168v. There is a whole list of the minor local officials of the Palatinate who were involved in this altercation.

These attacks on the bishop's authority within his own territory were not random. Palatine officials were especially concerned to prevent Catholic "innovations"—Tridentine reform measures—from taking root. Crosses outside the villages, more frequent processions, and restrictions on non-Catholics, especially on their burial in the village cemetery, all brought action from the Palatinate. Palatine officials even exercised some influence over the appointment of Catholic priests. In 1615 the Cathedral Chapter removed a graduate of the Alumnat, presumably a "reformed" priest, from the parish of Heiligenstein. The villagers had complained of his behavior and the canons feared he "might cause even greater trouble with the Electoral Palatinate."[60] Political and military power meant that even the elector's implicit desires had to be respected. The Palatinate wanted a docile, nonconfrontational bishopric. To this end, it supported the status quo in Catholic villages and hindered the progress of Tridentine Catholicism.

The inability of the bishop of Speyer to resist the attacks of the Palatinate became more apparent after 1600. In 1609, two thousand Palatine soldiers occupied Bruchsal, the most important town in the Hochstift, in order to free several peasants imprisoned by the bishop's officials as leaders of a rebellion in the village of Odenheim. In the same period, Palatine troops occupied several villages in an attempt to take over areas that had long been governed for the emperor by the bishops of Speyer.[61] The rising tensions between Protestants and Catholics in this region peaked in 1618 when troops from the Palatinate, Württemberg, and the city of Speyer razed the unfinished fortification at Philippsburg, a fortification Bishop Sötern was building to defend his principality from further Palatine attacks.[62]

At the village level, for practical reasons, relations between Catholics and Protestants were much more cordial. Economic and social ties that had existed for centuries were not easily broken. Bernard Vogler has claimed that in Protestant territories there was between 1555 and 1619 "a profound transformation of the people's mentality because of the efforts of a determined clergy supported by civil authority." According to Vogler, this new mentality included "confessional consciousness" and a rooted Protestantism in the middle Rhine region (the *pays rhénan*).[63] Yet Vogler also recognizes that

60. GLAK 61/10955, p. 121v.
61. Remling II, pp. 431–32. These areas included the town of Waibstadt and the "Ritterstift villages" of Odenheim, Landshausen, Tiefenbach, Eichelberg, and Rohrbach.
62. Remling II, pp. 460–61.
63. Vogler, *La vie religieuse en pays rhénan*, p. 1310.

there were often close relations between Catholic and Protestants, especially in the countryside. Mixed marriages never stopped, nor did the participation of Catholics in Protestant baptisms (and vice versa). Journeymen and servants seem to have moved around the region without regard to confessional frontiers.[64] Vogler's study of Protestant territories indicates that by the Thirty Years' War the clergy, the townsmen, and the "notables" had developed a Protestant consciousness that included a strong dose of anti-Catholicism. The majority of the population, however, tolerated other Christian faiths and were perhaps indifferent to religion in general.[65] Indicative of this view is the statement of one group of Lutheran villagers that "they do not criticize [anyone's] faith, all beliefs are good and of value, they do not want to scorn any of them, because each person will be saved by his own [faith]."[66]

Religious toleration was probably greater in the Catholic villages than in Protestant ones. Whereas Protestant officials tried to emphasize confessional division, especially at the time of the Reformation centennial in 1617, Catholic authorities were afraid to push a strong anti-Protestant policy. They discouraged the priests from giving vehemently anti-Protestant sermons and winced when the Jesuits did so. As the minority confession, Catholics favored religious toleration and coexistence; they were too weak to use confessional conflict for the purpose of strengthening the Church.

Weil der Stadt: A Catholic Imperial City

Weil der Stadt was a tiny imperial city with a population of around fifteen hundred. It was completely surrounded by the powerful Duchy of Württemberg, one of the leading Lutheran states in the empire. In the 1570s Weil der Stadt was officially Catholic, but it had an active, influential, and probably growing Protestant minority. Weil provides an example of Tridentine reform in a Catholic territory outside the direct secular rule of the bishop.

The years between 1570 and the Thirty Years' War were difficult ones for the city council of Weil. Two serious dangers jeopardized the town's internal peace and its political independence. The first was the constant menace of Württemberg, which threatened to use the

64. Ibid., part 3, chap.1, sec. 3.
65. Ibid., pp. 1268–69.
66. Ibid., p. 1268.

defense of the Lutherans in the city as an opportunity to invade. The second danger was the Counter-Reformation, as promoted by the Jesuits and the bishops of Speyer. As in Speyer, militant, anti-Protestant Catholicism threatened the fragile civic peace, the city's control of its ecclesiastical institutions, and its independence from Württemberg.

It is a reflection of the strength of the local Church and of the weakness of the bishops that the Rat was able to maintain the traditionalist Church establishment and the city's independence. Despite this traditionalist focus, the Jesuits had more impact on the city than the bishop, giving the Counter-Reformation in Weil a more radical tone than elsewhere in the Bishopric of Speyer. The Jesuits were willing to exploit social divisions within the city to advance their goals, a tactic that was foreign to the bishop's officials. While the Jesuits forged alliances in Weil, the bishop remained an outside power seeking to expand his rights and was therefore viewed with suspicion.

Religious conditions in Weil in the late sixteenth century were similar to those in many other German cities. The Peace of Augsburg gave legal protection to religious minorities in imperial cities, and even in territorial cities Protestants and Catholics lived together peacefully. In Münster, in the principality of the bishop of Münster, a traditionalist Catholic city government tolerated a Protestant minority, favoring communal loyalty over religious conflict.[67] In the imperial cities of Augsburg and Speyer (among others), Lutheran magistrates tolerated Catholic minorities.[68] The Protestant citizens of Weil also considered their religion protected by the Peace of Augsburg. In 1579, in an appeal to Württemberg, they stated that the Augsburg Confession was protected in the empire and that Lutherans could not be forced against their conscience to give up the "religion, belief, church practices, ordinances or ceremonies" of their choice. They pointed out that Catholics and Lutherans had lived peacefully together for a long time in Weil as they did in other cities.[69]

The Catholic majority tolerated the Protestants but refused to concede them any further rights. In 1579 the Protestants attempted to obtain a Lutheran preacher for the city. Although Württemberg supported this effort, the city council refused. The Rat was conciliatory, however, confirming the right of Protestant citizens to serve in

67. Hsia, Society and Religion in Münster.
68. Warmbrunn, Zwei Konfessionen in einer Stadt.
69. HStA.St. A208/Bü.661.

the city government, to go to Württemberg villages for services, and to be buried in the town cemetery. The councilors even reprimanded the Catholic priest for some anti-Protestant statements.[70] The city council itself included some Protestant members, and the magistrates did not want any serious religious conflict in their city.

The Catholic Church in Weil was completely under the control of the city government. The council hired the priest for the city's one parish without any involvement of the bishop. Apparently the city regularly appointed married priests, often men who had been disciplined for concubinage in more "reformed" areas. The chaplain serving in Weil in 1593 had been removed from the parish of Neutart in the Bishopric of Speyer, came to Weil with his concubine and children, married, and obtained citizenship. The Rat also controlled all the financial resources of the local parish.[71] There is little information about religious practice in Weil in the sixteenth century, although we know that the council refused to publicize any of the reform ordinances of the bishops and resisted any outside interference. This was traditional Catholicism, where clergymen were members of the community (and even legally citizens), the magistrates completely controlled clerical appointments and discipline, and ecclesiastical discipline was less important than communal peace. In a sense, conditions in Weil were similar to those in the villages of the Bishopric of Speyer. Because the city was politically independent of the bishops, however, it was less responsive to reform; and because it was threatened by religious division, the city government was not interested in the Counter-Reformation.

Although details are sparse, the first Jesuit mission to Weil seems to have shattered the status quo in the city. Two Jesuits traveled to Weil in 1573 to handle pastoral duties temporarily. The fathers' stay was cut short, however, over their interference in a marriage. Perhaps the Jesuits attempted to reform traditional marriage practice in Weil, or possibly they prohibited Protestants from participating in the wedding, thereby incurring the opposition of local authorities.[72]

Whether influenced by political conditions or by the Jesuits, by 1580 a group of Catholic citizens was advocating harsh measures against the Protestant minority. In March of that year this group held several meetings in the Augustinian monastery and presented the

70. HStA.St. A151/Bü.15.
71. HStA.St. A151/Bü.16, no. 1426.
72. St.A.MZ 15/402. The record only says that the Jesuits were expelled after involvement with the sacrament of marriage. It is also possible that the fathers wanted to require the posting of banns, or tried to have a marriage dispute adjudicated in Speyer.

Rat with a series of demands. These "radicals" demanded the removal of all non-Catholics from the council, the arrest of the Protestant town secretary, and the conversion of all Protestants. They suspected the secretary (*Stadtschreiber*) of being a spy for Württemberg, and they were correct if the voluminous correspondence he maintained with Württemberg officials is any evidence. The Catholics also demanded that the city gates be locked on Sundays in order to prevent the Protestants from going to services outside the city.[73]

The city council was caught between the demands of this radical group of Catholics and the Protestants. The Protestants had the support of Württemberg and could not be ignored. Furthermore, the Protestants were quite confident of their position in the city. As many as nine of the twelve city councilors were Lutherans (or at least sympathetic to the Lutherans), and many of the wealthier people in Weil were among those who attended Protestant services in neighboring villages. Some Protestant townsmen even verbally ridiculed their Catholic neighbors as they went to Mass. This, the city council reported to Württemberg, "drove the Catholics to disorder."[74] The Protestants were, of course, certain of the support of Württemberg; some of them, like the stadtschreiber, hoped that the Lutheran duchy would take over the city. Perhaps out of fear of the Counter-Reformation, perhaps out of overconfidence, the Protestant minority exacerbated the religious tensions in Weil der Stadt.

In 1587 a new Jesuit mission, this time with the support of Bishop Eberhard, came to Weil. At Easter two priests from Speyer, one of them a Jesuit, offered to preach and perform services. Although short of priests, the Rat refused to open the church to the visiting clergymen. The priests defied the magistrates and preached, conducted a burial, and administered the sacraments. On leaving, the "Speyer priests" (as the Weiler Protestants called them) left several books in the church, including a collection of sermons and several copies of Canisius's small catechism. The Protestants stated that "since their [the Jesuits'] departure, the papist townsmen are more unruly than ever before" and had been insulting Protestants in the streets.[75]

The city council found itself increasingly trapped. Its members correctly suspected that Bishop Eberhard wanted to increase his power over the clergy in Weil. In June 1587 the bishop ordered the council to get rid of a recently hired priest who lived with a concubine. The Rat refused and insisted on its right to hire anyone it

73. HStA.St. A151/Bü.15, 21 March, 22 March, May, July 1580.
74. Ibid., 17 March 1581.
75. Ibid., 17 May 1587.

wanted.[76] Meanwhile, Württemberg and several other Protestant powers pressured Weil to allow a Protestant preacher into the city. The councilors refused, claiming that they feared the reaction of the Catholic mob.[77]

This fear reveals an important element of the Counter-Reformation in Weil der Stadt. The Jesuits pitched their appeal in Weil to the lower classes. The magistrates, who controlled the traditional Church, had close social ties with the Protestants as well as important economic ties with Württemberg and therefore had little interest in reforming the Church. At least some of the poorer people, however, seem to have hoped that the Jesuits and the bishop of Speyer might help them gain some political influence. The Württemberg representative in Weil reported that "the poor people have been led around by the nose by the bishop of Speyer's [officials] and have been fooled [by] their magnificent promises."[78]

Both the Protestants and the city council overestimated the danger posed by the poor people of Weil. Although the radical Catholics were fairly well organized, the conservative/traditionalist group kept a tight hold on the reins of power. In 1592, at the height of the religious conflict, the bürgermeister (who was Protestant) was reelected easily.[79] This result seems to indicate that the radical Catholic party was either quite small or without significant influence among the ruling classes. But it is indeed possible that the disenfranchised portion of the population tried to use religious reform to gain political power.

In November 1593, an imperial commission came to Weil to resolve the religious conflict instigated by the radicals. Württemberg, the Margravate of Baden-Durlach, and three Protestant cities sent representatives to the hearings, as did the bishop of Speyer. The reform party in Speyer clearly considered this an important event, since the Speyer delegation was headed by the dean of the Cathedral Chapter, Andreas von Oberstein, and included the vicar general, Beatus Moses.[80] The commission essentially ordered a restoration of the status quo. Although it paid lip service to the rights of the bishop and ordered the city to install "exemplary Catholic priests," actual control of the local Church remained in the hands of the city council. The commission affirmed Catholicism as the only official religion in the city but ordered the city to respect the legal rights of all citizens,

76. Ibid., 23 June 1587.
77. Ibid., 10 January and 15 January 1592.
78. Ibid., no. 84.
79. Ibid.
80. HStA.St. A151/Bü.16, no. 138.

regardless of religion. This was a limited victory for the radical Catholics. All new citizens had to be Catholic, and no new members of the city council could be Protestant.[81] This clause, however, did not force the existing Protestant minority out of Weil. Instead it prevented the Protestants from growing in numbers and influence and left the traditionalist Catholics in control. The Protestants were left a permanent minority, and Weil became a secure Catholic haven in the middle of Württemberg. As a result a number of Catholics emigrated from Württemberg to Weil.[82]

The city council also came to a compromise agreement with the bishop. The Rat kept control of two key areas, clerical appointments and Church finances. The bishop obtained the right to investigate the qualifications of new priests but could not appoint his own candidates. The council could also remove unsatisfactory priests, as long as it officially operated through the bishop's institutions. Finally, the bishop acquired the right to conduct visitations in the city and was given jurisdiction over marriage cases.

In some ways this agreement was a success for the Catholic reformers and the bishop. The bishop gained powers in Weil he had never held before. In addition, the Jesuits were very active in Weil after 1594. They conducted at least five missions to the city between 1595 and 1617. As usual, the fathers badly frightened the Protestant minority, who claimed in 1598 that under Jesuit influence radical Catholics were intimidating the moderate majority and polarizing the city along religious lines.[83] The Jesuits also encouraged processions, especially on Corpus Christi day, which brought the Catholic townsmen into conflict with Württemberg officials, who used troops to keep the processions from entering Württemberg territory.[84]

Yet the efforts of the Jesuits and the new powers of the bishop did not lead to the imposition of Tridentine Catholicism in Weil. As the Jesuits reported in 1600, the reform had a long way to go. The fathers complained that marriage practices did not agree with the decrees of the council of Trent. The town church was in a state of disrepair, and the townsmen had let the Catholic paintings and images deteriorate. The Jesuits got along well enough with the parish priest, but the city council did not cooperate with them.[85] It appears that episcopal

81. HStA.St. A208/Bü.656, 15 November 1594, 9 July 1597.
82. HStA.St. A151/Bü.16, no. 198. In 1594 there were eighty-one citizens of Weil who had been born in Württemberg or other Protestant territories and had moved to Weil der Stadt.
83. HStA.St. A208/Bü.656, (1 November 1598).
84. HStA.St. A208/Bü.659.
85. ARSJ Rh.Inf.48, pp. 105r–105v. Once again, the Jesuits gave no specifics on the "abuses" in marriage practice in Weil. I suspect they objected to the participation of Protestants in the ceremonies.

authorities in Speyer lost interest in Weil after 1600. The imposition of episcopal authority there remained very difficult. There is, for example, no record of marriage (or related) cases from Weil coming before the bishop's council (*Hofrat*), nor did episcopal authorities discipline any priests from Weil. In practice, then, the city maintained its independent local Church and its traditional Catholicism.

The history of Weil der Stadt provides a telling example of the interplay of the various forces within the Catholic Church around 1600. Traditional Catholicism in Weil was supported by the city council and the majority of the Catholic population of the city. The Tridentine Church was represented by the Jesuits and supported by some of the townsmen. In many ways, the bishop of Speyer was caught between these forces. Episcopal authorities hoped to use the opportunity of reform to increase their control over the Church in Weil. At the same time, however, they were more hesitant than the Jesuits to attack the traditionalist authorities. The Speyer authorities were also very sensitive to regional political realities and did not want to antagonize Württemberg.

An agreement made in 1616 between the Protestant and Catholic citizens of Weil reflects the nonmilitant policy of Speyer. Acting as arbitrators for this agreement, the bishop's officials conceded the right of Protestant citizens to be baptized and to marry outside the Catholic Church. Protestants could take a special oath of citizenship that did not include a Catholic confession of faith. Church officials even conceded the right of Protestants to act as godparents in Catholic baptisms.[86] These concessions no doubt confirmed existing practice in Weil, but their acceptance by episcopal authorities is somewhat surprising. Once again, Catholic authorities in the Bishopric of Speyer temporized, stopping well short of a complete application of the Counter-Reformation.

Other Catholic princes, magistrates, and noblemen defended a local and territorial Catholic Church as vigorously as did the magistrates of Weil der Stadt. The margraves of Baden-Baden, for example, energetically supported Tridentine reform measures while simultaneously resisting episcopal interference in the Badenese Church.[87] Indeed, the government of Baden-Baden pushed a more aggressive and thorough reform than did Bishop Eberhard, especially in the 1570s and 1580s and again in the 1620s. The bishops of Speyer and

---

86. HStA.St. A208/Bü.661.
87. For Catholicism in Baden-Baden see Horst Bartmann, "Die Kirchenpolitik der Markgrafen von Baden-Baden im Zeitalter der Glaubenskämpfe, 1535–1622," *Freiburger Diözesan-Archiv* 81 (1961); Köhler, *Obrigkeitliche Konfessionsänderungen in Kondominaten*, esp. chap. 2.

the upper clergy in Speyer demonstrated a general lack of interest in the situation in Catholic territories such as Baden-Baden. Between 1560 and 1650, neither the Cathedral Chapter nor the bishop's council dealt regularly with religious conditions, or even their juridical and financial rights, in Baden. The ecclesiastical establishment in Speyer took a narrow view of its responsibilities. The Margravate of Baden-Baden was beyond the influence of the bishopric.

Throughout the sixteenth and seventeenth centuries, the Catholic Church in Weil der Stadt, Baden-Baden, and several smaller Catholic territories remained quite different from the Church in the bishop's territory.[88] None of these areas had the large, wealthy, and generally traditional clerical establishment that so influenced conditions in Speyer. As a result, Catholicism in Weil remained traditional in its religiosity and communal in its organization owing to its proximity to the powerful Protestant state of Württemberg. The territorial Church of Baden-Baden, by contrast, was very open to the Counter-Reformation because the secular, reform-minded government was not hampered by a powerful, traditionalist clergy. Here the Jesuits exercised a strong influence over the rural clergy and popular religious practice, which gave Catholicism in Baden-Baden a very different flavor from what it had elsewhere in the Bishopric of Speyer.

The two themes of this chapter, confessional conflict and the limits of episcopal authority, are closely related. The militant, anti-Protestant Catholicism that developed in some parts of Germany in this period needed strong, centralized leadership. The political fragmentation of the region meant that there was no single powerful Catholic prince, as there was, for example, in Bavaria. Leadership of the Catholic party in the middle Rhine valley fell to the bishops of Speyer, who were too weak to support an aggressive policy.[89] In the view of most of the upper clergy, the religious peace of 1555 operated reasonably well. In embracing the Counter-Reformation, these men sought to reform the Church internally. They had no interest in destroying the political or religious status quo. At this regional level, the Catholic Church avoided confessional conflict.

The unwillingness and inability of the bishops and their officials to extend episcopal authority into Weil der Stadt and other Catholic territories allowed Catholicism to retain its local character in the

---

88. One such territory was a group of villages governed by the von Gemmingen family.
89. By contrast, the bishops of Würzburg and Münster, and the archbishop of Mainz (to name several examples), although they focused on reform in their secular territories, were also regional leaders of the Church in the years before the Thirty Years' War.

bishopric.[90] Outside influences made their mark on these areas, as they did in the Hochstift, but they were sporadic and lacked institutional permanence. Only a variety of effective episcopal institutions could have imposed the sort of consistent policy that would have created a truly centralized, unified Tridentine Church. Although some of these institutions (ecclesiastical court, vicar general, rural chapters, and so on) existed, they did not function outside the territory directly governed by the bishops. The local focus of Catholicism remained a vital characteristic of the region throughout the early modern period.

90. This was also the case in the villages governed by the von Gemmingen family. These Kraichgau villages almost never figure in the records of the bishopric. The von Gemmingen family resisted even the slightest interference on the part of the bishop. In 1588, one priest wrote to Speyer, saying that Wolff Dietrich von Gemmingen had forbidden him to apply to Speyer for investiture in his parish. It had never been the custom in his village (Tiefenbronn) for the bishop to invest the priest (GLAK 229/105737).

5

The Thirty Years' War and the Failure of Catholicization

In many parts of Catholic Germany, indeed throughout Catholic Europe, the Counter-Reformation began with an effort to convert Protestant populations to Catholicism. In Würzburg in the 1570s, officials of the prince-bishop forced Protestants to convert or emigrate.[1] Elsewhere in the empire Catholic princes followed similar policies in the decades before the outbreak of the Thirty Years' War, exacerbating political and religious tensions.[2] These policies were an integral aspect of Tridentine reform as well as part of the attempt to strengthen state power.

In Germany, the Thirty Years' War gave further impetus to this aspect of the Counter-Reformation. Catholic military victories in the early 1620s allowed the Church to reintroduce Catholicism in many areas and seemed to threaten the survival of Protestantism in a Habsburg-dominated empire. The thorough and often brutal Catholicization of Bohemia after the Battle of White Mountain (1620) became the symbol of the Counter-Reformation at its most violent and oppressive.[3]

---

1. Rublack, *Gescheiterte Reformation*.
2. See especially Heckel, *Deutschland im konfessionellen Zeitalter*, part 4.
3. I prefer to call the process of converting Protestant regions "Catholicization" rather than "Recatholicization." First, this term is less awkward. Second, the process of establishing Catholic practice in areas that had been Protestant for three or more generations meant

Catholic victories even brought Catholicization to the Bishopric of Speyer. This was a new focus, for the Catholic establishment in Speyer had never considered the conversion of Protestants a part of Church reform. Catholic armies, however, dominated the Rhine valley for most of the war, and the defeat of the Protestant Electoral Palatinate removed one of the political restraints on the policies of the Catholic reformers in this region. In the 1620s the Catholics attempted to reintroduce Catholicism in Protestant villages and, even before the Edict of Restitution in 1629, sought to restore the monasteries to Church control.

This effort to convert Protestant areas failed for three fundamental reasons. The first was the determined resistance of rural communes to religious change, which they understood as a threat to both their political and religious autonomy. By the 1620s, Protestant religious practices had become traditional in Palatine villages and the introduction of Catholic services an innovation. It is never easy to impose new practices on an unwilling population.

The second reason for the failure of Catholicization in the Bishopric of Speyer was that it was never carried out forcefully. A thorough Catholicization, as practiced in some places in Germany during the war, was a three-stage process. First, Catholic priests were installed in the parishes. Second, there was an effort to persuade or convert the population to the benefits of the new religion. The third step was to devise and enforce legal restrictions on dissenters (and even waverers), such as punishments for failing to attend services and restrictions on the civil rights of those who resisted religious change. Eventually, these punishments could include imprisonment, banishment, or death for the most stubborn non-Catholics. In Speyer the local Catholics, led by the Cathedral Chapter, considered such an ambitious course too risky. Instead, they favored a conservative policy designed to preserve the status quo. They were willing to support the first two stages in the process but feared the consequences of more coercive measures.

For many Catholics in Germany, a determined Catholicization also implied the domination of the Jesuits, and the papacy, as well as the complete acceptance of Tridentine Catholicism. The latter suggests the third reason for the failure of Catholicization in Speyer: many in the local Church were highly skeptical of reformed Catholicism. As a result, they focused on the restoration of the most tradi-

---

building from the ground up. "Recatholicization" implies the (simple, easy) restoration of a previously existing condition, which was not the case.

tional institutions, the monasteries. Many churchmen resisted pro-
posals to use monastic incomes for pastoral purposes, fearing this
was the first step in an attack on the privileges and incomes of the
chapters.

There were other reasons for the failure of Catholicization in general. One was the division of the Catholic party. The various occupying powers of the Palatinate, the Bavarians, Austrians, Spanish, and
French all had different policies. None wanted to give the bishop
more authority. The bishop of Speyer, Philipp Christoph von Sötern,
was not a church reformer and was much more interested in increasing his political power and financial resources. In any case, his interest in Speyer faded after he was elected elector-archbishop of Trier in
1623.

For much of the war, the Bishopric of Speyer was an important
campaigning area. The destruction caused by marauding soldiers, the
constant forced levies and quartering of troops, and the extensive
population loss severely hurt the Church. The economic problems
associated with the war, especially in the 1630s and 1640s, forced the
authorities to cut the salaries of the parish priests and made it impossible to hire new ones. By the late 1640s there was a severe shortage of
priests, even to serve the reduced population. Clearly, this lack was
an impediment to continued reform within the Catholic villages as
well as to the conversion of Protestant villages.

It is possible, however, to exaggerate the long-term damage done by
the war.[4] Although the population loss was enormous, it was also
temporary. The recovery of the region in the late 1640s was striking,
rapid, and free of major structural disruption. In the Bishopric of
Speyer the organization of village life, the economic position of the
Church, and the power of the village communes retained their prewar character.

For the Counter-Reformation, the Thirty Years' War provided an
opportunity to Catholicize Protestant areas, but it also weakened the
Church financially and slowed the internal reform of Catholicism.
Significantly for the long-term course of the Counter-Reformation,
the failure of Catholicization convinced Catholic authorities that
confessional divisions were permanent in this part of Germany. The
long and destructive war reinforced the conservative and traditional
tendencies of the local clergy, which included a skeptical attitude

4. Günther Franz, *Der dreißigjährige Krieg und das deutsche Volk. Untersuchung zur
Bevölkerungs- und Agrargeschichte* (1940; reprint, Stuttgart: Gustav Fischer Verlag, 1979),
esp. the introduction and chap. 1.

toward Tridentine reforms and a growing dislike of religious fanaticism. Already by the 1630s, churchmen demonstrated a focus on the institutional survival of the Church and a pragmatism that bordered on religious indifference.

Impact of the War and the Decline of the Reform Impulse

Most studies of religious reform in Germany end with the Thirty Years' War. This holds true especially for studies of the institutionalization of the Protestant churches and of the Counter-Reformation.[5] Studies of the Counter-Reformation in France have a different chronological perspective; French historians have often argued that the final implementation of Tridentine reforms only came in the seventeenth and even eighteenth centuries.[6] The history of the Counter-Reformation in Germany would also benefit from this longer perspective, since the effort to reform the Church continued both during and after the war. The continuities in Church organization, in the policies of episcopal authorities, and in the responses of the laity to these policies during the whole early modern period were more important than the discontinuities caused by the war. Indeed, the war reinforced some of the most important characteristics of Catholicism in the Bishopric of Speyer, especially the conservatism of the upper clergy and the influence of the communal church.

Bishop Philipp Christoph von Sötern, 1610–52

The election in 1609 of Philipp Christoph von Sötern as coadjutor and successor to Bishop Eberhard was a sign of the weakness of the reform party in the Cathedral Chapter.[7] Sötern had a deserved reputation as an influential and politically adept churchman, but he had few of the personal qualities of a Tridentine bishop.[8]

5. Vogler, *La vie religieuse en pays rhénan*; Molitor, *Kirchliche Reformversuche*. Studies of the Counter-Reformation that take the long view include Hsia, *Social Discipline in the Reformation*, and Ortner, *Reformation, katholische Reform, und Gegenreformation im Erzstift Salzburg*. Ortner's history includes part of the eighteenth century.
6. See especially Hoffman, *Church and Community in the Diocese of Lyon*; and Châtellier, *Tradition chrétienne et renouveau catholique*.
7. The coadjutor was an assistant bishop with the right of succession. By 1609, Eberhard had been sick for a long time and the chapter wanted an active bishop.
8. Sötern was not the candidate of the reformers in Speyer and had made enemies in Speyer as early as 1594 by maneuvering his entrance into the Cathedral Chapter in Speyer at

Sötern's career followed the pattern of many aristocratic church-men in the Tridentine German Church. He began his clerical career in the traditionalist Ritterstift in Bruchsal and by 1600 had accumu-lated an impressive number of prestigious and well-endowed bene-fices in the middle Rhine region.[9] Like his opponents, the reform-minded canons, he had received a Jesuit education and was a dedi-cated Catholic. His interests, however, were above all political, as demonstrated by two reports he sent to the pope (1616 and 1623).[10] The 1616 report discusses the economic problems of the Hochstift, the Palatine threat and the political dependence of the bishopric on the emperor, and Sötern's building projects, especially the construc-tion of the fortress at Philippsburg. In addition to these political concerns, he reports on the successes and expansion of the Jesuit and Capuchin orders.[11] In the 1623 report, sent during a period of Cath-olic victory, Sötern emphasizes the economic problems caused by the war and the possibility of Catholicizing the Palatinate. In both re-ports, he is self-confident and even self-promoting, but in neither does he concern himself with the internal reform of the Church.

His election in 1623 as elector-archbishop of Trier allowed him to play an important role in imperial politics. He was a strong supporter of militant political Catholicism and an early champion of the Cath-olic League. As ruler of Trier and Speyer, he also saw himself as the leader of the anti-Habsburg Catholic party. Both in Speyer and in Trier he followed an independent policy.[12] Concern about the expan-sion of Habsburg power and conflicts with the Spanish led Sötern to conclude an alliance with France in 1632, which brought French troops into the empire, and when imperial forces captured Trier in 1635, earned him twelve years in imperial prisons in Belgium and Austria.[13]

Nationalist German historians have judged Philipp Christoph von Sötern harshly for "playing the French card." Ranke's comment that Sötern "only worked for territorial power and religion, but had no idea what the fatherland was" is anachronistic but not far from the

---

the expense of reforming dean Oberstein's candidate. See Stamer III/1, pp. 149–50. See also Press, "Das Hochstift Speyer," pp. 266–67.

9. Hermann Weber, *Frankreich, Kurtrier, der Rhein, und das Reich, 1623–1635* (Bonn: Ludwig Röhrscheid Verlag, 1969), 15–16.

10. Ibid., pp. 16–17; Schmidlin, *Die kirchlichen Zustände in Deutschland*, vol. 3, *West und Nordwestdeutschland*, p. 97. The reports to the pope are in Remling *UB*, pp. 653–60, 665–70.

11. Stamer III/1, pp. 150–51; Remling *UB*, pp. 653–60.

12. Weber, *Frankreich, Kurtrier, der Rhein, und das Reich*, esp. pp. 24–26.

13. Remling II, pp. 490–96.

truth.[14] Sötern, like many of the upper clergymen who dominated the Church in seventeenth-century Germany, worked to expand Catholicism. At the same time he was imbued with aristocratic ideals, politically narrow-minded with an essentially regional focus, and traditional enough to exploit the Church for his and his family's financial benefit. The Counter-Reformation did not break the hold of the traditional Reichskirche on the German Church. Sötern's pro-French and anti-Habsburg policy was a reaction against the centralizing trends of the imperial court as well as a reaction against the growing political power of the emperor.[15]

The War and Catholic Reform

The Bishopric of Speyer lay in the middle of an important war zone. The presence of the strategically vital fortress of Philippsburg, the importance of the Rhine river as a line of communications, and the wealth of the region made the Hochstift a target for marauding armies of both sides. The bishopric suffered two periods of sustained campaigning, the first during the so-called Mansfeld War (1621–23) and the second during the Swedish invasion (1631–32).[16] The French entrance in the war put Speyer and the Palatinate on the front lines, as would be the case throughout the seventeenth century. There were periodic campaigns in the 1630s and 1640s, but most of the destruction in this period was caused by foraging armies of both sides. Neither the loyalty of the Cathedral Chapter to the emperor nor the alliance of Bishop Sötern with the French spared the bishopric the exactions of the various armies.

It is almost impossible to estimate the demographic effect of the war. There is no question that all the inhabitants of some villages fled. This was especially the case on the left (west) bank of the Rhine. Some parts of the Palatinate lost over 75 percent of their inhabitants, and the overall population loss in the Rhine valley has been estimated at 66 percent.[17] The assessment of the bishop's council in 1644 that the population of the Hochstift had declined during the war from thirteen thousand to one thousand, however, probably overesti-

14. Paraphrased in Weber, *Frankreich, Kurtrier, der Rhein, und das Reich*, pp. 13–14.
15. Robert Bireley, S.J., *Religion and Politics in the Age of the Counterreformation: Emperor Ferdinand II, William Lamormaini, S.J., and the Formation of Imperial Policy* (Chapel Hill: University Press of North Carolina, 1981). Bireley emphasizes the close ties between the most militant Counter-Reformers (especially the Jesuits) and the emperor.
16. Remling II, p. 468. Bishop Philipp Christoph von Sötern estimated that three quarters of the population of the bishopric had fled or been killed during the "Mansfeld War."
17. Franz, *Der dreißigjährige Krieg und das deutsche Volk*, pp. 46–52.

mates the losses.[18] The population decline was, however, significant. Even on the right bank of the Rhine, which was somewhat less exposed to foraging armies, one group of Catholic villages reported a population loss of over 80 percent.[19]

The effect of the war on the local economy is obvious. As the population declined, agricultural production plunged, as did tax receipts and tithes. Especially between 1635 and 1648, peasants stopped farming marginal land. The collapse of trade particularly reduced the profits from wine production.[20] These developments were extremely damaging to the Catholic Church in Speyer. Most of the income that supported both the rural and the urban clergy came from tithes, interest on loans to the peasantry, and the profits on the wine and grain trade. Income from all these sources collapsed during the war. Just as the population explosion of the period before the Thirty Years' War had enriched the clergy, the war and the drop in population impoverished them.

The Thirty Years' War also caused a setback in the effort to reform the clergy and bring Tridentine Catholicism to the Catholic population of the bishopric. The Church faced difficult choices in the allocation of scarce resources. Those institutions that had been founded during the period of prosperity in the late sixteenth century were the first to suffer as revenues declined. These were precisely the institutions that had been founded to further reform, among them the Jesuit college and the Alumnat. Financial difficulties affected the rural clergy as well, cutting incomes and making it impossible to hire new priests. The number and quality of priests and services fell, and the influence of the Church in the countryside weakened.

One consequence of the war was the collapse in 1636 of the Alumnat, which had been training parish priests since the 1560s. In the 1620s, perhaps anticipating a demand for priests in newly Catholicized regions, the Cathedral Chapter admitted several new students to this seminary.[21] At the same time, however, the income of the Alumnat was declining. In 1623, it had a "debt" of three thousand gulden, which meant that it had been operating beyond its own

18. Joseph Baur, "Das Fürstbistum Speyer in den Jahren 1635 bis 1652," *Mitteilungen des historischen Vereins der Pfalz* 24 (1900): p. 104–5. Baur accepts these figures, which probably underestimate the population before and after the war.

19. GLAK 153/149. (1645 figures from 13 villages in Amt Kißlau). The population loss may have been somewhat lower, because the villagers overestimated the prewar population in an effort to show that the villages had been overcrowded before 1620.

20. Kuno Drollinger, *Kleine Städte Südwestdeutschlands. Studien zur Sozial- und Wirtschaftsgeschichte der Städte im rechtsrheinischen Teil des Hochstifts Speyer bis zur Mitte des 17. Jahrhunderts* (Stuttgart: Kohlhammer Verlag, 1968), 117.

21. GLAK 61/10957, pp. 51–52, 69–70, 249, 290, 319, 361, 446, 541, 787–88.

endowment on funds provided by the chapter.[22] The students had to live on very little, and by 1629 this situation began to affect their behavior and discipline. The canons complained that the students were not obeying the rules and suggested that it might be better to close the Alumnat entirely.[23]

The final collapse of the Alumnat in 1635–36 reflects the serious problems that faced the Church during the war. The Alumni had become increasingly disobedient, refusing to attend services in the Cathedral and being insolent to their teacher. The Cathedral Chapter felt that it was too expensive to support the students and decided to close the school. At the same time, however, there was such a shortage of priests in the countryside that the canons decided to send these half-trained priests out to the parishes to fill vacancies.[24] Not only had the Alumnat (which was originally conceived as a Tridentine seminary) fallen apart, but the wartime situation had forced the Church to lower its standards for rural priests.

The shortage of priests grew more serious as the war progressed. Through the 1620s, it was the physical destruction caused by passing armies that caused the greatest number of problems. The priests reported serious damage to churches and parsonages. The pfarrer in Geinsheim wrote to the Cathedral Chapter that Mansfeld's troops had destroyed an altar, windows, pictures of the Virgin and Saints Peter and Paul, and the pulpit in his church.[25] The destruction forced the patrons to cut the salaries of rural priests in half, at least in the first half of the 1620s.[26] By 1626 conditions had improved. The pfarrer in Geinsheim received 42 malter (c. 63 hectoliters or almost 190 bushels) of grain from the Cathedral Chapter, which was close to his peacetime allotment of 48 malter.[27] Nevertheless, priests found it difficult to survive on reduced resources and kept a lookout for better parishes. The priest in Bauerbach, Vitus Volck, left this poorly endowed parish for Baden in 1628. In 1629, the pfarrer in Geinsheim requested a position in the city of Speyer and, when none was available, asked to be transferred to the town of Landau.[28] This priest was concerned about his physical safety in the countryside as well as about his impoverishment.

22. Ibid., p. 60.
23. GLAK 61/10959, p. 206v.
24. Ibid., p. 570r; GLAK 61/10961, pp. 34v–35r, 91v–92r, 96v.
25. GLAK 61/10957, p. 93–94.
26. Ibid., pp. 294, 524. Also see Häusser, *Geschichte der rheinischen Pfalz*, p. 483. Häusser mistakenly says that Catholic officials reduced only the income of reformed pastors in the Palatinate in an effort to drive them out. In fact, all clergy had to take a pay cut in the 1620s.
27. GLAK 61/10957, pp. 900–901.
28. GLAK 61/10959, pp. 20v, 211 (Bauerbach), pp. 188v, 206v (Geinsheim).

After the Swedish invasion of 1631–34, the shortage of priests became acute. Church officials were forced to send monks out from Speyer to hold services in the villages around the city. This was not a new practice. Before the war two parishes had been served by Franciscans, but in the 1630s and 1640s, as many as nine parishes were served by Franciscans, Carmelites, Dominicans, and Capuchins. Because they continued to live in the city and were not trained as parish priests, the quality of service provided by the regulars was poor.

Those parish priests who continued to serve despite invading armies, plague, and food shortages were compelled to handle several parishes. Whereas before the war almost all priests served one parish, by 1640 most priests had two and sometimes three to take care of. Between 1635 and 1650, thirty-two parish priests appear in the records, and these held services in fifty-seven different parishes.[29] Those pfarrer who stayed in the villages did not live well. In 1641, Hartmann Stibius, the priest in Deidesheim, commented that he had lived in poverty for more than ten years.[30] Many priests survived by farming. The priest in Königsbach was forced to give up his parish in 1637 because (probably due to age) he was no longer physically able to farm the parish property.[31]

The villagers frequently complained that the priests did a poor job. No doubt this failing was to a great extent the result of serving too many parishes. The shortage of priests also made it unwise for episcopal authorities to discipline neglectful ones. The pfarrer in St. Leon tried to justify his failure to administer the sacraments and say Mass by pointing out that his income was small and he had two parishes to oversee. His parishioners were not sympathetic, and the Cathedral Chapter reminded him that as he was a graduate of the Alumnat they expected better of him.[32]

Many villages had no priest and no services. There were no priests, for example, in the Lauterburg *Amt* in the late 1630s, an area that had nine before the war.[33] In 1640, the mayor and council of the town of Lauterburg complained that no priest had resided there in three years.[34] The villagers of Langenbrücken withheld the tithe the same

29. These priests are mostly found in the minutes of the Cathedral Chapter and in the Bishop' Council minutes. There were probably others (GLAK 61/10959 to 61/10969, GLAK 61/11499 to 61/11504, GLAK 229).
30. GLAK 61/10963, p. 284r.
31. GLAK 61/10961, p. 345r.
32. Ibid., p. 285v–286r.
33. GLAK 61/11499, pp. 244v–245r.
34. GLAK 61/10963, p. 86r.

year in an effort to get the patrons to appoint a priest. The amount of the tithe was so small (about three gulden) that the patrons, the Gregorian Vicars of the Cathedral Chapter, decided not to press the villagers. No priest was appointed.[35]

The shortage of clergy, the general disorganization of both secular and spiritual administration, and the disruption of rural life led to a serious setback in the efforts of the Church to discipline the laity. Wartime conditions jeopardized even the limited prewar gains of the reformers, especially in Church attendance and respect for Sundays and holidays. Although no records of Church attendance could be kept, there is evidence that villagers increasingly neglected services and worked in the fields instead.[36] The clergy's interest in disciplining the people was limited before 1620. During the war it was nonexistent.

Another unmistakable sign of the declining importance of Tridentine reform was the deteriorating relationship between the Jesuits and the Cathedral Chapter during the war. In part problems developed because financial constraints forced the chapter to reduce the support it gave the Jesuits. More important, local churchmen opposed the militant anti-Protestant policy favored by the Jesuits and feared the growing influence of the order in Germany. Like many German Catholics, some in Speyer accused the Jesuits of being overinvolved in politics, too powerful at the imperial court, too ambitious, and (perhaps most important) too closely linked to the papacy.[37] In 1644, for example, the cathedral canons lamented the influence the Jesuits wielded in Rome and Vienna. Using this leverage the fathers had acquired the income of the former Cistercian monastery in Klingenmünster, at a time when the bishopric could have used the money.[38] The somewhat imperious tone taken by the rector of the college with church officials did not improve relations between the order and the local Church. Even the general aggressiveness of the Jesuits bothered the canons. In 1636, the fathers asked to take over several damaged and vacant chapels in the Cathedral. The

35. Ibid., pp. 143r–143v, 162r, 163r.
36. Ibid., p. 359r; GLAK 61/10965. pp. 139v–140r. These are both examples from the village of Ketsch, where a diligent, but nonresident, priest reported on the *fahrlessigkeit* (neglectfulness) of his parishioners.
37. Bireley, *Religion and Politics in the Age of the Counterreformation*, chap. 7. Many Catholics suspected, not without justification, that the Jesuits planned to take over the bulk of the monasteries restored by the Edict of Restitution.
38. GLAK 11501a, p. 211. The Jesuits also appealed to the emperor to force the Cathedral Chapter to pay what it owed the college in Speyer (GLAK 61/10957, pp. 607–8, 611, 743–44, 754, 792–93).

canons hesitated, commenting, "Once they [the Jesuits] are let into the Cathedral Chapter, they will be hard to get out again."[39]

These conflicts and financial difficulties caused the number of Jesuits in the Speyer house to decline as the war progressed. In the early 1620s there were thirty to thirty-five Jesuits living in Speyer (peaking at thirty-six in 1621) whereas in the 1640s the number hovered between twelve and eighteen.[40] In part the numbers of Jesuits declined because of their unpopularity with the French, who increasingly dominated the region. Perhaps more important, however, was the sense among the local clergy, especially in the Cathedral Chapter, that the Jesuits represented outside forces (the papacy and the emperor) and had little interest in the welfare of the local Church. This view was confirmed when Jesuits refused to accept gracefully a reduction in income, at a time when the whole Church was suffering.[41] The Jesuits' attitude gave them a reputation for selfishness and arrogance that stayed with them for the whole seventeenth century.

One result of the war, then, was a perceptible weakening of the impetus for reform in the Bishopric of Speyer. In a very practical way, the Thirty Years' War reduced the resources available for the Jesuits, the Alumnat, and the rural clergy. In a broader sense, the political insecurity of the period, especially after the Swedish invasion, reinforced the conservative tendencies of the local churchmen and reduced their enthusiasm for the Counter-Reformation.

The Postwar Consequences

Conditions in the postwar period accentuated the traditionalist tone of Catholicism, especially by strengthening the communal church. This strengthening was a consequence of the rapid economic recovery of the region. A French diplomat who passed through the area in both 1646 and 1658 commented at the time of his second visit that the villages and fields were in such good shape that it appeared as if there had never been a war.[42] There are strong indications that

---

39. GLAK 61/10961, p. 117r.

40. ARSJ Rh.Inf.48, pp. 226v, 257v; ARSJ Rh.Sup. 29, pp. 118r, 121r, 127r, 133r, 137r, 141r, 146r; ARSJ Rh.Sup. 31, pp. 4r–5r, 32r, 46v, 51r, 178v, 208v.

41. The Jesuits kept careful track of all money, grain, and wine owed them and bombarded the Cathedral Chapter with requests for support. See for example GLAK 61/10959, p. 560, GLAK 61/10961, pp. 187v–188r.

42. Häusser, Geschichte der rheinischen Pfalz, p. 588. Production began to increase in the 1640s. In 1646, for example, the Cathedral Chapter collected a tithe of 85 malter of grain from the town of Landau. In 1649 the Landauer paid 120 malter. On a smaller scale, the

those who survived were better off than they had been before the war, for quite simple reasons. In general, villages had been overcrowded in the prewar period, and in the 1650s the population recovered at a lower level. In the late seventeenth century, the villagers of Ostringen reported a population of 180 but claimed that it had been over 300 before the "great war." In the prewar period, they said, the village had been overcrowded, with several families living in each house. Every village in the two districts (*Ämter*) of Rotenburg and Kisslau reported similar figures and informed the bishop's officials that they did not want a return to the conditions of the early part of the century.[43]

This was a prosperous region, and the postwar recovery made the survivors comfortable. The smaller population did away with the overcrowding, the farming of marginal lands, and the impoverishment of some segments of the rural population that had existed between the 1590s and the 1620s. After 1650, previously landless peasants acquired property, while the shortage of landless laborers forced wealthy peasants to plant less land. There was a decline in social differences within villages and a resultant easing of social tensions. This situation, combined with the disorganization of secular and spiritual authority, strengthened village unity and local communal institutions.[44]

As a result, village communes continued to have an important role in local Church affairs and even expanded their influence in the late 1640s. The residents of Lauterburg, for example, appealed several times to the Church authorities in Speyer for a resident priest. In 1649, not having obtained satisfaction through the proper channels, the townsmen, working with local officials, appointed their own.[45]

In 1648, the gemeinde of Edesheim wrote to the Cathedral Chapter that the parish was vacant and that the chapter could not appoint a new priest "without allowing the commune, as tradition and practice prescribe, to confirm him."[46] The chapter was quite hostile to this

---

peasants in Rödersheim, which in the mid-1630s was completely abandoned, paid one malter in 1646, five malter in 1649 (GLAK 61/10967, pp. 165–81, 933–66; GLAK 61/10961, p. 57v). Towns recovered rapidly as well. See Drollinger, *Kleine Städte Südwestdeutschlands*, pp. 114–21.

43. GLAK 153/157. See above, note 19.

44. There is no evidence of a weakening of communal institutions or of the loyalty of the villagers to the gemeinde, either before or after the war, as Robisheaux has found for Hohenlohe and Rebel for Upper Austria. See Robisheaux, *Rural Society and the Search for Order*, esp. chap. 3; Rebel, *Peasant Classes*, esp. chap. 5. See also Wunder, *Die bäuerliche Gemeinde in Deutschland*, chap. 5.

45. GLAK 61/10967, p. 1020.

46. Ibid., p. 546.

idea, commenting that "the Cathedral Chapter as patron . . . should examine the qualities of the priests, and not (against all laws) the commune."[47] The canons also suspected that the outgoing priest, Jost Gerber, was responsible for this letter, which they found "passionate," impertinent, and criminal. They did not, however, punish Gerber or the villagers. A priest was hired from a neighboring village, but it is not clear if he was the choice of the Cathedral Chapter, the villagers, or both.[48] In any event, the gemeinde had openly claimed extensive rights over the local church.

A long-running feud between Johan Lammit, pfarrer in Neipsheim, and his parishioners further illustrates the villagers' power over the clergy. In the summer of 1648, Lammit and the Cathedral Chapter's agent in Neipsheim personally collected the tithe in the fields—a clear break with tradition, since the Cathedral Chapter had always negotiated with the commune and collected the tithe through the village representatives. The priest and his helper apparently followed the example of Protestant clergy in neighboring villages, a clear indication that Catholic communes traditionally had a greater role in Church affairs than their Protestant neighbors. The bishop's council, while conceding that the Cathedral Chapter had a right to collect tithes as it wished, argued that the method used by Lammit only served to alienate the villagers from the Church.[49] The council further lamented the failure of the vicar general to adjudicate the dispute, fearing that the conflict would cause the villagers to boycott services and endanger their souls.[50]

In 1649, the bishop's officials expressed even greater disgust with Lammit's behavior. The pfarrer had, in effect, excommunicated the village mayor and his wife. He had taken this drastic step after a confrontation with the mayor's wife, who tore out some of the priest's hair. Lammit announced to the villagers in church that "any lay person who strikes a priest or cleric is damned to hell."[51] The bishop's council once again blamed the priest for his "scandalous and very dangerous actions" and suggested that the vicar general treat him severely.[52]

The incident in Neipsheim indicates several subtle but important effects of the war on the relationship between the communes and the

47. Ibid., p. 547.
48. Ibid., p. 558.
49. GLAK 61/11503a, pp. 148r–148v.
50. Ibid., p. 219r.
51. GLAK 61/11503b, p. 43r: "Der seye in abgrundt der höllen verdambt."
52. Ibid., p. 44r.

Church. The self-assurance of the villagers in their conflict with the priest is evidence of their strength. The disruption of war had forced them to rely on local initiative for everything from poor relief to military defense. Furthermore, the sympathy for the villagers shown by the bishop's officials suggests that the elites in the bishopric were not unified. Perhaps in an effort to attract immigrants, officials tried to tone down the activities of overzealous priests. Finally, the heavy-handed behavior of Lammit is a sign that the quality of the rural clergy had declined during the war.

Catholicization: The Monasteries and the Palatinate

The Thirty Years' War forced Catholics in the Bishopric of Speyer to face the issue of Catholicization. Whereas before the war Catholics had political authority over few Protestants, the defeat of the Protestant Palatinate in the early 1620s made the restoration of Catholicism in large areas of the region a possibility.

Some Catholic powers in the Empire moved quickly to Catholicize thoroughly areas brought under their control. In the 1620s the Austrians cleared Bohemia of Protestants efficiently and brutally. Bavarian policy in the Upper Palatinate was similarly effective in making the formerly Palatine province completely Catholic. Both powers used military means and property confiscations to convert or drive out Protestant elites and forced Catholic practice on the populations, often by sending soldiers into the villages.

Catholic authorities in Speyer did not share the enthusiasm of their colleagues in Vienna and Munich for such a ruthless policy. After seventy-five years as the minority and politically weaker religion in the middle Rhine valley, the local Church had difficulty grasping the consequences of Catholic victory. Having based their political and financial security on the religious peace of 1555, many of the Catholic elite in Speyer hesitated to seize the possibly short-lived fruits of victory. During the war, the Swedish invasion in the early 1630s confirmed this view. Rather than attempt a thorough Catholicization of the bishopric, the local Church sought more limited gains for Catholics, especially hoping to restore certain legal and financial rights "usurped" by the Palatinate.

When examining the process of Catholicization in the Bishopric of Speyer, one must consider the restitution of the monasteries and the Catholicization of the Palatinate. Because the Palatinate had taken over the monasteries after the Peace of Augsburg, their incorporation into the Electorate had always been of dubious legality. As early as 1622, Bishop Sötern attempted to gain control of the income of the monasteries.[53] The Catholicization of the Palatinate as a whole was now possible because the emperor stripped Elector Frederick V of his principality and assumed direct imperial control. Without such legal justification, however, Catholic authorities in Speyer did not attempt to Catholicize other Protestant areas in the bishopric, such as the Principality of Zweibrücken, the Margravate of Baden-Durlach, or the Imperial City of Speyer.

Catholicization proceeded very haphazardly. Financial and political problems caused by the war made expediency more important than long-term policy. There were serious divisions among the various Catholic powers (the Austrians, Bavarians, and Spanish) occupying the Palatinate, as well as between these powers and the episcopal authorities. Bishop Sötern and the Cathedral Chapter were rarely in agreement, especially after the bishop's French alliance and subsequent imprisonment. Ultimately, it was the reluctance of the local Church to undertake a major Catholicization program that determined Catholic policy. By the 1650s it was apparent that the war had done little to change the confessional geography of the region. Although a few Catholic minorities could be found in Palatine territory, religious divisions closely resembled those of 1620.

The Restitution of the Monasteries

Some German Catholics did believe that Protestantism could be eradicated in the empire. Emperor Ferdinand's Jesuit confessor, William Lamormaini, even wrote to the pope, "Perhaps even all of Germany may be led back to the old faith."[54] Catholic militants considered the restoration of Church lands that had been taken by Protestants since the Peace of Augsburg an essential first step in this process. Robert Bireley has argued that some leading Catholics, especially in Bavaria and Vienna, considered the Edict of Restitution as only the beginning of a Catholicization of all of Protestant Germany.[55] The precise practical connection between the restitution of

---

53. Stamer III/1, p. 160; Remling II, pp. 471–72.
54. Quoted in Geoffrey Parker et al., *The Thirty Years' War* (London: Routledge and Kegan Paul, 1984), 94.
55. Robert Bireley, S.J., *Maximilian von Bayern, Adam Contzen S.J. und die Gegenreformation in Deutschland 1624–35* (Göttingen, Vandenhoeck und Ruprecht, 1975); idem, *Religion and Politics in the Age of the Counterreformation.*

Church property and the conversion of Protestant populations was never clearly formulated. It seems that the Jesuits in particular hoped that the recovered property would be used to support more Jesuit colleges and missions as well as other Counter-Reformation measures, such as the education of Catholic clergy. These measures in turn would facilitate the conversion of Protestant populations.

Bishop Sötern did not view the restitution of the monasteries as part of an attempt to restore the Church to its pre-Reformation condition or even to the situation in 1552, before the secularization of the monasteries. He hoped above all to gain episcopal control of monastic rights and incomes. Although he favored using some of the monastic revenues for a new episcopal seminary, most of the new income was to be used to support his ambitious political plans as prince-bishop of Speyer and elector-archbishop of Trier.

As soon as Catholic armies conquered the Palatinate, Sötern attempted to take possession of the monasteries. In November 1622, Pope Gregory XV gave the bishop his support for this plan, but the opposition of Emperor Ferdinand delayed the project.[56] A year later the bishop asked Gregory's successor, Urban VIII, to assign the incomes of the monasteries of Limburg, Eußerthal, and Seebach directly to the bishop of Speyer. The new pope turned down this request, instead giving most of the Palatine monasteries to Archduke Leopold of Austria for two years. Sötern gained possession only of the small former Augustinian chapter in Hördt.[57] In the early 1620s, as one historian has emphasized, "what was urgent for the Emperor . . . and for the Bishop of Speyer was not so much the Recatholicization of the conquered land, as the restitution of the clerical foundations."[58] In other words, financial and political concerns outweighed religious ones.

The Edict of Restitution (March 1629) accelerated the process of recovering the monasteries for the Catholic Church, greatly increased the number of institutions involved, and caused serious conflicts within the Catholic party. The edict provided (among other things) that all ecclesiastical institutions incorporated by Protestant authorities since 1552 be returned to the Church. Within the Bishop-

---

56. Stamer III/1, p. 160; Remling II, pp. 471–72.
57. Stamer III/1, pp. 160–61; Remling II, pp. 472–73, 477. Remling points out that Sötern also took benefices of the bishopric for his own use, including the primissary in Schifferstadt. This was an attempt to channel church resources to political and military uses.
58. Karl Lutz, "Fürstbischöfliche und kaiserliche, österreichische und französische Rekatholisierung im südlichen Speiergau, 1622–1632, und ihre reichs- und kirchenrechtlichen Begründungen," Archiv für mittelrheinische Kirchengeschichte 20 (1968): 281.

ric of Speyer, in addition to the Palatine monasteries, the Catholics now claimed five monasteries and chapters in Württemberg, two in Baden-Durlach, and one in Zweibrücken.[59] Who was to control the monasteries and their considerable incomes and how these resources were to be used remained in dispute.

One program was to use the newly acquired resources to promote Catholic reform measures and the conversion of Protestants. This may have been the policy favored by Emperor Ferdinand II when he promulgated the edict, and it also had supporters in Speyer.[60] Sötern himself used the income of the chapter in Hördt to help support a small seminary in Philippsburg. He even hoped to use the revenue of some of the monasteries to fund a large episcopal seminary in Speyer. The bishop also wrote to Rome proposing the transfer of various rural monasteries and chapters to places where their resources could be used for pastoral purposes.[61] It is perhaps possible to dismiss these plans as window dressing devised by a bishop who ultimately wanted the resources of the monasteries for military and political purposes. In any case, the Swedish invasion and wartime dislocations put an end to these plans.

The Jesuits benefited from the Edict of Restitution, although not to the extent they might have anticipated. Between 1623 and 1646 two Jesuits resided in the former Cistercian convent of Heilsbruck. The fathers not only managed the convent's property but used Heilsbruck as a base for missions to convert the local population. In 1646, however, the Jesuits lost a long court battle with the Cistercians and had to turn the convent over to the nuns.[62]

The conflict over Heilsbruck was similar to those fought all over Germany between the Jesuits and the old orders. In 1630 the Jesuits presented a plan in Vienna, calling for the establishment of ninety new Jesuit colleges. Many of these were to be missionary outposts dedicated to the conversion of Protestants, and all were to be supported by the resources of the monasteries. The Society argued that especially the income of female houses should go to the Jesuits, for the nuns did no pastoral work. These ambitious plans were quashed

59. Stamer III/1, pp. 161–62.
60. Bireley, *Religion and Politics in the Age of the Counterreformation*, chaps. 4 and 5.
61. Stamer III/1, p. 165. Sötern proposed the monastery of Limburg be moved to Deidesheim, Hornbach to Lauterburg, Hördt to Philippsburg, and Klingenmünster to Landau. These were all safer locations and put the monasteries closer to the seat of episcopal government in Philippsburg. See also Remling II, pp. 477–78; Remling *UB*, pp. 668–69.
62. Stamer III/1, p. 163; Duhr II/1, p. 170; St.A.MZ, 15/400, 1637.

by a strong anti-Jesuit reaction within the Church. Ultimately, it was monks from the old orders who took possession of the monasteries.[63]

In the Bishopric of Speyer the Benedictines returned to Hornbach and Limburg, the Cistercians to Eußerthal, and the Augustinians to Hördt. In each case the old orders were able to send only a couple of monks to establish their possession of the monasteries. None of these orders had the manpower or initiative to establish a strong presence in the countryside.[64] The monks of the old orders did nothing to support the Counter-Reformation or help Catholicize Protestant areas. In fact, peasants of all religions were traditionally quite hostile to the monks, whom they considered parasites. Where they were active, the Jesuits and Capuchins developed better relations with the rural population.

Finally, the Catholic powers who occupied the Palatinate were eager to use the resources of the monasteries to help defray the costs of the war. The Austrians gained control of several monasteries in the 1620s for this purpose. The Spanish were very reluctant to allow the bishop or the orders to administer clerical property in their zone of influence.[65] In the 1630s, the episcopal authorities had a drawn-out dispute with the Bavarians over control of the small chapter in Sinsheim.[66] All these conflicts only underscore the divisions within the Catholic party that turned out to be especially significant for the failure to Catholicize the Electoral Palatinate.

Catholicization in the Countryside

The campaign to Catholicize Protestant villages, especially in the Palatinate (*Kurpfalz*), was unsuccessful over the long term for three reasons. The divisions among the Catholic powers meant that Catholicization proceeded haphazardly and without clear direction. The episcopal authorities in Speyer had little prewar experience in converting Protestant regions, nor indeed much confidence in the success of such an endeavor, and therefore did not press Catholicization very energetically. And finally, the disruption of war and the shortage of trained priests meant that neither the funds nor the manpower was available to accomplish the task in any case.

63. Bireley, *Religion and Politics in the Age of the Counterreformation*, chap. 7, esp. pp. 134–36.
64. Stamer III/1, pp. 162–65.
65. GLAK 61/11497/II, p. 363v.
66. GLAK 61/10961, pp. 8v–9r, 17r–17v, 69v, 193v.

The local Catholic authorities had some prewar experience trying to convert Protestant villagers, and this experience gave them little reason to expect the easy success of Catholicization during the war. Between about 1580 and 1620, Catholic officials moved to convert the people of two regions on the edges of the Hochstift with large Protestant populations. The first was the region of five large villages under the nominal secular rule of the Ritterstift in Bruchsal. The second was the lordship of Dahn, an episcopal fief that returned to the possession of the bishop at the extinction of the von Dahn family in 1603. This holding included six villages that had been Protestant for many decades.[67]

The Catholicization of these regions proved very difficult. Catholic authorities instituted the first two steps in this process, establishing legal authority in ecclesiastical affairs and installing new clerics in the parishes. There followed an effort to persuade or convert the population to the benefits of Catholicism. This, however, was the extent of it. The third, more coercive stage of Catholicization was not undertaken. No restrictions were successfully placed on the Protestant inhabitants of these villages, and no effort was made to evict non-Catholics. This moderate policy toward Protestant villagers dovetailed with the relatively restrained policy of the Church toward Catholic popular religion and popular culture.

Above all, however, the villagers themselves prevented the Catholicization of these regions. The Protestant inhabitants of Dahn and the Ritterstift villages exploited the moderation of the local Counter-Reformation, used the political support of the Palatinate, and maintained their strong traditions of local political autonomy and communal control of the Church. Lengthy lawsuits and even armed resistance restricted the impact of Catholicization. In the long run, all these methods allowed the Protestant villagers to practice their religion inside the Catholic Hochstift.[68]

During the war, local Catholic authorities applied this experience to the attempt to Catholicize the Palatinate. The process was quite straightforward. Catholic priests were in short supply, but when possible Protestant clergymen were removed from the parishes. The religious orders, especially the Jesuits, supported the secular clergy

67. For background on the Ritterstift villages, see Chapter 1. For Dahn see Stamer III/1, p. 218.

68. For the Ritterstift villages see Feigenbutz, *Kurzer Abriß der Geschichte von Odenheim*, p. 21. See also GLAK 94/392; GLAK 61/5341, pp. 41–46, 48–59, 777–78; GLAK 61/5342, p. 117v; for Landshausen see GLAK 229/57523, 229/57524; for Odenheim see 229/79246, 229/79260; ARSJ Rh.Inf.48, p. 104v. For Dahn see Stamer III/1, p. 218; LASp. D2/348; ARSJ Rh.Inf. 48, p. 160v.

with missions and pastoral work. By 1625, episcopal authorities had decided that they would pay the remaining Protestant pastors in the conquered territory half of their salary (Catholic priests were no better paid) and that pastors illegally serving parishes would not be paid at all. The parish patrons were not to fill vacancies unless the villagers wanted a Catholic priest.[69] The Cathedral Chapter, as patron of a number of parishes in Palatine territory, appointed about eight priests to serve in Protestant villages in the 1620s. The secular authorities also appointed priests to serve in the villages. In 1626, the Habsburg archduke Leopold, who governed the area around Germersheim, ordered all Protestant clerics out of the area and moved to hire Catholic priests.[70] The Spanish government, based in Kreuznach, began to install Catholic clergy in the parishes in 1625, albeit slowly. By 1627 there were twenty-two priests working in the areas under Spanish rule, although few of them within the Bishopric of Speyer.[71] The Bavarian government in Heidelberg also installed priests in the villages on the right side of the Rhine, especially after 1625.[72]

Not surprisingly, the Jesuits actively supported the Catholicization of the Palatinate. The fathers set up several small establishments in Palatine territory, in Germersheim (1628–31), Bretten (from 1625), and Neustadt (1625–32, 1638–50). In all three locations, the Jesuits held services, worked to convert the residents of the three towns, and did pastoral work in neighboring villages. The Jesuits supplemented the work of these "standing missions" with irregular missions to Protestant areas. As always, they claimed considerable success, especially in the area around Neustadt, once an important Calvinist stronghold.[73] Undoubtedly Jesuit influence in the Bishopric of Speyer peaked in the 1620s, especially in the countryside, where they were more active than ever before.

All the Catholic powers in the Palatinate installed Catholic priests in the villages and supported the efforts of the Jesuits and other

69. GLAK 61/10957, pp. 536–37; Stamer III/1, p. 166.

70. Karl Lutz, "Fürstbischöfliche und kaiserliche, österreichische und französische Rekatholiserung," pp. 282–83.

71. Anna Egler, *Die Spanier in der linksrheinischen Pfalz, 1620–1632. Invasion, Verwaltung, Rekatholisierung* (Mainz: Selbstverlag der Gesellschaft für mittelrheinische Kirchengeschichte, 1971), 126–44, 154.

72. Häusser, *Geschichte der rheinischen Pfalz*, pp. 481–84.

73. Duhr II/1, pp. 171–74; St.A.MZ 15/400, 1636–38, 1640, 1641. See also ARSJ Rh.Sup. 31, p. 5r. Over five hundred people took communion in the Jesuit church in Neustadt in 1646. According to the fathers, this was a large number given the size of the Catholic population. See also Meinrad Schaab, "Die Wiederherstellung des Katholizismus in der Kurpfalz im 17. und 18. Jahrhundert," *Zeitschrift für Geschichte des Oberrheins* 114 (1966): 170–71.

orders to convert Protestants. There was no unanimity, however, on the extent to which harsh, coercive measures should be used to force the population to attend Catholic services. Anna Egler, in her study of the Spanish occupation of the Palatinate, has shown that Spanish policymakers were primarily interested in safeguarding their political and military position in the area. Fearing a mass emigration of the Protestant population, Spanish authorities refrained from instituting harsh anti-Protestant ordinances, especially in the 1640s, when the population loss was severe and eventual Catholic victory doubtful.[74] The Spanish had no long-term interest in governing this part of the Palatinate and considered the occupation temporary. For this reason they avoided strong Counter-Reformation measures that risked antagonizing the population.

The Bavarian authorities had more extensive goals than the Spanish. As a reward for his service to the Catholic cause, Duke Maximilian of Bavaria received the Palatine Electoral dignity as well as large pieces of Palatine territory. Maximilian hoped to make these gains permanent. Partly in order to break the loyalty of the inhabitants of the Palatinate to their Calvinist rulers (now in exile in Holland), Maximilian favored an aggressive anti-Protestant policy. Maximilian's strong Catholic faith, the influence of the Jesuits at his court, and his personal antipathy to Calvinists, whom he blamed for the war, further contributed to this policy.[75] In 1625 the Bavarians banished all Protestant clergy, and in 1628 they ordered all citizens to convert. These measures could be enforced only in the towns, but the 1628 ordinance caused an exodus of a number of prominent citizens, especially from Heidelberg.[76]

The Bavarians also hoped to use the resources of the University of Heidelberg to support a secondary school, a seminary for the education of priests, and a Jesuit college. The bishops of Worms, Würzburg, and Speyer, whose dioceses all included Palatine territory, considered this an effort to create a Bavarian territorial Church in the Palatinate. The bishops also hesitated to give the Jesuits further influence and distrusted their close ties to Maximilian. As Volker Press has pointed out, the three bishops feared Bavarian domination and "were not ready to sacrifice their fundamental claims [to ecclesiastical jurisdictions and properties] in exchange for the renewal of Catholicism in the Palatinate."[77]

74. Egler, Die Spanier in der linksrheinischen Pfalz, esp. p. 154; Schaab, "Die Wiederherstellung des Katholizismus," p. 154.
75. Bireley, Maximilian von Bayern, (Göttingen, 1974), esp. pp. 7–8 and chap. 4.
76. Häusser, Geschichte der rheinischen Pfalz, pp. 481–84.
77. Volker Press, "Kurfürst Maximilian I. von Bayern, die Jesuiten und die Universität Heidelberg im dreißigjährigen Krieg 1622–1649," in Semper Apertus, Sechshundert Jahre

The Swedish invasion in 1631 shattered the confidence of the Catholics in the middle Rhine region, especially the episcopal authorities in Speyer. The new situation caused the Cathedral Chapter to work throughout the 1630s and 1640s to protect the Hochstift from outside powers of all religions. The canons realized that a return to the prewar religious division of the region was likely and, taking the long view, pursued a moderate policy *vis-à-vis* Protestant areas. With the postwar situation in mind, local Catholics focused on strengthening the legal and financial rights of the Church in Protestant territories and ignored opportunities to spread Catholicism.[78]

Even the Bavarians followed a more moderate policy after the Swedish invasion. In 1641, the governor in Heidelberg wrote to Maximilian that it was no longer expedient to force people to go to Catholic services.[79] The French, who occupied most of the left bank of the Rhine, installed Catholic priests where they could, but the shortage of priests greatly hindered any consistent policy of Catholicization in the war-torn region. In the 1640s, depopulation, poverty, and general war-weariness all diminished interest in Catholicization. For local officials and churchmen, the war had proved the danger of the ambitious, independent policies of Bishop Sötern and the uselessness of the endeavor to restore the monasteries and Catholicize the Palatinate.

The attempt to uproot Protestantism and restore Catholic unity during the Thirty Years' War was undoubtedly disorganized and chaotic. The reasons for this chaos—the disruption of war, financial limitations, and divisions within the Catholic party—are also clear. Of perhaps greater importance, however, was the context of traditional confessional relations in the Bishopric of Speyer. The local Catholic elite, in the chapters and in the bishop's administration, were not prepared to exploit Catholic dominance. Accustomed to a policy based on the defense of specific rights (such as territorial rights, patronage of parishes, and legal exemptions), these men were unable and unwilling to attempt anything more ambitious.

Did the Catholicization, however haphazard it may have been, have any long-term effect on Protestant-Catholic relations in the

---

Ruprecht-Karls-Universität Heidelberg 1386–1986 (Berlin: Springer Verlag, 1986), 338–41; Schaab, "Die Wiederherstellung des Katholizismus," p. 173.

78. Some examples: the Cathedral Chapter's neglected its right of patronage in Barbelroth (GLAK 61/10963, p. 333r) and its alternate right of patronage in Lußheim (GLAK 61/10961, p. 135v). In 1636, the Cathedral Chapter wrote to the emperor about political and jurisdictional issues, but not about Catholicization (GLAK 61/10961, pp. 131v–132r).

79. Häusser, *Geschichte der rheinischen Pfalz*, p. 565.

bishopric? It is difficult to determine the percentage of Catholics in the *Kurpfalz* at the end of the war. In the most aggressively Catholicized part of the Palatinate, the part governed by Bavaria, Catholic officials estimated that in 1640, "barely one third [of the population] are truly in their hearts Catholic."[80] The Austrian government in Germersheim reported in 1626 that the local people were "soft" (*weich*) in their religious beliefs and attended Catholic services as ordered.[81] They appear to have returned just as quickly to Protestant services. In other places, however, there was resistance, both passive and active, to Catholicization. After the Peace of Westphalia (1648) the Palatinate returned to the Elector Karl Ludwig, son of Frederick V. Karl Ludwig placed Calvinist clergy in the parishes but also tolerated religious minorities, including Catholics. The wartime Catholicization, the postwar immigration of Catholics to the devastated but fertile Palatinate, and religious toleration all contributed to the establishment of a small but significant Catholic minority in the Palatinate.[82]

Yet the Palatinate remained predominantly Protestant and did not tolerate public Catholic services. The confessional geography of the middle Rhine valley did not change significantly as a result of the Thirty Years' War. In the 1650s, the Catholics were once again the minority religion and the politically weaker confession.

Catholicization in the Villages: Oberöwisheim

The history of the village of Oberöwisheim between 1623 and the mid-1650s illustrates the process of Catholicization and the resistance faced by Catholic authorities within Protestant villages during the Thirty Years' War. Just as elsewhere in the Bishopric of Speyer, neither Catholic military and political domination nor the presence of Catholic priests achieved the conversion of the Protestant population of this village in the Kraichgau. During the war the villagers passively resisted authorities by refusing to attend Catholic services and secretly holding Protestant ones. As soon as the war ended, the villagers frustrated Catholic claims more actively, pressing lawsuits, withholding the tithe to force the support of a Protestant pastor, and appealing to Protestant powers for assistance.

80. Schaab, "Die Wiederherstellung des Katholizismus," pp. 153–54.
81. Stamer III/1, pp. 168–69.
82. Schaab, "Die Wiederherstellung des Katholizismus," pp. 154–55; Stamer III/1, p. 170.

Authority in Oberöwisheim was extremely fragmented. Secular power was shared by the Cathedral Chapter in Speyer and two free imperial knights, Herr von Helmstatt and Herr von Sternenfels. Each lord held approximately one-third of the villagers as serfs (*Leibeigene*). The three lords, or their representatives, held regular court sessions together. The Cathedral Chapter possessed the patronage of the village parish. The net effect of this division of power was to allow the villagers extraordinary influence in local government and to leave power over religious matters to the politically dominant confession.

Before the Thirty Years' War, both von Helmstatt and von Sternenfels, like most of the Kraichgau nobility, were Lutherans. Because of the power of the Palatinate and the residence of von Helmstatt in Oberöwisheim, the Cathedral Chapter appointed and paid a Protestant pastor. In fact, no Catholic services had been held in the village since the 1520s or 1530s, and the villagers were firmly Protestant. The war, however, changed the political situation and made it possible for the Cathedral Chapter to install a Catholic priest and attempt to Catholicize the village. The fragmentation of authority, while it made Catholicization possible, also restrained it. The ability of the chapter to enforce its policy depended on the cooperation of the other two lords of the village; for obvious reasons such cooperation was not often forthcoming.

The ebb and flow of the war also hindered Catholicization in Oberöwisheim. Catholic armies dominated the area around the village from 1621 to 1631 and again after 1636. But, between 1631 and 1636, the Swedish invasion allowed the Protestants to reestablish Lutheran services. During the 1640s, because of the decline in population, the reluctance of the villagers to pay the tithe, and the inability of the Cathedral Chapter to enforce its claims, no clergyman (of any religion) lived in Oberöwisheim. Consequently, most of the people attended Protestant services in neighboring villages.

Catholicization in Oberöwisheim, as elsewhere in the Bishopric of Speyer, failed because of the fragmentation of authority, the problems of war, and the resistance of the villagers. It also failed because of the limited program of the Cathedral Chapter. Like episcopal officials in the Palatinate, the canons viewed the Catholic domination as a chance to assert and strengthen their juridical rights in Oberöwisheim, especially that of patronage. These rights, of course, carried financial benefits. Only between 1628 and 1631, however, was there any attempt to encourage Catholic practice in Oberöwisheim. Otherwise, the canons were mainly intent on acquiring and maintaining "possession" of the parish. After a series of postwar conflicts, the Catholics did succeed in attaining this limited goal, but they were never able to change the religious practice of the villagers.

Methods of Protestant Resistance

The Catholicization of Oberöwisheim went through very clear stages. Between 1623 and 1628, the Cathedral Chapter, as patron of the parish, installed a Catholic priest and tried to maintain him against the hostility of the villagers. Beginning in 1628, the chapter tried to force Catholic practice on the villagers. After the Swedish invasion, the Cathedral Chapter returned to a limited policy of asserting its juridical rights in Oberöwisheim. Finally, after the Peace of Westphalia in 1648, the Catholics worked to keep these juridical rights and tried to prevent the return of Protestant pastors.

If the Catholic bid to convert the villagers of Oberöwisheim was implemented inconsistently, the local Protestants, for their part, resisted Catholicization with single-minded tenacity. Once again, the tradition of local autonomy and communal control of the village church provided the villagers with an effective defense against outside authorities. Furthermore, the villagers aptly played each lord off against the others, leaving the gemeinde as the only institution uniting the village. Protestant opposition to Catholicization was led by the gemeinde, by the two Protestant noblemen, von Helmstatt and von Sternenfels, and by the Protestant pastor. Although the Protestants had to keep a low profile during much of the war, at the end they still controlled village institutions and stood united to restore open, public Lutheran worship.

Catholicization began in 1623 when the Cathedral Chapter, asserting its right as patron of the parish, refused to appoint a new Lutheran pastor and ordered the priest from the bishop's village of Zeuthern to perform services in Oberöwisheim. This priest had a difficult time in Oberöwisheim, especially with Marquard von Helmstatt. Imperial law protected von Helmstatt's personal religious practice because he was a free imperial knight. As one of the lords of Oberöwisheim, he also had a certain immunity in his dealings with the Cathedral Chapter. In 1623, he prevented visiting Catholic priests from using the church, arguing that the Cathedral Chapter could not appoint Catholics to the parish. Apparently disregarding the presence of Catholic armies in the area, von Helmstatt gave the schoolteacher's benefice to a Protestant pastor and demanded that the Cathedral Chapter pay him. These efforts, however, failed to end Catholic services, and the Cathedral Chapter appointed a resident priest to maintain a presence in the village. Von Helmstatt, however, did make it possible for a Lutheran pastor openly to hold Protestant services until at least 1625.[83]

From 1623 to 1628, both Catholic and Protestant services took place in Oberöwisheim. In August 1623, the Catholic priest, Johan Beuerlin, reported that he was diligently doing his services, but that a Protestant preacher came regularly to preach, baptize children, and visit the sick. By November, von Helmstatt was no longer harassing Beuerlin, but the nobleman had appointed a Protestant pastor as resident schoolteacher.[84] The Cathedral Chapter accepted this division of the benefices in Oberöwisheim, albeit somewhat reluctantly, because it gave the chapter "possession" of the parish.

If the Catholics had possession of the parish, it was almost purely a legal position. In 1649, when an imperial commission was investigating conditions in Oberöwisheim during the war, the villagers reported that in January 1624 "the Catholic priest's sermons were heard by no person in the community, as a result he preached to no one except the walls, chairs, and benches . . . [there was] no Catholic practice . . . by the subjects of the village."[85] There is little evidence to contradict this report. In 1649, the Catholics argued that services did not require an audience to be considered *Exercitium* under the provisions of the peace treaty, implicitly conceding that there were few, if any, practicing Catholics in Oberöwisheim in 1624.[86]

It seems that the Cathedral Chapter hoped to encourage at least its own serfs to convert to Catholicism. To this end the canons tried to protect them from the depredations of the Bavarian troops in the area. The practical benefits of being Catholic may have led to some conversions. In 1625, the canons protested to von Helmstatt that the Lutheran pastor had insulted the Catholic religion in general and those in the village who went to Mass in particular. Von Helmstatt, recognizing the power of the Catholics, forced the pastor to apologize for calling the Mass "the devil's work."[87] By all indications, however, the vast majority of the villagers remained Protestant. Throughout the war they attended services in neighboring Protestant villages when necessary and regularly found a pastor to bless weddings, per-

83. GLAK 61/10957, pp. 34, 68–69, 85, 99–100, 102–4, 108, 287–88, 301, 111–12.
84. Ibid., pp. 141, 185, 190, 259.
85. GLAK 229/82623, 26 October 1649 ("Restitutions Sachen"): "Er [hat] Niemand anderst alss den wänden, Stühlen und bänckhen gepredigt."
86. GLAK 229/82623, 26 October 1649 ("Protokolle der Commission, Bönnigheim").
87. GLAK 61/10957, pp. 367, 441, 541, 543, 564–65, 596.

form burials, and baptize children. These methods allowed the villagers to avoid direct confrontation with the Catholics and prevented the suppression of Protestant practice.

In early 1628, the Catholics instituted a more aggressive policy. Interestingly, it was a newly appointed priest, Bartolomeus Vogt, who pushed for a more extensive Catholicization of Oberöwisheim. Vogt presented a detailed proposal to the Cathedral Chapter. His first goal was to get rid of the Protestant pastor. Vogt argued that the pastor's presence was illegal, since the noblemen had installed him after the religious peace of 1555. Although Vogt's chronology was inaccurate and his evidence shaky, he went on to argue (somewhat inarticulately) a more persuasive point.

> As my lords [the canons of the Cathedral Chapter] are the patrons . . . it would now be the best time, since the imperial soldiers are in the region and this is a good opportunity that otherwise might be lost, . . . and he would like, with great eagerness, to build up something good. [Having] studied and done other things unfortunately without result, he would like also to teach school and the catechism at no extra cost and stay a while, until slowly the numbers [of Catholics? or people?] grow.[88]

Vogt expressly argued that the political and military situation provided an opportunity that should not be neglected. His proposal for a more active policy in Oberöwisheim received the support of the canons, although with some hesitation. The canons warned Vogt above all to respect the rights of the two noblemen to hold Protestant services in their homes. When Vogt complained that the villagers did not show him proper respect, the canons responded: "The pfarrer's enthusiasm in religious matters is to be commended, but he should be reminded to behave somewhat more modestly with the people. Heretics are converted by good example, not by bloodshed."[89] The chapter suspected that Vogt's aggressive style was the cause of his disputes with the villagers.

Notwithstanding their hesitation, Catholic authorities barred the Protestant pastor from the church and ordered the villagers to attend Catholic services and stop going to neighboring villages to baptize their children.[90] In an attempt to enforce these regulations, the Cathedral Chapter refused to intercede on behalf of Oberöwisheim with the Bavarians. The canons would not prevent further quartering of

88. GLAK 61/10959, pp. 14r–14v.
89. Ibid., pp. 36r–36v.
90. Ibid., pp. 18r–18v, 22v–23v.

troops unless the villagers were "more reasonable" toward the Catholic religion. At least seven times between 1628 and 1631 the canons threatened to have troops sent to Oberöwisheim if the villagers did not put an end to their stubbornness in regard to religion. Using the carrot as well as the stick, the canons also promised to reduce taxes and levies if the villagers became Catholic.[91] These threats and promises had little effect on the villagers; they probably realized that the canons in Speyer had little influence with the Bavarians, who were likely to tax and force levies on the villagers no matter what religion they practiced.

The Swedish occupation ended this period of vigorous Catholicization. From 1632 to 1635 there was a resident Lutheran pastor in Oberöwisheim, and no Catholic services were held.[92] Beginning in 1636, the Catholics sent a neighboring priest to perform services "so that we stay in religious possession." But attendance was low, and the Cathedral Chapter complained that "few peasants come to church, only a few women."[93] No clergyman, Protestant or Catholic, lived in Oberöwisheim in the 1640s, making it easier for the villagers to attend services elsewhere. Most continued to go to Protestant villages, especially for baptisms. The disruption caused by the war in this period also made any consistent policy of Catholicization difficult. Many villagers died or fled Oberöwisheim, and those who stayed could not support a priest or pastor. The Cathedral Chapter was unable to find a priest for the village and the priests in neighboring areas refused to conduct services there without being paid.

Catholic policy during all but three years of the Thirty Years' War was limited to restoring and maintaining the Cathedral Chapter's patronage of the village parish. The canons most likely understood this policy as a way to increase the financial resources of the chapter, especially by collecting the priest's income when the parish was vacant. Yet they also appeared to believe that if Catholic services took place in Oberöwisheim, the villagers might eventually be converted to Catholicism. The Peace of Westphalia did not change this goal. In fact the peace treaty, by setting January 1, 1624, as the "normative date" for religious matters, legalized the presence of a Catholic priest in Oberöwisheim.[94]

91. Ibid., pp. 22v–23r, 28r, 64r–64v, 76r–76v, 91v, 216v–217r, 380r.
92. GLAK 229/82623, 26 October 1649 (Oberöwisheim).
93. GLAK 61/10961, p. 127r.
94. Parker et al., *The Thirty Years' War*, p. 182. The "normative date" of 1 January 1624 generally benefited the Protestants. In the Palatinate, where the Catholics had begun Catholicizing in the early 1620s, it helped the Catholics, although not in the Electoral Palatinate itself, where the son of Elector Frederick V was fully restored to power.

The imperial commission that investigated the religious situation in Oberöwisheim in October 1649 concluded:

> Because the Protestants were also there in 1624, they should stay . . . both the Protestants and the Catholics should have their services, and neither [religion] should hurt the other, but instead [they should] live peacefully together. Neither should publicly or privately attack the other in religious matters . . . and both should have their services in the church.[95]

The commission (made up of the bishop of Constance and the duke of Württemberg) ordered the creation of a biconfessional village. This plan caused new problems because after the war the Protestants wanted a full restoration of the *status quo ante*—a difficult matter since the religious peace protected the Catholic priest. Furthermore, the political balance within Oberöwisheim had changed: in 1641 a Catholic branch of the von Helmstatt family came into possession of the family's rights in Oberöwisheim.[96] The Protestants were not pleased with the decision of the imperial commission of 1649, but they accepted it and were determined to make the Cathedral Chapter obey it as well.

The most problematic part of the commission's decision related to the payment of the two clergymen. The commission required that the Cathedral Chapter, which held the tithe, pay both the Catholic priest and the Lutheran minister. Not surprisingly, the chapter was reluctant to comply, recognizing that splitting the tithe lowered the income so much that it might be impossible to fill the post. To prevent this eventuality, the chapter could have cut its own take from the tithe, but this solution did not appeal to the canons. Furthermore, the commission did not spell out how the tithe was to be collected and then disbursed. Under the pretext of this confusion, the Cathedral Chapter refused to support the Protestant pastor, and, in retaliation, the villagers refused to pay the tithe.

The village council organized the withholding of the tithe in 1649, 1650, 1651, and 1652. The goal was clear. In October 1650, for example, the villagers forcefully took the tithe wine from the Cathedral Chapter's keller and delivered it to the Lutheran pastor.[97] In August 1651 the villagers defied a second imperial commission, which or-

---

95. GLAK 229/82623 ("Protokolle der Commission"): "Keiner dem andern in Religions Sachen publice vel privatim nach reden."
96. GLAK 61/10963, p. 335v.
97. GLAK 61/10969, p. 435.

dered them to pay the tithe to the Cathedral Chapter, and delivered the grain directly to the pastor. Soon after, they closed the church to the Catholic priest.[98]

The villagers of Oberöwisheim continued to withhold the tithe despite the orders of an imperial commission, a mandate from the Reichskammergericht, and the periodic application of military force by the Cathedral Chapter. The most serious confrontation took place in July 1652, when a Cathedral canon and twenty musketeers arrived in Oberöwisheim to collect the tithe. A crowd of peasants gathered in front of the barn where the grain was stored. The canon, Herr von Frenz, was on horseback and tried to force a passage to the barn. A villager challenged the canon and von Frenz clubbed him over the head with his pistol, apparently killing him. The troops then took away the tithe and arrested two peasants.[99]

A second method of resistance was to appeal to neighboring Protestant powers. One villager said in 1649, "[The canons] will have soldiers take our property, now they deprive us of our salvation too. We should make sure that the Cathedral Chapter will have not only the entire nobility of the Kraichgau on its back, but also the military might of the Duke of Württemberg."[100] The support of these Protestant powers, especially Württemberg, was very important for the villagers and discouraged the Cathedral Chapter from severely punishing the organizers of the various "tithe strikes" in the 1650s.

By 1655, in fact, the disputes over the tithe had become routine. In July the Cathedral Chapter's agent in Oberöwisheim refused to pay the Protestant pastor, citing the religious peace. The peasants then took the tithe from him and gave it to the pastor. The chapter protested, commenting that there was little else it could do.[101] These disputes continued without resolution into the 1660s. In practice, however, conditions closely resembled what the imperial commission had ordered in 1649. Both religions had a resident clergyman in Oberöwisheim, the schoolteacher was a Protestant, both religions used the church, the whole community used the "old calendar" (as the Protestants did), and the Protestants held all the positions on the village council.[102]

Protestant resistance had succeeded. Even though two of the three lords of the village were Catholic after 1641, Protestant villagers

---

98. GLAK 61/10971, pp. 83–84, 166.
99. Ibid., pp. 274–75.
100. GLAK 61/10967, p. 866.
101. GLAK 61/10971, pp. 587–88.
102. GLAK 229/82623, 8–19 November 1649. (Oberöwisheim).

continued to control the village. In Oberöwisheim as elsewhere it was not possible to force Catholicism on a Protestant population without a massive application of force. Such a policy was never contemplated by churchmen in Speyer and was, in any case, beyond their powers.

The Murder of Peter Kranz, Priest of Oberöwisheim

On May 8, 1653, Christopher Saposius, the Lutheran pastor of Oberöwisheim, sent his maid, Anna, to a kitchen garden to gather some vegetables for supper. As she worked in the garden, Anna was confronted by the Cathedral Chapter's agent in the village, the keller, who told her the pastor had no right to use the garden. The keller struck Anna, knocking her down.[103]

This episode was part of a long dispute between the keller and the pastor. The keller claimed the garden belonged to the Cathedral Chapter, while the pastor argued it belonged to the parish. Upon hearing Anna's story, Saposius grabbed his newly purchased pistol and, ignoring his wife's pleas to seek help from the mayor and other members of the village council, rushed to the garden. There he confronted the keller: "You rogue (*Schelm*), why did you knock my maid down? I will shoot you!" The keller responded, "Go right ahead, I am standing on my lords' property."[104]

A brawl broke out, with the keller getting the upper hand. Onlookers attempted to break up the fight, telling the keller that he had done enough. Both combatants were on the ground when Peter Kranz, the Catholic priest, attempted to pry the two men apart. Suddenly the pastor's gun went off and Kranz fell to the ground dead. The keller, apparently unaware someone had been hit, continued to pound the pastor until someone cried, "O lord Jesus, stop it, the priest has been shot."[105]

All the witnesses to the event testified that the shooting had been an accident. The priest and the pastor had a civil, if distant, relationship. It was the Cathedral Chapter's keller and the pastor who had repeatedly battled over property and religious issues. Saposius, how-

---

103. The story of the murder of Kranz comes from two sources: GLAK 229/82734, pp. 8–11, which includes the evidence of five witnesses to the events of May 9; and GLAK 61/10971, pp. 373–80, which is the report received by the Cathedral Chapter.
104. GLAK 229/82734.
105. Ibid.: "O herr Jesu, Amptman hörst doch auff der Probst ist geschossen."

ever, did not wait to see if the courts would find Kranz's death accidental. The night after the shooting he and his family fled, leaving most of their property behind.

The shooting itself, which demonstrates the level of tensions within the village in the 1650s, is not as interesting as the aftermath. First of all, the corpse of the priest behaved strangely. Catherine Holtz, a widow, had helped to wash it. An excitable witness, she was unable to recall the events of the shooting due to "fear," but she discussed the behavior of the corpse in gory detail. First the body sweated through the bullet hole, then it started bleeding again the next day. Two days after the shooting the corpse started sweating from the mouth and nose to such an extent that Catherine Holtz could not clean it. Clearly there was something unusual, perhaps supernatural, about the body of the dead priest.

The Cathedral Chapter was determined to exploit the shooting to the fullest. The canons discussed the burial and decided "that a funeral sermon [should] be given, using the opportunity to admonish the subjects as to the effects of rebellion and disobedience."[106] The funeral itself was an attempt to demonstrate the special status of the priest. The funeral procession included three neighboring parish priests, two sacristans, a Dominican friar, and an Augustinian father from Speyer. All arrived in Oberöwisheim in full clerical regalia and followed the coffin into the church singing.

This was no ordinary funeral. Not only was there a large and impressive clerical presence, but all the villagers attended as well as many from neighboring villages. Representatives of all three lords were present. Herr Zacharias Meyer, the pfarrer in Odenheim, gave such a good sermon that everyone stayed to the end. Finally, six Protestant members of the village council served as pallbearers for the priest, a clear attempt to defuse confessional conflict.

If the funeral was in part an attempt to calm the tensions within Oberöwisheim, it succeeded. Reports from late 1653 indicate that the villagers had solved their religious disputes "among themselves."[107] But the Cathedral Chapter and the Catholics also had a second goal. The carefully organized attendance of Catholic clergy from neighboring villages and from Speyer served to remind the Oberöwisheimer Catholics that they were part of a wider community, not just a minority within their village. Of course the Church

---

106. GLAK 61/10971, p. 376.
107. GLAK 229/82734, p. 12v.

was also not averse to exploiting the propaganda victory afforded it by the murder of an innocent man. Finally, it did not hurt to demonstrate the power and beauty of Church services to the villagers.

The funeral of pfarrer Kranz is also indicative of the growing confidence of Catholics in the middle Rhine valley after the Thirty Years' War. This confidence was warranted in Oberöwisheim. Although the villagers who survived the war were almost all Protestants, many of the postwar immigrants to Oberöwisheim were Catholics. By 1652, sixteen Catholics had settled in the village.[108] In 1660 Herr von Helmstatt claimed there were one hundred Catholics in Oberöwisheim.[109] The Catholic community grew because two of the three lords of the village were now Catholic and did not allow the immigration of non-Catholics. As the seventeenth century progressed, the population of Oberöwisheim became increasingly Catholic.

Ultimately, then, the modest gains of the Catholics in Oberöwisheim during the Thirty Years' War were significant. By establishing Catholic services and maintaining a priest in the village, the Cathedral Chapter made the later formation of a Catholic community possible. Because one of the lords remained Protestant, however, and because Protestant practice was also protected, the village remained biconfessional. It is somewhat ironic that the effort to force Catholic unity in the village in fact created religious diversity.

The attempt to Catholicize Protestant areas was never the central thrust of the Counter-Reformation in the Bishopric of Speyer. Efforts before the war to convert the Ritterstift villages and the villages of Dahn were circumscribed. The Church establishment was unwilling to go beyond the initial steps of solidifying its juridical position and installing a Catholic priest in the villages.

The Catholic victories in the early years of the Thirty Years' War changed the political context but did little to change the policies of the local Church. Pressured by other Catholic powers and seeking new financial resources, Speyer officials participated in the attempt to Catholicize the Palatinate and recover the monasteries for the Church. Protestant resistance at the village level, wartime dislocation, and the resulting financial problems and shortage of priests all frustrated this effort.

The war, which crippled the bishopric's finances and destroyed the region economically, was more of a setback than a boost for the

108. GLAK 61/10971, p. 241.
109. GLAK 61/10973, p. 394.

Counter-Reformation. Indeed, it threatened to remove many of the gains of the years from 1580 to 1620—a more educated and celibate rural clergy, a reform-minded upper clergy, and better Church attendance in the villages. Rural communes were able to maintain and even increase their control of local churches, reversing the prewar period's tentative trend toward centralization.

Ultimately, the surprisingly rapid recovery of the region after the war restored the economic health of the bishopric. Economic recovery, the restoration of the Palatinate to Protestant control, and the election in 1652 of a reformer, Lothar Friederich von Metternich, as bishop, all contributed to a return to prewar conditions. The Counter-Reformation in the Bishopric of Speyer was characterized by considerable temporizing and hesitancy to use force, despite the opportunities the war offered, at the outset at least, to replicate the successes of the Bavarian and Austrian Catholics elsewhere in the Empire. However lacking in apparent coherence, was this not a policy of the art of the possible?

6

The Tridentine Clergy and the Communal Church, 1650–1720

The period after 1650 was decisive both for the Counter-Reformation and for the development of distinct confessional cultures in Germany. As we have seen, the Thirty Years' War was more of a watershed in imperial politics than in local and regional religious conditions. Efforts to reform the Catholic Church continued after the Peace of Westphalia in the Bishopric of Speyer, as they did in the rest of Catholic Europe. Recent research, in fact, has emphasized that reformed Catholicism did not take hold in the countryside until the late seventeenth and eighteenth centuries.[1] To what extent did Tridentine Catholicism penetrate to the villages around Speyer?

Religious reform in this part of Germany was a dynamic and complex process, and few of the basic dichotomies often used to explain the religious sociology of early modern Europe are helpful when applied to these local conditions. Historians of the Reformation era, for example, focus on the conflict between elite and popular culture.[2] Some Counter-Reformation scholars view Tridentine reforms as part of the long-standing conflict between the laity and the clergy for control of the Church;[3] yet recent syntheses propose that a clerical

1. Châtellier, *Europe of the Devout* and *Tradition chrétienne et renouveau catholique*; Bücking, *Frühabsolutismus und Kirchenreform in Tirol*; Ortner, *Reformation, katholische Reform, und Gegenreformation im Erzstift Salzburg*.
2. Strauss, *Luther's House of Learning*; Burke, *Popular Culture in Early Modern Europe*; Robert W. Scribner, "Ritual and Popular Religion in Catholic Germany at the Time of the Reformation," *Journal of Ecclesiastical History* 35 (1984):47–77.
3. Bücking, *Frühabsolutismus und Kirchenreform in Tirol*.

and lay elite worked together to impose reformed religion on traditionalist populations.[4] While each of these themes played a role in the Counter-Reformation in Speyer, a more complete social analysis is necessary.

It is useful to consider the three groups that determined the nature of Catholic practice and belief in the Bishopric of Speyer. First, there was the Church hierarchy, including the bishops, top episcopal officials such as the vicar general, the ecclesiastics of the Cathedral Chapter, and the canons of the smaller chapters. They made policy at the highest level in the bishopric. The second group, the parish clergy, had the responsibility of providing services for the Catholics in the countryside. Finally, there were the Catholic people of the bishopric, especially those village notables who had power and influence in communal institutions.[5]

For each of these three groups, the reforms of Trent meant something different, and in the decades after the Thirty Years' War their various attitudes changed. A reform party still existed within the upper clergy, but it was now weaker than it had been in the late sixteenth century. Furthermore, the reformers no longer dominated the Cathedral Chapter but worked instead in the episcopal administration. Meanwhile, the Cathedral Chapter and the smaller chapters became increasingly conservative and indifferent to religious issues in the late seventeenth century.

As the upper clergy became more conservative, the parish priests became the leaders of the Counter-Reformation. Educated and ambitious young priests, eager to serve the faithful, came to Speyer in ever larger numbers, especially in the years after 1700. Their presence changed the relationship between the rural priests and their parishioners. The new priests still had to deal with the same strong village communes that their sixteenth-century predecessors had found so obstinate. Church and governmental institutions in the bishopric remained weak, and frequent wars with their resulting economic dislocation prevented any centralization of state power. In this context, village communes maintained their control of local parishes. This situation in turn limited the influence of the "new" priests and continued to prevent the imposition of many Tridentine reforms, especially those that involved disciplining lay behavior.

Yet the villagers and the parish priests also agreed on the need for

---

4. Bossy, *Christianity in the West, 1400–1700*; Delumeau, *Catholicism between Luther and Voltaire*; Hsia, *Social Discipline in the Reformation*.

5. On social differences within communes, see Rebel, *Peasant Classes*; and Robisheaux, *Rural Society and the Search for Order*.

regular religious services and an active clergy. This desire sometimes led to clashes with the inactive and traditionalist chapter clergy, whom the villagers and rural priests alike considered parasitic. Ultimately however, the parish priests were the only group that favored major religious reform. The strength of both the aristocratic Church and the village communes meant that even in the presence of reform-minded parish priests, Catholicism in the Bishopric of Speyer remained highly traditional.

Political conditions were also changing in the middle Rhine region in the second half of the seventeenth century. Conflicts between the Palatinate (*Kurpfalz*) and Speyer continued after 1650 but lost much of their religious content. Even this pressure on the Hochstift eased after the Catholic dynasty of Pfalz-Neuburg took over the *Kurpfalz* at the end of the century. If political restraints on the Counter-Reformation weakened, several major wars, especially the devastating French invasion of 1688–89, caused economic disruption in the region and hindered the progress of Church reform.

The main focus of this chapter is on the reform of the clergy and the relationship between the rural priests and their parishioners. When the priests attempted to reform traditional practices or change lay behavior, they had trouble with the villagers. The priests also clashed with the traditionalist chapter clergy, which retained considerable power in the bishopric. The canons, along with the powerful village communes, had little interest in Tridentine reform after 1650. The chapter clergy and the village communes remained the mainstays of the traditional Catholicism that continued to dominate the Bishopric of Speyer despite a reformed rural clergy.

The New Political and Religious Setting

The political situation in the middle Rhine valley in the late seventeenth and early eighteenth centuries differed from the situation before the Thirty Years' War. Between 1560 and 1620, the region had been prosperous and peaceful, enabling the Church to expand its organization, for example by bringing the Jesuits to Speyer. After 1650, by contrast, constant wars, some of them very destructive, hampered the reform of the Church. In the late sixteenth century, although the peace held, the Catholics in the region had lived in constant fear of attack by the Protestant Palatinate. After the Peace of Westphalia, relations between Speyer and the Palatinate improved, giving Catholics some security, but also reducing the sense of urgency for reform. Finally, for most of the period the Bishopric of Speyer did not have a resident bishop and was only an adjunct of the larger and more important archbishoprics of Trier and Mainz. This factor also hindered any consistent implementation of reform.

The rising power of France was felt nowhere more keenly than in the Rhine valley. The French presence protected Catholics in the area, at least as long as peace lasted. There was, however, little peace. French ambition caused three long wars between 1674 and 1712. The French attack on Holland in 1672 led to a European-wide war. Because of the French control of the fortress of Philippsburg, the Bishopric of Speyer was a major battleground between 1673 and the Peace of Nijmegen in 1679. In 1676 French troops burned the episcopal town of Bruchsal to the ground, leaving only thirty-six of over five hundred houses intact. The villages around Philippsburg also suffered extensively during the imperial siege of the fortress (April–September 1676).[6]

The impact of this war was limited compared to the destruction caused by the French invasion of 1688–89. During this so-called "Palatinate War," the French burned the cities of Speyer, Worms, Mannheim, and Heidelberg and much of the countryside. Louis XIV ostensibly fought this war in order to make his brother elector of the Palatinate (a claim based on his brother's marriage to the daughter of Elector Karl Ludwig), but in fact French policy was to create a demilitarized buffer zone between France and the Empire. French armies destroyed all fortifications, including the militarily obsolete walls of cities and towns, and then burned the most important cities.[7]

The effect of this invasion on the region was probably greater than that of the Thirty Years' War, especially in the Rhine valley between Speyer, Worms, and Heidelberg. The city of Speyer itself lay vacant for ten years, and the Cathedral Chapter and episcopal administration resided in five different cities before returning to Speyer in 1699.[8] Much of the rural population fled during the destruction, only to return to burned fields and crops. Naturally the clergy suffered as well. The destruction was extensive; the great cathedral in Speyer was badly damaged, as were many rural churches and parsonages.

In the late 1690s, as a result of the invasion, the Speyer Church faced the same problems it had dealt with during and after the Thirty

---

6. Remling II, pp. 559–62.
7. Kurt von Raumer, *Die Zerstörung der Pfalz von 1689, im Zusammenhang der französischen Rheinpolitik* (1930; reprint, Bad Neustadt a.d. Saale: Verlag Dietrich Pfaeler, 1982), esp. chap. 4.
8. Press, "Das Hochstift Speyer," p. 274.

Years' War. Many parish priests had fled during the French invasion and, because of low incomes, never returned, for in November 1689 the Cathedral Chapter was forced to halve the incomes of all the rural clergy.[9] The result was an acute shortage of priests. In 1692 only two priests served in the rural chapter of Deidesheim, and six years later the priest in Deidesheim complained that he was forced to administer three parishes.[10]

The region recovered from the French invasion in the first two decades of the eighteenth century, despite the campaigns of the War of Spanish Succession (1701–15). The economic and demographic recovery of the bishopric allowed the full restoration of the clerical establishment. The cathedral was slowly repaired and new parish priests hired. The invasion and destruction of 1688–89, in fact, marked an important turning point for the Counter-Reformation in the Bishopric of Speyer. The almost complete turnover of the rural Catholic clergy brought a new generation of educated, "reformed" priests into the villages. This group served with remarkable longevity in many parishes between the 1690s and 1720. Perhaps for the first time, the Church in this area enjoyed a steady and loyal parish clergy.

The policies of Protestant princes had always influenced the progress of Catholic reform. After 1650 confessional relations, especially between the Hochstift Speyer and the Electoral Palatinate, became much calmer. Confessional peace stabilized religious boundaries and allowed the solidification of religious cultures. Catholics, however, remained the minority. Elector Karl Ludwig restored Calvinism as the official religion of the Palatinate, but unlike his father he was a religious pragmatist. Karl Ludwig gave tax incentives and promised religious toleration to immigrants in an effort to restore his devastated principality.[11] A practical man, the Calvinist elector even required his daughter, Elisabeth Charlotte, to marry the Catholic brother of Louis XIV, hoping (in vain) to protect the Palatinate from French aggression. At the local level, Karl Ludwig sought financial concessions from the Bishopric of Speyer but rarely interfered in religious affairs in Catholic areas.

Between 1685 and 1705, the political and religious balance in the region changed dramatically. In 1685, the Catholic dynasty of Pfalz-Neuburg took over the Electoral Palatinate. Especially after 1697, this dynasty officially encouraged Catholic practice in the villages of

9. GLAK 61/10979, p. 70v.
10. Ibid., p. 337r; Stamer III/2, p. 52.
11. Häusser, *Geschichte der rheinischen Pfalz*, vol. 2, pp. 586–87.

the Palatinate. Although never pursued with great vigor, this policy was partially successful. The political influence of Protestant powers, above all Brandenburg, prevented a thorough recatholicization and brought about a unique religious agreement in the Palatinate.[12]

The *Kurpfälzische Religionsdeklaration* of 1705 granted freedom of worship to the three Christian confessions in the Electoral Palatinate and gave two-sevenths of the village churches to the Catholics, five-sevenths to the Calvinists. In cities and towns, Protestants and Catholics were each given a church. In towns where there was only one church, the confessions were required to divide the building, the Catholics taking the choir, the Protestants the nave. This agreement recognized the gains made by the Catholics in the years after 1685, but it also acknowledged the strength of Protestantism and the inability of the Catholic electors to enforce the principle of *cuius regio* after 1648.

These changes in the confessional politics of the Palatinate had a important impact on the Bishopric of Speyer. Tensions between the electors and the bishops declined considerably even before the accession of the Catholic dynasty in 1685. At the regional level princes and their officials undoubtedly had learned the lesson of the Thirty Years' War and downplayed the religious element in political relations. For Church reformers, the decline in confessional tensions allowed a freedom from Palatine interference that their predecessors in the period from 1580 to 1620 had not enjoyed.

The presence of the French in the southwestern part of the bishopric also contributed to the new confessional balance. Between 1682 and 1697, the French controlled the Palatine district (*Amt*) of Germersheim and aggressively Catholicized the area. Especially in the 1680s, they removed Protestant pastors and schoolteachers, encouraged conversions, forbade interfaith marriages, and ordered severe punishments for relapsed converts to Catholicism. The Capuchins, Augustinians, and Jesuits participated actively in this process, while the episcopal authorities in Speyer played only a small role. By 1700, this policy had helped build Catholic minorities in many villages of the area under French influence.[13]

The changed confessional balance in the Bishopric of Speyer ap-

12. Stamer III/2, pp. 21–25; Schaab, "Die Wiederherstellung des Katholizismus," pp. 150–51.

13. Stamer III/2, pp. 12–21; Press, "Das Hochstift Speyer," pp. 273–74; P. Archange Sieffert, "Die Kapuziner zu Weißenburg (1684–1791) und die katholische Restauration beiderseits der Lauter. IV. Die Kapuziner-Missionspfarreien in der Südpfalz (1684–1800)," *Archives de l'Eglise d'Alsace*, n.s. 5 (1953–54), 135–78.

pears to have given Catholic authorities more self-confidence. Certainly the sense of crisis that pervaded the minutes of the Cathedral Chapter and the Bishop's Council in the sixteenth century was no longer present in the late seventeenth century. The more secure position of the Hochstift, and of Catholicism in general, might have led to a renewal of the reform impulse. Instead it led to a certain complacency in the Church hierarchy and to what Volker Press has called "a strengthened aristocratic tendency."[14] One reason for this complacency was a lack of strong leadership from the bishops. An active, resident bishop governed Speyer only between 1652 and 1673. Through most of the period from 1650 to 1720, the bishopric was an adjunct of the neighboring archbishoprics of Trier and Mainz. The lack of forceful leadership hindered the progress of internal Church reform and tended to leave the Cathedral Chapter and the smaller chapters considerable influence.

The episcopate of Lothar Friedrich von Metternich, a member of the family that had long opposed Bishop Philipp Christoph Sötern, was an exception to this pattern. Metternich's election demonstrated the desire of the Cathedral Chapter for a resident and energetic bishop. Metternich also had close ties to the archbishop of Mainz, Johan Philipp von Schönborn, a leader of the postwar Catholic Church in Germany.[15] An active, hands-on reformer, Metternich reorganized the episcopal administration and ordered visitations of the chapters.[16]

Metternich became archbishop of Mainz in 1673, and his successor, Johann Hugo von Orsbeck (bishop, 1675–1711) was simultaneously archbishop of Trier. Orsbeck made only one short visit to Speyer during his thirty-six-year episcopate.[17] The day-to-day administration of the bishopric fell to Heinrich Hartard von Rollingen, who served as administrator and vicar general from 1676 to 1711 and as bishop in his own right from 1711 to 1719. Rollingen was a hardworking and reform-minded administrator, but without full episcopal authority he could neither break the power of the traditionalist chapters nor institute any kind of territorial centralization.

In general, then, the improved political and religious situation of the Catholic Church in the middle Rhine valley did little to foster a forceful Counter-Reformation. Perhaps most important, the destruction of the wars, the lack of a resident bishop, and the influence of

14. Press, "Das Hochstift Speyer," p. 274.
15. Remling II, p. 547.
16. Remling II, pp. 233–39.
17. Press, "Das Hochstift Speyer," p. 273.

traditionalist aristocratic clergymen meant that local Counter-Reformers could not make Church reform part of a process of territorial consolidation. However, two important goals of the Counter-Reformation, the installation of a "reformed" clergy and the development of a Catholic consciousness in the population, occurred without the cooperation of a strong secular power.

The Establishment of a Tridentine Rural Clergy

Curiously, the history of the Catholic clergy in Germany after 1650 has received little attention. The traditional distinction between the Counter-Reformation, which is seen to end with the Peace of Westphalia, and "baroque Catholicism" has caused historians to overlook the continuing reform of the clergy. Studies of baroque Catholicism focus on the laity, for this was the period of the revival of popular piety, the founding of confraternities and congregations, and the explosion of pilgrimage piety.[18] The Jesuits, Capuchins, and other reformed orders led this movement, not the secular clergy. Yet there is no question that for the mass of the Catholic population, the most notable development of the period after 1650 was the education and improvement of the rural clergy.

A dramatic change occurred in the educational level and professional performance of the rural clergy of the Bishopric of Speyer. Many of the priests were now trained in seminaries in Mainz or Fulda and came to the bishopric from all over Catholic Germany. These men had a personal and professional commitment to Tridentine Catholicism and an understanding of the reform within the Church. The "new" priests had the self-confidence of a professional class.

This self-assurance often caused the priests to view the chapter clergy with a certain disdain. In the later seventeenth century, the cathedral chapters in Germany and even the smaller chapters in Speyer became increasingly aristocratic and exclusive. The canons lost interest in Church reform and, like many members of their class, focused on political and administrative activities.[19] By the eighteenth century, the parish priests and bishops, not the chapter clergy, would dominate the Church in Speyer.

18. Hsia, *Social Discipline in the Reformation*, pp. 90–104; Albrecht, "Gegenreformation und katholische Reform" and "Die Barockzeit" in Spindler, ed., *Handbuch der bayerischen Geschichte* II, esp. pp. 733–34.
19. Press, "Das Hochstift Speyer," p. 274.

Yet the reformed priests, whose hallmark was dedication to personal piety and to discipline of the laity, as well as to the new forms of Tridentine religiosity, had a limited impact on the people of the bishopric. Economic problems prevented the establishment of a complete parish network, leaving some villages without a permanent priest. Furthermore, the traditionalist upper clergy maintained their influence in the upper levels of both the spiritual and the secular administration of the Bishopric of Speyer. The priests did not receive the kind of consistent support from secular and episcopal officials that was needed to impose strong discipline on the laity. Finally, village communes continued to shape local religious life, both by resisting unwanted changes and by supporting what they considered positive developments. The parish priests had to adapt themselves to this situation.

Rebuilding the Church (1650–89)

Between 1650 and the French invasion of the late 1680s, the Catholic Church in Speyer focused its efforts on recovering from the Thirty Years' War. Although the material damage of the war was repaired fairly quickly, it took longer to restore the Church administration and, above all, to find enough qualified priests to serve the rural parishes. The relative poverty of the bishopric caused it to suffer a shortage of priests throughout the second half of the seventeenth century. Incomes were low in the rural parishes, and episcopal authorities lacked the resources to train new priests. Economic stagnation made it impossible for either the bishops or the Cathedral Chapter to found a seminary or even restore the Alumnat to its prewar function.[20] But after 1700 the economic situation eased enough for the Cathedral Chapter to give stipends to five students to study at the pontifical seminary in Fulda. The first episcopal seminary in the Bishopric of Speyer was founded in Bruchsal in 1729.[21]

The Cathedral Chapter attempted periodically to reestablish the Alumnat. In the 1650s the dean lamented the lack of income that made it impossible to support even two students.[22] The canons were

20. While Germany, unlike France, did not suffer demographic and economic decline in the period from 1650 to 1740, growth was slow, especially after the initial postwar recovery period. In the middle Rhine region, the cities of Speyer and Worms, which were already in decline in the late sixteenth centuries, became economic backwaters in the seventeenth and eighteenth centuries. See Rudolf Vierhaus, *Staaten und Stände. Vom westfälischen bis zum Hubertusburger Frieden, 1648 bis 1763* (Berlin: Propyläen Verlag, 1984), 63–75.
    21. Ammerich, "Formen und Wege der katholischen Reform," pp. 302–5; Stamer III/2, p. 53.
    22. GLAK 61/10973, pp. 427, 472, 535, 559, 608.

aware of the need for a training institution: "The dean reminded the lords [the canons] of the great lack of parish priests in the countryside and, when a parish is vacated due to death, one is forced to take just about anyone. [This situation] makes it necessary to [re]establish the seminary [i.e., the Alumnat]."[23] In 1668, the canons commented that they had "often discussed" the restoration of the Alumnat, but "up to now nothing concrete had come of it."[24] In 1672, the Cathedral Chapter gave the former residence of the alumni to the Jesuits, conceding that it was not possible to reestablish a school for parish priests in Speyer.[25]

The lack of a seminary in Speyer forced the Church to appoint priests trained elsewhere, and these priests were not necessarily the best available. One popular saying was that "all the good-for-nothings (*Taugenichtse*) from other dioceses come to the Bishopric of Speyer."[26] Episcopal authorities had great difficulty checking the qualifications of these "foreign" priests. Johan Caspar Mülheim, for example, arrived in the vacant parish of Riedseltz in August 1680 and, without presenting any evidence of his previous employment, was invested as parish priest. Within two months, Mülheim's neglect of his duties and his overall behavior (he drank, swore, stole Church funds, and had a concubine), led the villagers to demand his removal. It turned out that Mülheim had been banished in 1679 from the Bishopric of Strasbourg for immoral behavior.[27]

Many priests had to serve more than one parish. In the 1680s, at least seventeen priests (of about sixty) served two or more parishes.[28] In some cases the parishes had been combined for centuries, but most of these mergers had first taken place during the Thirty Years' War. By the 1680s this situation had become permanent in many places, especially in a whole group of villages around Bruchsal.[29]

There was a rapid turnover of priests, especially in the 1650s and 1660s. Between 1652 and 1655, five different priests served in Hainfeld.[30] Poor incomes meant that the resident priests were always on the lookout for better parishes. Rural priests often complained of poverty, and the patrons had trouble finding priests for the poorest

23. GLAK 61/10973, p. 324.
24. GLAK 61/10974a, p. 75 1r.
25. GLAK 61/10975, pp. 106v–107r.
26. Stamer III/2, p. 52.
27. ADBR 19 J 396, nos. 1–14; Louis Kammerer, *Repertoire du clergé d'Alsace sous l'ancien régime, 1648–1792*, vol. 1 (Typescript, Strasbourg, 1985), 227.
28. See especially the visitation of 1683.
29. The episcopal authorities also continued to employ monks as parish priests, especially in the villages around Speyer itself.
30. GLAK 61/10971, pp. 314, 355, 391, 397, 527, 596.

parishes.[31] Contrary to one of the goals of Trent, many priests had to support themselves by farming. In 1668, the Cathedral Chapter reprimanded the pfarrer in Deidesheim for being overly involved in the wine trade.[32] In 1682, the priest in Landshausen said that he was poor and reported that most of his income was from the land he farmed himself.[33]

Many wartime expediencies, such as priests serving multiple parishes, the expectation that priests should support themselves by farming, and the employment of poor quality "foreign" priests and monks, remained features of the rural Church into the late seventeenth century. All these measures had the effect of reducing the influence of the rural clergy in the countryside. Even the most dedicated priests could do little to inspire their parishioners when they had to serve multiple parishes and were tied down by farming duties. Of course poorly trained transient priests and nonresident monks had even less impact on the religious life of the laity.

In the 1670s the shortage of priests became somewhat less acute. As early as 1666 the Cathedral Chapter even informed the rector of the seminary in Fulda that there were no vacancies in the chapter's patronage parishes.[34] Another sign of improvement is that episcopal officials appointed priests to the chaplaincies in Deidesheim, Hambach, and Jöhlingen. Just as before the war, the young priests who held these positions assisted the parish priests and received training for parishes of their own.[35] By 1680, the Cathedral Chapter was also able to avoid the haphazard hiring practices of the 1650s. The canons appointed and promoted priests in a more organized way, rewarding hard-working and popular priests with better-endowed parishes. In 1680, for example, the canons removed a priest from the wealthy parish of Hambach for disciplinary reasons and transferred three different priests. The priest in Edesheim moved to Hambach, the priest from the small parish of Bauerbach went to Edesheim, and the chaplain in Deidesheim took over Bauerbach.[36] A clear and logical pattern of appointment and promotion was important for the morale of the priests and for the stability of the rural clergy. The expectation of promotion out of the poorer parishes kept priests from leaving the bishopric and gave them an incentive to do a good job.

31. Ibid., pp. 427, 490, 592; GLAK 61/10974a, p. 458.
32. GLAK 61/10974a, p. 718r.
33. GLAK 61/5344, pp. 871–87v.
34. GLAK 61/10974a, p. 445.
35. GLAK 61/10975, pp. 9v, 14r, 153r, 241r, 386r.
36. GLAK 61/10977, p. 24v.

As the number of available priests grew, the Church was able to enforce stricter discipline among both the rural and the chapter clergy. Episcopal visitations served this purpose best. Although neither Bishop Metternich nor his successors ever instituted regular visitations of the diocese, at least two and perhaps three partial visitations took place between 1650 and 1689.[37] Two complete visitations took place in the early eighteenth century, one in 1701–2 and the second between 1718 and 1721.[38] Yet none of these was as probing of the clergy and the laity as the survey of 1583–88 and none of them led to the sort of outburst of disciplinary activity that had occurred in the 1580s and 1590s. The visitation of 1683, conducted by the Jesuits, was more of a rural mission than an inspection of the clergy, and the two surveys of 1701–2 and 1718–21 have left only rather laconic documentation consisting of catalogues of names, qualifications, and incomes of parish priests.

Even in the immediate aftermath of the Thirty Years' War, when episcopal officials hesitated to enforce tight discipline, they quickly removed priests found guilty of concubinage or adultery. In 1660 the pfarrer in Rödersheim was imprisoned for the latter offense.[39] In 1668 the priest in Rülzheim fled to the Palatinate after the bishop's officials found him guilty of concubinage and infanticide. He had killed his maid's baby and buried it in his cellar.[40] There are four or five cases of clerical concubinage in the documents for the period from 1650 to 1680, certainly a small number compared to the sixteenth century.

Beginning in the mid-1660s, the bishop and his vicar general began to enforce other regulations more strictly. In 1665 the pfarrer in Deidesheim was fined for neglect of his duties. He had stayed in Speyer on Easter evening and had been unavailable to perform a baptism in Deidesheim.[41] The patrons of the parishes also began to inspect the papers (especially the *dimissoriales*, which were evidence of honorable dismissal from the previous post) of new priests. In 1676 the vicar general discharged the priest in Bauerbach because of vague rumors that he associated frequently with neighboring Prot-

---

37. GLAK 229/34853, 1667; GLAK 78/711, 1675; GLAK 61/11263, 61/11264, 61/11265, 1683.

38. GLAK 61/11266, 61/11267, 1701–2; GLAK 61/11269, 61/11270, 61/11271, 61/11272, 61/11273; LASp. D2/306/6, 1718–20.

39. GLAK 61/10973, p. 454.

40. GLAK 61/11507b, pp. 183–84, 192, 204. According to the bishop's council, the maid was let off easy. She was convicted of homicide, pardoned, whipped "three times," and banished from the bishopric.

41. GLAK 10974a, p. 385.

estant pastors.[42] By the 1680s, in fact, the number of disciplinary cases declined, indicating that the priests generally behaved well.

In the four decades after the Thirty Years' War, the rural clergy of the Bishopric of Speyer gradually improved in quality, quantity, and discipline. Furthermore, by the time of the French invasion in 1689 the administration and financial condition of the Church had improved. This difficult recovery period meant, however, that the Church did little to discipline the laity or change popular religious practice. The shortage of quality priests continued to restrict the ability of the Church to control, or even greatly influence, the religious beliefs and practices of the Catholic population.[43]

Limits to Episcopal Authority

The upper clergy functioned as a brake on reform after 1650. Even the canons of the Cathedral Chapter had little interest in continuing Tridentine reform measures. The sense of crisis that had created a strong reform party between 1560 and 1610 was no longer present after the Thirty Years' War. The Peace of Westphalia clearly guaranteed the survival of the ecclesiastical states and stabilized the confessional situation in Germany. The fear of mediatization by the Palatinate and the loss of Church benefices no longer threatened the nobles who sat in the chapters. The religious indifference that had marked the later stages of the war remained important as well. Few canons demonstrated an interest in the pastoral or religious aspects of their position, few were ordained as priests, and many were absent from Speyer for long periods, often because they held more lucrative positions in other chapters.[44]

When it came to Church administration, however, the canons of the Cathedral Chapter in Speyer were neither inactive nor disinterested. The voluminous minutes of the chapter show that they continued to deal with a wide variety of issues, often handling minute problems at the village level. This sort of involvement also made the canons meticulous and determined defenders of the chapter's privileges and autonomy. In conflicts with bishops, the chapter often succeeded in maintaining its rights by passively resisting the more ambitious bishops and expanding its power under absentee or weak

---

42. GLAK 61/10975, p. 260v.

43. Châtellier's conclusions about Strasbourg in 1680 are similar (*Tradition chrétienne et renouveau catholique* p. 182).

44. See especially Hersche, *Die deutschen Domkapitel im 17. und 18. Jahrhundert.*

bishops. This strategy worked, for example, between 1650 and 1720, when there was a resident bishop for only thirty years.

Despite this trend within the hierarchy, Bishop Metternich, more than any other bishop of Speyer in the Counter-Reformation era, tried to widen episcopal authority and weaken the power of the chapters. Elected bishop in 1652 at age thirty-five, he had been educated in Lorraine and had close personal and family ties in Mainz and Trier. He no doubt hoped to restructure the Bishopric of Speyer according to the models of its more centralized northern and French neighbors. Being young and energetic, he succeeded in some areas, but he found that the Cathedral Chapter and the smaller chapters had great powers of resistance. Just as they had done in the sixteenth century, the canons resisted intrusions into their traditional jurisdictions and defied the bishop's attempts to interfere in the internal discipline of the chapters.

Metternich maintained good relations with the Cathedral Chapter. After all, he and his family had been prominent members of the chapter for decades. The canons in turn appreciated his efforts to rebuild the bishopric.[45] In 1657, however, Metternich violated the traditional immunity of the chapter and personally inspected the cathedral, questioning each canon on his duties. Just the threat of this "visitation," which had been mandated by the pope, prompted the chapter to improve internal discipline before the bishop's arrival.[46] By anticipating the changes the bishop might order, the chapter kept control of its internal discipline.[47]

If the Cathedral Chapter continued to resist episcopal centralization, at least it maintained a high level of internal discipline and a competent administration of its affairs. The same cannot be said of the three smaller chapters in Speyer or the chapters in Weißenburg and Bruchsal. The lack of clerical discipline and general disregard for pastoral duties in these chapters indicate a failure of the Counter-Reformation to change these traditional institutions. As patrons of many rural parishes, the chapters were highly visible throughout the bishopric. For most Catholics, the traditionalist chapters and not, for example, the Jesuits, still exemplified the institutional Church.

45. Remling II, p. 543.
46. Ibid., pp. 536–37.
47. There were also conflicts between the bishop and the Cathedral Chapter over jurisdiction in the villages. See GLAK 61/10973, pp. 61, 110, 265; GLAK 61/11505, pp. 3831–384v (Rights of the Provost); GLAK 61/10973, pp. 829–30 (patronage parishes); GLAK 61/10974a, p. 276 (vicar general removed the pfarrer in Niederlauterbach in 1664 without the involvement of the chapter).

A letter from the city council in Weißenburg to the bishop protest-ing the conditions in the chapter illustrates the situation in all the smaller chapters.[48] The chapter in Weißenburg was required to pro-vide a priest for the Catholic parish in the predominantly Lutheran town. The magistrates reported that among the twelve canons and three vicars, none was capable of serving the parish and certainly not of preaching. The canons, they pointed out, took the income of the parish but failed to check if their parishioners took Easter commu-nion, did not teach catechism class or observe the feast days, ne-glected services, and never visited the sick and dying. The Rat pro-posed that one or more of the chapter's benefices be awarded to a "competent, exemplary, and educated person" rather than to a use-less canon. Catholics in Weißenburg, including prominent French officials, considered the chapter worthless for pastoral purposes, a parasitic institution, and damaging to the reputation of the Church in a Protestant area.

Serious problems also arose in the chapters in Speyer, especially in the poorest of the three, the Allerheiligen *Stift*. During the 1650s, Allerheiligen was racked by internal dissension and suffered a se-rious decline in discipline. The behavior of the dean, Heinrich vom Berg, appears to have caused many of the problems. Vom Berg refused to allow two newly elected canons into the chapter. The rest of the canons responded by deposing the dean and selling his horse, divid-ing the proceeds among themselves. The two sides in this dispute traded accusations of moral turpitude and appealed to the Cathedral Chapter and to the bishop. Although the cathedral canons helped work out a reconciliation, they also commented that vom Berg had a deserved reputation in Speyer as a troublemaker.[49] Several years later, vom Berg, by then an elderly man, was arrested and thrown in prison for further misconduct.[50] In 1653 an episcopal visitation conducted by the dean, a sexprebendary of the Cathedral Chapter, and a Ca-puchin father found a lack of discipline and "corrupt morals (*mores depravati*)" at Allerheiligen. The bishop ordered a major reform, but unfortunately the records give no information on the impact of these measures.[51] The canons clearly had little interest in reform and

48. P. Archange Sieffert, "Die katholische Pfarrei St. Johann zu Weißenburg im achtzehn-ten Jahrhundert," *Archiv für elsässische Kirchengeschichte* 4 (1929): 177–78. This "schrift-liche Beschwerde" was sent 9 October 1700.

49. GLAK 61/10969, p. 563; GLAK 61/10971, pp. 58–59, 63–64.

50. Remling II, pp. 535–36.

51. GLAK 78/1552.

surely did not "set a good example" for either the parish clergy or the Catholic laity.

Bishop Metternich, like many of his predecessors, had great trouble bringing the Ritterstift in Bruchsal under episcopal control. During the 1650s, Metternich clashed repeatedly with the aristocratic chapter. These conflicts centered on two issues: the right of the bishop to conduct a visitation of the chapter, and the authority of the bishop over the rural parishes under the chapter's patronage. The parish priests in the chapter's villages exploited these disputes to avoid the control of the vicar general, sometimes refusing summons to the bishop's court or even resisting dismissal. Only in the 1690s did the Ritterstift reluctantly accept episcopal jurisdiction over the parishes.[52]

The canons of the Ritterstift had never accepted the bishops' right to investigate conditions in the chapter itself. In the 1650s, the dean of the chapter, Johan Rudolph von Flaxslandt, refused to allow several visitations.[53] Furthermore, von Flaxslandt attempted to dismiss the chapter's preacher, Peter Nobs, whom the bishop had appointed personally. Nobs had clashed with the canons after trying to improve and reform services in the chapter church in Bruchsal.[54] Although episcopal officials eventually succeeded in visiting the Ritterstift, legal battles between the chapter and the bishop lasted into the 1670s.[55] A papal bull ultimately reinforced episcopal jurisdiction over the chapter, but other legal conflicts continued well into the eighteenth century.[56]

The conflicts between the Ritterstift and Bishop Metternich demonstrate the continued strength of the chapters in the Bishopric of Speyer. One hundred years after the Council of Trent, much of the Church in Speyer did not accept the Tridentine model of a centralized bishopric under an all-powerful bishop. Indeed, the disruptions of the Thirty Years' War and the failed attempt to recatholicize Germany under the leadership of the Habsburgs and the Jesuits rein-

---

52. Vicar general refused permission to check the qualifications of the priest in Odenheim (GLAK 229/79230 I, pp. 19r, 20r). Priest in Odenheim is cited at *Fiscus* (GLAK 61/5343, pp. 106r, 106v–107r, 134r–134v, 141v). Ritterstift accepts episcopal jurisdiction (GLAK 229/79230 I, pp. 33r, 35r, 36r, 37r; GLAK 61/5345, pp. 50v, 91r–91v).

53. Remling II, p. 534; GLAK 94/274; GLAK 61/11505, pp. 80r–80v, 80v–81r, 81v–82r, 91v, 123v–124v.

54. GLAK 94/439, 5 April 1653. Nobs also tried to end the singing of German hymns in the church (GLAK 133/461).

55. Remling II, pp. 534–35; GLAK 94/271, pp. 3r–5r.

56. For later conflicts between the bishop and the Ritterstift, see GLAK 65/11604 ("Ausführlicher Bericht von dem Ritter-Stifft Bruchsal").

forced the particularist tendencies within the Church in southwest Germany. The Peace of Westphalia further strengthened this local focus by securing the survival of the ecclesiastical states. No strong bishops ruled Speyer in the period from 1673 to 1720, allowing ecclesiastical institutions to maintain considerable independence. The upper reaches of the local Church did not support Tridentine reforms and at times hindered their implementation.

The Arrival of the Tridentine Rural Clergy (1700–1720)

While the upper clergy remained conservative and traditional, the parish priests increasingly represented Tridentine Catholicism in the Bishopric of Speyer. As the bishopric recovered from the devastation of the French invasion of 1688–89, a new generation of priests arrived to fill the many vacant parishes. Young, hard-working, often seminary-educated, and coming from all over Catholic Germany, these men came close to exemplifying the Tridentine ideal.

Tridentine reformers demanded that the "reformed" priest supervise the parish, administer the sacraments, and deliver inspired sermons. Perhaps more important, they expected him to be a living example of Counter-Reformation piety in the countryside. The Tridentine priest wore the cassock at all times, confessed frequently, fasted correctly, and lived a personal life above reproach. According to the Council of Trent, priests were to avoid "luxury, feasting, dances, gambling, sports, and all sorts of crime and secular pursuits."[57] The Church also hoped that all priests would be trained at a seminary and encouraged even the poorest rural priest to maintain a library. The goal was to place a competent, educated, and effective elite in the countryside.

It was difficult to meet the stringent demands of this ideal, and before 1700 many parish priests in the Bishopric of Speyer did not even try. The priests who arrived in the bishopric beginning in the late 1690s were different. For several reasons, this was the first group that truly aspired to meet the standards of Trent. First, many of these priests had been trained in seminaries before coming to Speyer. More than ever before, they came from parts of Germany where Tridentine reforms had taken better hold than in Speyer. Economic conditions in the bishopric also improved dramatically after 1700, making it

---

57. Schroeder, ed., *Canons and Decrees of the Council of Trent*, p. 153; Hoffman, *Church and Community in the Diocese of Lyon*, esp. chap. 3.

possible for many priests to live in the style befitting a Tridentine clergyman. Finally, many arrived in their new parishes as young men and stayed for long periods, giving them the time to establish a mode of behavior and an identity within the community.

The rural clergy was already changing in the decades after 1650. The parish priests favorably impressed the two Jesuit fathers who visited 150 parishes in the bishopric in 1683.[58] Of the thirty-one priests from the Hochstift mentioned in surviving reports, only one was harshly criticized by the visitors—the pfarrer in Rauenberg, Johan Jacob Meyer. Meyer had a drinking problem, which caused him to neglect services, sleep late, behave "scandalously" during processions, and socialize too much with the villagers, especially the women. The visitors recommended that he be transferred to another parish, where he could make a fresh start.[59] Otherwise the priests were, according to the visitors, "vigilant, modest, prudent, and zealous [and] neglect nothing."[60]

The two Jesuit visitors in 1683 focused on the missionary aspect of the visitation, that is, on increasing the religious understanding and enthusiasm of the population, rather than on the clergy. In their somewhat cursory examinations of the priests, the visitors concerned themselves with the quality of services, personal behavior, and the priests' domestic arrangements. They found that the priests rarely neglected weekly services and provided the sacraments as required. Only the nonresident monks who served the parishes around Speyer were not always available to perform baptisms or visit the sick. With the exception of Meyer, none of the priests drank excessively, nor were they overly familiar with their parishioners. The visitors reported no concubines and found that all the priests either lived alone or had elderly women or relatives as housekeepers.

The findings of the visitation of 1683 indicate that the priests were much closer to the Tridentine ideal than they had been in the 1580s.[61] It should be noted, however, that the visitors tolerated a number of lesser failings. Many priests, for example, neglected to "assist" young couples, that is, question and advise them on their

---

58. One of the visitors, Wilhelm Osburg, had extensive experience as a visitor and missionary in the Archbishopric of Trier before coming to Speyer. Apparently the priests in Speyer matched those in Trier in quality. See Sieffert, "Die Kapuziner zu Weißenburg (1684–1791) und die katholische Restauration beiderseits der Lauter," *Archives de l'Eglise d'Alsace*, n.s. 3 (1949–50): 248–52; Duhr III/2, pp. 621, 660–64.

59. GLAK 61/11263, p. 41.

60. Ibid., p. 23. This referred to the priest in Odenheim, Willibrod Beck.

61. Stamer III/1, p. 206; Ammerich, "Formen und Wege der katholischen Reform," pp. 309–12.

impending marriage. The pfarrer in Ostringen did not hold catechism classes, and the visitors accepted his excuse that the villagers refused to send their children.[62] Finally, the visitors did not expect a high level of education from the priests or feel that it was necessary. They reported favorably on the priest in Rot, who was "a simple and sincere man, who satisfies his office and his parishioners."[63] Only three of the thirty-one priests had studied at a seminary. It seems that in the late seventeenth century the parish clergy of the Bishopric of Speyer was slowly rising to meet the Tridentine ideal. The French invasion in the late 1680s gave this process a jolt.

The improving educational level of the clergy was perhaps the most important characteristic of the post-1700 generation. According to the visitation of 1718–21, over one-third of the priests in the bishopric (39 of 110) had a seminary education (see table 1). Of these, twenty-four were alumni of the pontifical seminary in Fulda. This seminary was founded in 1584 by Pope Gregory XIII and experienced a "second flowering" in the late seventeenth century. Run by the Jesuits, the seminary in Fulda turned out priests with a solid training in pastoral work and a self-consciously militant Catholic identity.[64] Although they represented only a minority of the priests who served in the Bishopric of Speyer, those trained in Fulda and in the seminary in Mainz (twelve in 1718–21) dominated the rural clergy in the period after 1700. In 1718–21, at least three of the five rural deans were Fulda alumni.

In the same period, there was also an important shift in the geographic origins of the priests who served in the bishopric. Traditionally, priests had been either local men or men from Swabia and the Rhineland.[65] To some extent, this was still the case in 1683 (see Table 2). There was a major change after 1700. Not only did the percentage of local priests decline, but the new priests now came from the Catholic centers of Germany. The most important new recruiting grounds were Trier, Mainz, Franconia (the bishoprics of Bamberg and Würzburg), Bavaria, and the area around Fulda. These solidly Catholic areas had successful seminaries and produced a surplus of priests. Although these "outsiders" had difficulty adjusting to conditions in Speyer, they also came from regions with a strong and confident Catholic tradition. They certainly brought a wider perspective to the Catholic villages in the Bishopric of Speyer. They may also have been more militantly Catholic and anti-Protestant

62. GLAK 61/11263, p. 37.
63. Ibid., p. 43 ("vir est sinceres et simplex, qui officio suo et parochianos satisfacit").
64. Stamer III/2, p. 53.
65. See Chapter 1.

Table 1. Numbers and education of parish priests in the Bishopric of Speyer

	Parishes	Priests	Seminary-educated	Monks	Priest/parish
1683	48	31	5	6	.645
1701–2	94	68	(1?)	6 (+7 ex-monks)	.723
1718–21	129	110	39	8 (+11 ex-monks)	.858

Table 2. Geographic origin of parish priests in the Bishopric of Speyer

	1683	1701–2	1718–21
Bishopric of Speyer	6 (28.5%)	13 (25%)	15 (17%)
Trier/Luxembourg	3	9	11
Swabia	3	7	4
Franconia	2	2	10
Rhineland	2	9	5
Alsace	—	1	5
Mainz	—	—	7
Switzerland	—	4	2
Westphalia	—	2	2
Fulda	—	—	4
Eichfeld	—	—	5
Bavaria	—	1	4
Holland	2	—	—
Other	3	4	2 (Freiburg im Breisgau)
Total identified	21	52	76

than the priests who came from such confessionally mixed areas as the Palatinate and Swabia.[66]

The new priests benefited from improving economic conditions. After 1700 the bishopric recovered well from the French invasion. By 1706 tithes in most areas had reached the levels of the 1680s, and they continued to increase until the 1720s. Several examples will suffice. In Jöhlingen, the Cathedral Chapter collected 437 malter of grain in 1687, before the French invasion. In 1698 it collected only 239 malter; in 1706, 374 malter; and in 1712, 411 malter. In Bauerbach the amounts were 236 malter in 1687, 47 in 1698, 226 in 1706, and 305 in 1712.[67] The priests as well as the chapters profited from

---

66. This was the case in Alsace (Châtellier, *Tradition chrétienne et renouveau catholique*, p. 104).

67. GLAK 61/10977, pp. 446, 449; GLAK 61/10981, pp. 251–271; GLAK 61/10983, pp. 94v–94r; GLAK 61/10985, pp. 544–47. These numbers are actually the estimates of the Cathedral Chapter early in the summer at the *"Zehent Verleihung"*. The actual amount of tithe collected was not recorded.

the economic recovery. In 1715 the Cathedral Chapter resolved to raise the incomes of parish priests.[68] The chapter also moved to repair parsonages in a variety of villages, allowing the priests to live with more dignity and making it possible to replace nonresident monks with resident secular priests.[69] Such replacements occurred in Oberhausen in 1718 and in Heiligenstein in 1719.[70] Stamer also claims that by the 1730s priests no longer found it necessary to farm.[71]

The number of priests per parish rose between 1701 and 1720 because fewer priests were expected to handle two parishes (see Table 1).[72] Whereas in 1701 one priest served both Obergrombach and Untergrombach, each parish had its own priest in 1719. This was also true for the neighboring parishes of Ostringen and Langenbrücken. Some parishes even had two priests by 1720. In 1709, for example, the priest in Jöhlingen could afford to hire a chaplain to assist him with this large parish.[73] These measures were the result of improving financial conditions and a new commitment within the Church to serve the rural parishes. The priests themselves often recognized problems in the parishes and pressured their superiors for improvements.

The rural chapters met more regularly after 1700 than they had at any time since the late sixteenth century, a sign of improved organization. The rural chapter in Bruchsal was especially active. Over twenty priests attended the June 1711 meeting, which served several purposes. Some of the priests used it as a forum to register complaints about their income, the condition of parish property, or the behavior of secular officials. The chapter disciplined a few priests for minor failings, such as doing business with Calvinists, and the dean announced several episcopal ordinances. Finally, the priests themselves suggested several reforms. One proposal was that all priests be required to use the older Mainz Agenda, because the "new one is very confusing."[74] The rural chapters gave the priests an opportunity to get together socially and professionally. For the first time they could

68. GLAK 61/10987, p. 292.
69. GLAK 61/10985, pp. 62, 417, 257.
70. GLAK 61/10989, pp. 303, 339.
71. Stamer III/2, p. 57.
72. Even after 1700, the number of priests per parish was very low in the Bishopric of Speyer. If one includes all the chapter clergy and the regular clergy in towns, there were certainly fewer than three priests per parish in the bishopric. This compares, for example, with between six and eight *secular* clergymen per parish in Brittany in the seventeenth century (Croix, *La Bretagne aux 16e et 17e siècles*, vol. 2, p. 1157).
73. GLAK 229/49542 (Jöhlingen).
74. GLAK 78/629.

act as a pressure group and operate in concert on issues of common concern. Regular meetings also meant that the priests, some of whom had known each other as students in Mainz and Fulda, were less isolated in the villages. The chapters contributed to the creation of a clerical elite, bound together by personal and professional ties.[75]

These ties were reinforced by the long tenures of the priests who arrived in Speyer after 1700. Of the seven priests serving in the Speyer villages of the rural chapter of Deidesheim in 1718, only one had served less than seven years, and three had served more than nineteen years.[76] This situation, which existed throughout the bishopric, gave the priests time to build personal bonds with their fellow priests as well as with their parishioners. The will of Andreas Rohrmoser, pfarrer in Bruchsal and dean of the rural chapter, shows his loyalty to the clerical estate. The executors of Rohrmoser's will were the parish priest in the neighboring village of Forst, a vicar from the Ritterstift, and the late priest's nephew. Rohrmoser left significant sums of money to his church and to the rural chapter. Although he bequeathed some of his property to his sister, Rohrmoser's family inherited only a small part of his estate.[77] His first loyalty was to the Church and his fellow priests, and he trusted his friends in the clergy with his property.

The Tridentine priests who came to the Bishopric of Speyer were a reforming elite. They had their own social network, reinforced by regular meetings, similar educational backgrounds, and a code of conduct that distinguished them from their parishioners. They became more detached from village life and more a part of an outside elite. Yet the separation of the clergy from rural society was not complete. The upper clergy of the bishopric never wholeheartedly embraced Tridentine models of clerical behavior and thereby undermined the position of Jesuit-trained rural clergy. Church institutions remained weak and relatively inactive, and thus parish priests could not count on support in conflicts with their parishioners. Left on their own, most priests understood that they had to accommodate themselves to the community around them. Their pastoral training, which taught them to maintain good relations with the villagers, reinforced this attitude.

---

75. Timothy Tackett argues that by 1750 the "Cantonal Conferences" (i.e., rural chapters) of the Diocese of Gap had helped to create a sense of teamwork and a "community of priests" (*Priest and Parish in 18th Century France*, p. 85).

76. LASp. D2/306/6, pp. 198r–226v.

77. GLAK 67/428, pp. 136v–139r. Compare the will of Johan Merckell, priest in Jöhlingen, from 1592, discussed in Chapter 1. Merckell left his estate to his grandchildren.

The New Priests and Their Parishioners

What was the impact of the educated, reform-minded priests in the villages? Did this clerical elite wrest control of the local church from the commune and transform the Catholic Church into an institution intent on disciplining the laity? Philip Hoffman has argued that by the late seventeenth century the clergy of the diocese of Lyon had become "agents of the Counter-Reformation" and helped the French state attack communal institutions and loyalties in their parishes.[78] The priest became an outsider in his parish, in constant conflict with the population.

The effect of the new priests in the Bishopric of Speyer was less dramatic than what Hoffman found in Lyon. In general, Counter-Reformation ideals had a limited influence on the people and clergy of the bishopric even after 1650. More specifically, the weakness of the episcopal administration and the lack of a strong state restrained the impact of the Tridentine clergy. Above all, the priests continued to operate within a local church dominated by the village commune.

The communal church (gemeinde kirche) remained very influential as an organizing force in rural Catholicism and in the relationship between the priests and the villagers. Some new conflicts arose between the pfarrer and their parishioners with the arrival of the Tridentine priests, but cooperation and compromise also continued to characterize this relationship. The gemeinde kirche not only weakened the Church's attempt to discipline the laity and reform popular religion, but also created the conditions that allowed popular Catholicism to thrive.

The Preservation of Communal Control

The circumstances that allowed the village communes to control the local churches in the sixteenth century were still present after 1650. Secular and ecclesiastical authority remained fragmented; Church institutions lacked permanence and authority; much of the upper clergy was complacent and inactive; and strong state structures did not exist. As a result, village communes continued to influence the appointment and disciplining of the clergy and to control important financial resources. Significantly, the rural communes never relinquished their role in the organization of popular religious life, especially processions and festivals. This situation allowed a

78. Hoffman, *Church and Community in the Diocese of Lyon*, chap. 4.

strong and vital popular Catholicism to flourish into the eighteenth century.

The most important realm of communal influence remained in the appointment and disciplining of the clergy. The villagers' leverage in this area allowed them to procure priests who met their desires and standards, at least within the framework of prevailing economic conditions and the basic requirements of the Church. The extent of this influence on appointments varied. Some village communes had strong traditions and recommended priests directly to the patron of the parish. This was the case in Edesheim, where the gemeinde proposed two candidates to the Cathedral Chapter in 1704. The canons accepted one of the two applicants.[79] In 1659 the villagers of Stundtweiler "presented" a priest to the chapter, which reluctantly rejected the candidate because he lacked proper papers.[80] The canons agreed to consider the villagers' candidate again the following year.

The "trial sermon" (*Probe Predigen*) also remained important. In 1662 the "keller, village council, and whole commune" of Deidesheim sent a written report to the Cathedral Chapter on the audition of a candidate for the parish in that village.[81] The process of appointing a new parish priest had not changed significantly since the pre-Tridentine period.

The villagers continued to take a leading role in the disciplining of parish priests. In some areas, especially on the edges of the bishopric, local communes even removed priests on their own authority. The villagers did not consider this a usurpation of episcopal authority but rather part of the local administration of village affairs. After all, village communes collected their own taxes, organized agricultural life, adjudicated local disputes, and kept public order, so it made sense for them to discipline incompetent parish priests as well. In 1654 the schultheiss and mayor of Odenheim, apparently with the support of the rest of the village, removed an unsatisfactory priest on their own authority. The ongoing conflict between the Ritterstift and Bishop Metternich meant that ecclesiastical authority in Odenheim was in dispute, and so the villagers decided to act on their own. The episcopal authorities eventually reinstated the priest, only to find him disobedient and argumentative.[82]

The villagers of Riedseltz, like those in Odenheim, had a long

---

79. GLAK 61/10981, p. 335v. Note that the commune of Edesheim claimed the legal right to examine all new priests. See Chapter 5.
80. GLAK 61/10973, p. 361.
81. Ibid., p. 830.
82. GLAK 229/79230 I, p. 19r, 20r, 21r–22r (Odenheim).

tradition of independent control of the local parish. In 1680 the Riedseltzers protested that the patron of the parish had rejected a priest recommended by the commune. Instead, the chapter in Weißenburg had appointed Caspar Mülheim, who turned out to be a renegade priest from Strasbourg. In August 1681, Mülheim came under suspicion of impregnating his maid. Without any ecclesiastical representative present, three villagers and the secular administrator of the village (which was under the lordship of the Teutonic Knights) interrogated the priest. As a result of this investigation, the villagers removed Mülheim and presented a new priest, whose appointment was confirmed by the episcopal authorities in Speyer.[83] The Teutonic Knights supported the villagers of Riedseltz at each stage, legitimizing the removal of Mülheim and the appointment of a new priest. The support of the Knights probably made it easier for the villagers to act on their own, but the Riedseltzers actively administered the village parish and did not appeal to outside authorities for help.

The villagers wielded their influence above all to improve the quality and availability of religious services in the parish. They complained about and quarreled with priests who failed to do their job. The villagers often approved of seminary-trained pfarrer because these priests met their expectations: that the priest reside in the village, provide the sacraments, and diligently perform regular church services. It was especially important to them that the priest be available at all times to perform baptisms and visit the dying. These expectations differed little from the desires of the villagers in the sixteenth century. By the late seventeenth century, however, the villagers had accepted the Counter-Reformation model of the priest to some extent. They expected their priests to be celibate and, although they were rather more tolerant than the official Church, their standards of personal morality were slightly higher for priests than for the rest of their neighbors. In general, however, the villagers still wanted the priests to be part of the local community and did not accept the clergy's claim of exemption from the usual village duties, taxes, or fees.[84]

The most frequent request was for a resident priest. The villagers made this demand most constantly in the 1650s, when the shortage of priests was especially acute, but pleas for resident priests were heard throughout the period. The village communes often took the

83. ADBR 19 J 396, nos. 8, 11, 12, 14, 16, 20, 24. Riedseltz and its traditions of community control of the parish church are discussed in Chapter 1.

84. The professional function of the priest remained more important than his personal morality. See Châtellier, *Tradition chrétienne et renouveau catholique*, p. 179.

initiative to improve pastoral care in the parishes, and the case of Langenbrücken is a good example. The villagers of Langenbrücken had always had poor relations with the patrons of the village, the Gregorian Vicars of the Cathedral Chapter. In the 1650s, the vicars failed to give any money either to the priest in a neighboring village to whom the villagers were going for the sacraments or to the Capuchins, who occasionally said Mass in Langenbrücken. The villagers retaliated by collecting the tithe and paying it directly to whoever performed pastoral duties in the village. In the following decades, they pressured the vicars to repair the parsonage, and in 1686 they thanked the bishop for his help in getting a resident priest to Langenbrücken.[85] It had taken the villagers over thirty years, but they finally succeeded.

In another case, the Cathedral Chapter objected to the somewhat devious attempt of the commune of St. Leon to attract a resident priest. These villagers shared a priest with the neighboring village of Rot, where the pfarrer lived. Hoping to get the priest to move to St. Leon, the villagers rebuilt the parsonage.[86] Although this plan did not succeed, it is apparent that village communes operated on their own initiative.

It had always been a goal of the Church to provide each parish with a resident priest, and the seventeenth-century villagers' pleas for priests were strikingly similar to such requests from the century before. In 1686, the villagers of Obergrombach asked for their own priest, citing a growing population of over three hundred, the danger of fire and theft when everyone left for services in another village, and the need for a resident priest who could visit the sick and dying.[87] It also appears that the visitation and Jesuit mission of 1683 had increased the villagers' awareness of the problems associated with a nonresident pfarrer. It was the villagers who were dissatisfied with the Church, not, as Delumeau would have it, the Church with the villagers.[88]

Villagers often objected to the use of monks in rural parishes, especially in Heiligenstein, which was served by the Carmelites for most of the seventeenth century. In 1655 the gemeinde complained that the Carmelites were "very neglectful."[89] In 1663 the villagers went into more detail: "The Carmelite fathers," they said, "have held

---

85. GLAK 229/57748, pp. 5, 6, 10, 13–15; GLAK 229/57751, p. 3.
86. GLAK 61/10977, pp. 385r–385v (1686).
87. GLAK 229/34848. This is strikingly similar to the request of the villagers of Riedseltz for a resident priest in the 1570s. See Chapter 1.
88. Delumeau, *Catholicism between Luther and Voltaire*, chap.4.
89. GLAK 61/10971, pp. 561–62.

services here for some years, but not completely, only every other Sunday or holiday."[90] The villagers found this pattern unacceptable and demanded weekly services. Like all nonresident priests, the monks were usually not available to perform emergency baptisms or to visit sick parishioners. As this example illustrates, they also had a reputation for neglecting services, although in general, the monks seem to have improved in this area. In 1666, for example, the Augustinians sent a priest out from Speyer to live in Schifferstadt during an outbreak of the plague, so as to be available in emergencies. This act was especially admirable since the city was much less afflicted by the contagion than the surrounding countryside.[91]

The villagers not only wanted a resident priest, they wanted him to do his job. Christoph Crass, pfarrer in Niederlauterbach, was not sufficiently accessible to his parishioners. In 1689 the villagers complained that Crass's house was always closed up and no one ever answered the door. "One can stand and knock, call out, or yell, and no one in the house appears to listen." According to the villagers, none of Crass' predecessors had behaved in this way.[92] The most frequent complaint was that the pfarrer neglected weekly services, or "poorly served" the parish.[93] If the priest held regular services, administered the sacraments, and was available for emergencies, he probably satisfied his parishioners.

Concubinage, which had been widely accepted in the rural parishes in the late sixteenth century, was no longer tolerated by Catholic villagers. There is little doubt that reform efforts had penetrated popular consciousness in this respect. The villagers in Scheidt, for example, objected to their priest's "household," no doubt a reference to the female company he kept.[94] In Waibstadt, the gemeinde was suspicious of the priest's relationship with his maid, although there was no evidence of misconduct. Furthermore, the gemeinde found the woman personally disagreeable and disruptive and said she gave the town a bad reputation among its Protestant neighbors.[95] Thus a major change in the popular view of clerical concubinage occurred between the 1580s and the late seventeenth century. Not only did the villagers no longer tolerate public concubinage, they were suspicious of any familiarity between priests and women. In this important area,

90. GLAK 61/10974a, pp. 11–12.
91. Ibid., p. 634v. The monks and priests were not allowed to go in and out of the city for the duration of the plague.
92. ADBR G5819, 26 March 1688.
93. GLAK 61/10974a, p. 669v; GLAK 61/10975, p. 119r.
94. GLAK 61/10975, p. 117r.
95. GLAK 229/108722, 1688.

the people had accepted the Tridentine model of a parish priest because it was now part of their Catholic identity to be served by a celibate priest, while the Protestants went to a married pastor.

The priests sometimes resisted the commune's influence over the local church, which ran counter to the ongoing effort of the Church to eradicate secular influence over Church offices, property, and practices. The Council of Trent had reinforced this view and had attempted to organize and centralize authority within the Church itself. The pope was, theoretically, all-powerful within the Church, the bishop within his diocese, and the priest within his parish. But conditions in the rural parishes in Speyer did not even come close to this model.

Some priests challenged the communes. In 1686 the pfarrer in Deidesheim tried unsuccessfully to influence the election of the *Kirchengeschworene*, or church wardens, who had always been chosen by the gemeinde.[96] Even a new ordinance relating to the church wardens published by episcopal authorities in 1689 only required that the parish priest be present at the election of the wardens. The choice of these officials remained in the hands of the village council.[97]

During the visitation of 1683, the visitors asked the villagers to comment on their relationship with the parish priest. Some of the responses seem to have caught the attention of the Jesuit visitors. The villagers did not consider the priest an authority figure. In Büchig they said, "He has no right to order us around."[98] In a similar vein, the villagers of Oberhausen and Rheinhausen commented: "The priest has his say in the church, and not outside [it]."[99] Finally, in an even more general statement, the villagers of Neipsheim asserted that "the priest must serve us!"[100] Such views did not change drastically between 1650 and 1720, even as the rural clergy increasingly reflected Tridentine values. The strong traditional attitudes of the villagers and their active assertion of communal control of the parish church at times clashed with the reforming views of the parish priests.

<hr>

96. LASp. D2/341b/2, p. 7r.

97. *Collectio processuum synodalium*, 24 November 1689; *Sammlung der Hochfürstlich-Speierischen Gesetze und Landesverordnungen*, vol. 1 (Bruchsal, 1789), 61–62. The episcopal authorities expected the priests to influence the election of the wardens.

98. GLAK 61/11262, p. 18: "Er hat ihnen nichts zu befehlen."

99. GLAK 61/11265(2), p. 178: "Der pfarrer hatt in ihr Kirchen zu sagen undt nicht daraußen."

100. GLAK 61/112632, p. 17: "Der pfaff muß unß wohl aufwarten."

Conflict and Cooperation:
The Priest in the Village

Even when the priest discharged his pastoral duties well, conflicts with the villagers sometimes arose. There was trouble when the priests aggressively asserted special rights and privileges within the villages and when they attempted to impose new standards of behavior on the villagers. The seminary-educated priests did not easily accept their position as servants of the village commune, and this attitude caused tensions in the rural parishes. Disputes arose over tax exemptions, fees for religious services, and the priest's obligations to the commune.

Tensions between priests and their parishioners over the special status of the clergy were not new. Starting in the 1680s, however, conflict over these issues increased. The priests asserted themselves more vigorously, demanding not only their legal privileges but personal respect from their parishioners. Some were shocked by the familiarity, and sometimes disdain, the villagers showed them. In 1681 the priest in Diedesfeld objected that one of the villagers had spoken "rudely to him with words of defamation and abuse."[101] The priest demanded that the offender be punished. The pfarrer in Rödersheim complained several years later that his parishioners were "impertinent."[102] To be sure, an extreme sensitivity to insults was common at all levels of society in this period, but some priests, conscious of their special status, demanded extraordinary deference from their neighbors.

The priests' insistence on their privileges carried over into their economic relations within the village. The pfarrer in Waibstadt, Johan Klein, objected to being treated like "a citizen of the commune (*gemeinen Bürger*)." In 1693 Klein had to pay all the taxes, some dues, and the fees for the town shepherd. "I am given no clerical immunity," he complained, "except that I am freed from the *Fron* (labor services) and guard duty."[103] Klein indicated to the bishop that he wanted to move to a different parish. He doubted the townsmen would make any concessions on these issues.

The villagers of Bauerbach held their priest to all the rules of the commune. In 1707 they protested to the Cathedral Chapter that the pfarrer was grazing more than his fair share of pigs in the common woods.[104] In 1710 the villagers complained again, this time that the

101. GLAK 61/10977, p. 152v.
102. Ibid., p. 391v.
103. GLAK 229/108725, 14 September 1693.
104. GLAK 61/10983, p. 182r. The priest was allowed to graze nine pigs in the woods.

priest's dogs had damaged the village vineyards, he had paid the wine dues incorrectly, and he had refused to pay the usual fee for use of the pasture.[105] In both cases, the Cathedral Chapter supported the villagers, telling them to shoot the priest's dogs if they were found in the vineyards. The economic exemptions and legal privileges of the clergy caused conflict everywhere, but in the Bishopric of Speyer, in contrast to other parts of Catholic Europe, the village communes often forced their priests to pay fees and taxes like any inhabitant.

Disputes between the priests and the villagers often involved the *jura stola* (or *Stohlgebüren*, surplice fees), the fees the priests charged for performing services, especially funerals and weddings. Villagers had traditionally opposed these charges, arguing that they paid the priest with the tithe and he should do all services as part of his occupation.[106] Many priests, however, needed these fees to supplement small incomes. The bishops of Speyer issued decrees regulating the *Stohlgebühren* in 1664, 1692, and 1706.[107] The goal of these ordinances was to set the fees at affordable levels and to limit them to funerals and marriages. Nevertheless, the *jura stola* remained a point of serious contention in the relationship between the villagers and the priests.

In Jöhlingen in the 1660s, the villagers engaged their newly appointed priest in a long conflict over these charges. After a year of petitions and counter-petitions, the Cathedral Chapter sent a commission to Jöhlingen to resolve the dispute. The villagers and the pfarrer agreed to fix the jura stola at the level of the 1650s.[108] The Cathedral Chapter canons demonstrated little sympathy for the priest in this conflict, indicating that his effort to collect fees was an illegal innovation. It appears that the final compromise was a victory for the villagers.

One of the goals of the visitation of 1683 was to determine what fees were collected in the bishopric. In almost all villages, the priests collected the jura stola only for funerals and marriages. The going rate was one or two gulden for a funeral and about half a gulden for a wedding.[109] These amounts were not significant, since most priests received an income of seventy-five to one hundred gulden a year. On the other hand, the priests did not receive fees for any other sacraments. There were few complaints from the villagers on this subject

105. GLAK 61/10985, p. 189.
106. Blickle, *Gemeinde Reformation*.
107. *Collectio processuum synodalium*, Ordinatus Variae, 1664; Decretus Jurae Stolae, 1692; Synod of 25 August 1706.
108. GLAK 61/10974a, pp. 697v, 699r–699v, 708r, 735v, 759v, 772v–773r.
109. GLAK 61/11263, pp. 2, 4, 8. There are many more examples.

during the visitation. They were no doubt happy to have the visitors document present conditions and thus prevent priests from increasing the fees in the future.

The peasants reacted very negatively to priests who attempted to collect money for ceremonies other than burials or weddings, or who refused to perform services unless they were paid. In 1705 the residents of Bauerbach reported that their priest had refused to accompany the funeral procession from a dead man's house to the graveyard, as was traditional, but instead only performed the funeral service in the cemetery. The priest defended this behavior by saying he received "no salary for accompanying the corpse [to the cemetery] or for baptisms." The villagers reported that several years previously he had refused to perform a baptism unless he was paid first.[110] These two abuses headed a long list of problems the villagers had with this priest. Once again, we see that the laity continued to view the parish priest as someone who had duties to the village. As they had in the sixteenth century, the villagers kept a careful eye on the priest's performance in office.

Problems invariably arose in the rural parishes if the priest decided to correct the daily behavior and morals of his parishioners, as all Tridentine priests were in fact expected to do. Priests were told to improve the behavior and piety of their flock, above all by personal example, but also through sermons, teaching, and private and public admonition of their parishioners. Not surprisingly, the villagers of the Bishopric of Speyer did not respond positively to this sort of pedagogical endeavor. Furthermore, episcopal authorities often reprimanded priests who demonstrated a lack of "feel" for their parishioners. Ultimately, there were few of these conflicts.

Few controversies involving overly demanding priests appear in the minutes of the visitation of 1683. The visitors did suggest that the priest in Bruchsal was too excitable and should learn to adjust to local conditions. They complimented the priest in Jöhlingen on his diligence but suggested he shorten his three-hour sermons.[111] Beginning in the 1690s, however, there were more problems with overly zealous priests. In 1696 the villagers of Langenbrücken complained that their priest was too "severe and hard" in his pastoral duties.[112] They requested a new pfarrer. In 1705 the Cathedral Chapter chided the priest in Jöhlingen for publicly rebuking a villager for a crime that

---

110. GLAK 61/10981, pp. 410v–411r.
111. GLAK 61/11263, pp. 2, 13.
112. GLAK 61/57752, 13 September 1696: "Schwer und hart."

the canons had already punished. The canons felt this sort of humiliation was unnecessary and detrimental to public order.[113]

Two cases illustrate the confrontations between overzealous priests and self-assured village communes especially well. The first case involved Peter Mentenich, pfarrer in Rülzheim. In January 1700, the rural dean in Herxheim went to investigate conditions in Rülzheim. The villagers had complained repeatedly about Mentenich, saying that he "belittled" and "abused" them and was constantly "angry" and "contemptuous."[114]

> For the people (*vox populi*) [said], we pray to God that we could get rid of this quarrelsome and troublesome priest. We want to behave as good Catholic Christians should, but [all we get] from him is abuse, ridicule, and insults. What he hears all week long from his spies and other gossip-mongers [in the village] must be preached from the pulpit.[115]

Georg Jos, the rural dean, and longtime priest in Herxheim, sympathized with Mentenich. Jos commented that the income in Rülzheim was very low, that Mentenich had accumulated many debts, and that he was the poorest priest in the area. Jos respected and even liked Mentenich, whom he found "in general good enough, in fact, too good."[116] Menterich's problem, the dean said, was that he had no feeling for the villagers. Holding himself to high standards of personal behavior, Mentenich tried to impose these standards on the villagers. Furthermore, due to his poor income, he was no doubt bitter. His parishioners refused to change their conduct and did not accept his public interference in their lives. Jos recommended that Mentenich be transferred to another parish. By 1701 he had left Rülzheim.

The second case involved Georg Krug, the priest in Langenbrücken in 1713. Krug's parishioners characterized him above all as "arrogant" (*hochmütig*), and he offended the villagers with a variety of public declarations. He was heard to say that there was no one in the village good enough to drink with him. Krug frequently demanded that the villagers show him special deference. "Show respect to a pfarrer" was one of his favorite phrases. He reprimanded villagers who failed to remove their hats when they passed him in the

---

113. GLAK 61/10983, p. 30r.
114. LASp. D2/466/1: "schmähung . . . veracht und verkleinert . . . Zorn."
115. Ibid.
116. Ibid.: "Sonsten ist herr Mentenig an sich selbsten guth genug, imo gar zu guth."

street.[117] The villagers' protests make it clear that they found this conduct haughty and unacceptable.

Krug's personal behavior was more than a matter of style. The pfarrer interfered in the commune's control of the parish, attempting to take possession of the offering box, the key to which was kept by the *Pfleger*, an official appointed by the commune. When the gemeinde resisted Krug, he shifted his attack to the schultheiß, the highest secular official in the village and the head of the village council. Krug moved the schultheiß's wife's chair from its privileged position in the church and put his gloves and stick on the schultheiß's chair. He then went on to insult the schultheiß and his family in front of the whole congregation, intimating that the schultheiß was secretly a Jew.[118]

Krug meddled in other areas that the villagers considered off limits. His examinations of couples intending to marry lasted three times as long as his predecessor's. Before the wedding of one couple, Krug asserted in public, without citing evidence, that he thought the bride was not a virgin. Finally, he intruded in the affairs of married couples. According to the villagers, Krug encouraged the wife of an innkeeper to take her husband to court for abuse. The pfarrer denied he caused dissension in the marriage but commented that the innkeeper did treat his wife badly. Krug felt it was part of his duty to improve the morals of his parishioners, and he said to an investigating commission that he hoped he was allowed to correct people.[119] The villagers clearly considered such "correction" an unwanted interference in village affairs. In their view, the priest's authority was limited to the church.

Krug only reluctantly participated in votive processions organized by the commune. It is unclear whether he considered these events theologically questionable or whether they were just an extra bother. In any case, he further alienated the inhabitants of Langenbrücken by causing trouble on these occasions. In the summer of 1713, the cattle in the village came down with an unknown disease, and the village council organized a procession to appeal for divine help to cure the cows. The pfarrer had initially agreed to allow a Capuchin to accompany the procession, but later, citing his parochial jurisdiction, he protested the father's participation. Krug did not allow the church bells to be rung and would not permit the Capuchin to take the

---

117. GLAK 229/57754, pp. 12r, 13r, 14r, 8r.
118. Ibid., pp. 13r–15r.
119. Ibid., pp. 12r, 7v, 8r, 4v, 28r.

consecrated host out of the church.[120] A similar confrontation occurred ten days later, when the villagers organized a second procession. Although he was unwilling or too lazy to participate, Krug did
not like the fact that the gemeinde organized the processions and
wanted to assert his authority over these events.

In August 1714, the episcopal authorities moved Krug to the village of St. Martin, on the other side of the Rhine. This case illustrates
more, however, than the ability of a village commune to drive out a
priest the people did not like. Krug's personal behavior and his performance as parish priest contradicted the villagers' understanding of
the nature of the local church and the role of the parish priest. They
wanted a priest who behaved like a member of the community, gave
them the services they wanted, and did not meddle in family or
communal affairs. A heavy-handed, arrogant Tridentine priest who
attempted to reform the behavior of the villagers and interfered with
local administration of the church could cause serious conflicts.
Most of the new priests, however, did not have such difficulties.
Many even cooperated with their parishioners to improve religious
life in the villages.

Village communes supported their priests' requests for increased
income, especially when the patron was an urban chapter with a
reputation for compensating parish priests inadequately. Thus the
gemeinde of Malsch appealed to the episcopal authorities in 1694 to
force the Allerheiligen Chapter to improve the pay of its priest. The
villagers reported that the priest was very diligent, visited the sick
day and night, and had remained in the village during the French
invasion. The chapter responded that it did not have the money to
pay him more but hoped the pfarrer would not leave, as he was very
popular with his parishioners.[121]

The villagers also worked to keep priests they liked. In the early
eighteenth century, the commune of Maikammer protested the appointment of a new priest to the village parish. The peasants were
happy with the performance of their current priest and feared that
the new one, Andreas Braun, was too young and inexperienced for the
large parish. Furthermore, Braun was a local man, and the village
council feared that some parishioners would be unwilling to confess
to him, for fear he would repeat what he had heard.[122]

Sometimes the villagers supported the priest against other govern-

120. Ibid., pp. 17r–20r.
121. GLAK 229/63939.
122. LASp. D2/412/3.

ment officials. In 1654, for example, the villagers of Dahn protested to the bishop that the keller was not paying the parish priest correctly. The villagers feared that the priest would quit his post, leaving the area without pastoral care.[123] In 1701 the commune and priest in Forst cooperated to remove an unsatisfactory schoolteacher.[124]

Parish priests, in turn, did not always enforce episcopal decrees diligently. As was the case before the Thirty Years' War, they often accommodated local practices and compromised with their parishioners. It is clear from the visitation of 1683 that few, if any, priests attempted to suppress what the visitors referred to as "superstitions and abuses." The Pfarrer, in fact, participated in some of these practices, for example by blessing farm animals and fields and leading processions that included heavy drinking.[125] The Cathedral Chapter reprimanded the priest in Bauerbach in 1716 for failing to fine several parishioners who had been found working on the feast of St. Joseph.[126] The canons, of course, were more concerned with collecting the fines than with the behavior of their subjects.

The priests clearly remained enmeshed in village life, even as they began to differ from their parishioners in educational and personal background. If some priests clashed frequently with their flock, most maintained good relations and even cooperated with the Catholic people of the bishopric. The villagers, in turn, had many reasons to be pleased with the reformed priests. These men were attentive to their duties, available and active in the parish, and above moral reproach. Especially after 1700, the population was served by a more effective clergy than ever before.

By about 1720, a Tridentine clergy operated within a rural church that was organized along traditional lines. Village communes still dominated local churches in the period from 1650 to 1720, and it was not in the interest of the priests or the Church hierarchy to challenge this control. Most priests were practical enough to realize that their parishioners would not listen to scoldings from the pulpit or respond positively to constant interference in their everyday lives. The villagers, for their part, often respected and honored the abilities of the priests. There were certainly tensions in the bishopric between Tri-

123. GLAK 61/11505, p. 220v.
124. GLAK 229/29163, pp. 13r–17r.
125. GLAK 61/11263, pp. 2, 7, 16, 33, 37.
126. GLAK 61/10987, p. 371. The Tridentine Church gave the feast of St. Joseph a new emphasis. Coming in March, this holiday interfered with important agricultural tasks, especially for farmers, like those in Bauerbach, who had vineyards.

dentine Catholicism, with its clerical elite, individualistic piety, and centralizing tendencies, and the more local and communally based traditional Catholicism of the region; but the essential characteristic of this relationship was compromise and understanding. In the long run the willingness of ecclesiastic authorities to accept many elements of traditional Catholicism had a positive effect on the relationship between the Church and the Catholic people of the bishopric. The Church remained entrenched in the countryside and continued to respond to the desires of the villagers.

7

The Growth of Catholic
Consciousness, 1650–1720

By the early eighteenth century, the Catholic villagers of the Bishopric of Speyer had a strong loyalty to Catholic religious practices and a basic understanding of the tenets of their faith. The people expressed this loyalty both positively, by conforming to certain Catholic practices and beliefs, and negatively, by opposing the Protestantism of their neighbors. Although daily association with Protestants continued, the easy relations that had characterized the sixteenth century ended. Catholics no longer readily accepted Protestant journeymen or permanent residents in their villages. The immigrants who helped repopulate the villages of the bishopric after the destructive wars of the seventeenth century came almost exclusively from the other parts of Catholic Germany. By 1720, even at the village level, the middle Rhine region was divided into two confessional cultures.

This important development did not result from aggressive and successful Tridentine reform. As we have seen, the Counter-Reformation in the Bishopric of Speyer was above all tentative, moderate, and limited. What little progress had been made on the reform agenda by 1620, especially the creation of an educated and active parish clergy, suffered a serious setback during the Thirty Years' War. The most significant reform came after 1650 when the Catholic Church successfully placed well-educated priests in the villages. Especially in the first two decades of the eighteenth century, a steady flow of "reformed" priests came to the Bishopric of Speyer.

Yet it was not these priests who created Catholic consciousness in the villages. There was no process of acculturation as described by Delumeau.[1] Both the traditionalist clerical establishment and the village communes prevented reformers from establishing new modes of behavior and innovative religious practices in the rural parishes. It is impossible to find a unified elite acting to acculturate the population.

If the growth of Catholic consciousness was not a consequence of acculturation, neither was it the result of confessionalization. Because the bishops of Speyer did not undertake a program of state-building, they did not employ Church institutions and the clergy to strengthen princely power and control, and made little effort to impose social discipline in the countryside.[2] Furthermore, although the bishops and their officials certainly understood Catholicism as a bulwark of their secular authority, they had little leverage over the religious life of the peasantry in the weakly governed principality. The villagers did not develop a confessional consciousness to avoid state coercion or to court princely favor.[3]

It was, instead, the traditional communal church that provided the basis for a Catholic revival after 1700. With the support of the Church, but not under its leadership, the villagers made Catholicism part of their communal identity and autonomy. In a region of religious fragmentation, confessional loyalty worked to reinforce local loyalties, rather than to encourage territorial integration as it did in larger states. Indeed, the moderation of the Counter-Reformation helped the Speyer Church. The inclination of the conservative Church hierarchy to tolerate and even encourage popular religious practices, while reforming many of the abuses of the clergy, meant that the Church did not alienate the population in Speyer as it had in other parts of Catholic Europe. Similarly, because Church institutions were not implicated in a process of state-building, the villagers continued to look on their village Church as a local institution, not as an outside power or an organ of the state.

To use John Bossy's categories, the villagers stressed the communal and ritualistic aspects of Catholicism, including regular Sunday services, processions, and pilgrimages, and tended to ignore or resist the more individualistic innovations promoted by the Tridentine

1. Delumeau, *Catholicism between Luther and Voltaire.*
2. Hsia, *Social Discipline in the Reformation*, p. 5.
3. This may have been the case in Austria and Bavaria and in some Protestant states (Hsia, *Social Discipline in the Reformation*, chap. 5). See also Rebel, *Peasant Classes*, esp. chap. 8; Ortner, *Reformation, katholische Reform, und Gegenreformation im Erzstift Salzburg.*

Church, such as confession and individual prayer. For this reason the villagers fiercely resisted the efforts of the most ambitious priests to change local practices and traditions or to force the villagers to confess more frequently and behave more "morally."

This locally focused Catholic consciousness did not exist in isolation from the rest of the Church. Certainly the parish clergy itself, with its national and even international perspective, had an impact on the religiosity of the villagers. Regular processions to nearby Catholic villages also reinforced an important sense of a larger Catholic community. Finally, the influx of immigrants, especially in the period after 1690, gave the villagers personal contact with the rest of Catholic Germany. Although these contacts served to strengthen confessional loyalty in the villages, rural communes did not allow the priests, the immigrants, or the Church hierarchy to control their religious life.

The decline in the popularity of the Jesuits and the simultaneous rise of the Capuchins gives us a good idea of the traditional nature of Catholic consciousness. The local Church favored the sympathetic attitude of the Capuchins toward popular religious practices over the Jesuit focus on elite religion. In addition, rising confessional tensions in the city of Speyer indicate a growing Catholic confidence and militancy, both in the city and in the surrounding villages. Catholic consciousness, however, was most important in the countryside; indeed, in the Bishopric of Speyer it was in the villages and the countryside that Catholic consciousness arose.

The Decline of the Jesuits and the Rise of the Capuchins

Every historian of the Bishopric of Speyer has recognized the importance of the religious orders in the Counter-Reformation. The poverty of the bishopric made it difficult for the local Church to meet even the basic pastoral needs of the Catholic population.[4] As a result, the Church depended heavily on the orders to assist in the parishes, undertake missions, and staff educational institutions. Although the Franciscans, Carmelites, Augustinians, and Dominicans were all active in and around the city of Speyer, it was the two Counter-Reformation orders, the Society of Jesus and the Capuchins, who operated

---

4. On the importance of the orders see especially Hans Ammerich, "Formen und Wege der katholischen Reform."

throughout the diocese. The Jesuits and Capuchins undertook almost all extraordinary missions to both Catholic and Protestant areas of the bishopric. Because of such endeavors, these two orders played a significant role in the development of confessional consciousness.

The Jesuits dominated the Counter-Reformation in Speyer until the Thirty Years' War. As the war dragged on, however, the local clergy began to view the Jesuits as dangerously extreme, self-serving, and arrogant. After the war, the Jesuits' influence dwindled in Speyer. Although Bishop Metternich supported the Society, the Jesuits lost the favor of the canons of the Cathedral Chapter, probably in part due to a protracted dispute over the income of the Jesuit establishment. These problems meant that the number of Jesuits based in Speyer declined, and the Jesuit presence in the bishopric, which peaked during the Thirty Years' War, waned. Jesuit fathers appeared in the countryside only on extraordinary occasions, such as during the visitation and mission of 1683. Meanwhile, the fathers of the reformed Franciscan order of Capuchins became a frequent, regular, and influential presence in the countryside.

The Capuchins first came to the Bishopric of Speyer in 1616, a half-century after the Jesuits. Although the Capuchins built up their position during the war, especially by founding a house in the city of Speyer to complement the original establishment at the pilgrimage shrine at Wagheusel, their greatest influence came to be felt after 1650. Working out of friaries in Wagheusel, Speyer, Weil der Stadt, Bruchsal, and Weißenburg, the Capuchins engaged in missions to convert Protestant areas and evangelize Catholic villages. They also served as parish priests and maintained shrines.

The Capuchins, unlike the Jesuits, had no difficulty with the Catholic establishment in Speyer, nor did they antagonize the Protestants to the same extent. Furthermore, they were successful and popular in the countryside—not surprisingly, since the order had been founded in the early sixteenth century for the purpose of returning to the simplicity of the early Franciscans.[5] The Capuchins, known as "the people's preachers," sought to exhort and encourage the population through preaching and personal example. In the villages, indeed throughout the bishopric, this method contrasted favorably with the Jesuit focus on austerity, discipline, and militancy. The Capuchins represented the strand within the Counter-Reformation that sym-

5. Father Cuthbert, O.S.F.C., *The Capuchins. A Contribution to the History of the Counter-Reformation*, 2 vols. (New York: Longmans, Green, 1929).

pathized with much of popular religion and culture. Their success in the middle Rhine region after 1650 reflects the dominance of this aspect of Catholic reform.

The Decline of the Jesuits

The Jesuits had always represented Tridentine Catholicism in its most rigorous form. Disciplined and austere, militant and elitist, the Jesuits served as both a model and a challenge to Speyer churchmen. By 1650 the Society of Jesus had been active in Speyer for over eighty years, and it was losing the support of the Cathedral Chapter. Financial and personal disputes with the canons began during the Thirty Years' War and continued long after. The canons and the Jesuits never resolved the financial problems caused by the war and the economic contraction of the seventeenth century. At the same time, the fathers antagonized the chapter by criticizing the canons' behavior and demonstrating a general lack of respect for the ecclesiastics. This friction was a symptom of the declining influence of the Jesuits and of the kind of Church reform they represented.[6]

Throughout the 1650s and 1660s, the Cathedral Chapter found it impossible to pay the Jesuits the full amount specified by the college's foundation. As the canons explained to the Jesuits in 1663, the chapter had previously paid the fathers out of the surplus income from loans (*Renten, pensiones*). Both the income and the capital of these investments had been lost in the war. Many of the benefices in the cathedral could not be fully funded, let alone the Jesuit college.[7] Naturally the Jesuits felt their college should be given a higher priority. In his letters to Speyer, the father general of the Society in Rome implied that tensions were high in Speyer but complimented the fathers on their patience with the Cathedral Chapter.[8] This correspondence also contains some veiled criticism of the chapter, including insinuations that the canons were holding back Bishop Metternich's reform efforts.[9]

The financial difficulties and poor relations with the local Catholics may have contributed to discipline problems that appeared in the college in the 1650s and 1660s. In 1656 these problems were severe enough to cause the transfer of the rector and the appointment of a new head of the Speyer college.[10] The Society always restored inter-

6. Châtellier, *Europe of the Devout*, chap. 10.
7. GLAK 61/10974a, p. 136.
8. ARSJ Rh.Sup.2, pp. 132, 153, 182, 183.
9. Ibid., pp. 267, 279, 361.
10. Ibid., pp. 291, 300, 335–36, 437, 518.

nal discipline quickly, but it was perhaps harder to restore morale in the Speyer house. A 1655 report from the college, for example, recounts gloomily the efforts of rather vague enemies (apparently the Protestants and the Cathedral Chapter) to drive the Jesuits out of the city.[11] This defensiveness contrasted sharply with the almost reckless confidence of the Jesuits during their first decades in Speyer and contributed to their less active role after 1650.

Just as during the war, the Cathedral Chapter found the Jesuits personally difficult. Their constant demands for payment of their income back to the 1620s clearly grated on the canons. One episode illustrates the strained relations between the chapter and the Society. In 1670, the chapter paid the Jesuits eight hundred gulden, a goodly portion of its debt to the fathers. A month later, however, the Jesuits complained that the chapter still owed two *Fuder* of wine, bringing an exasperated response from the canons that further payment was impossible.[12]

There were other problems. In 1654 a Jesuit delivered a sermon in the Cathedral that criticized the chapter clergy. The dean of the Cathedral Chapter found the sermon insolent and received an apology from the rector of the Jesuit college.[13] A decade later the canons complained that the Jesuits had introduced innovations in religious services in the Cathedral. The fathers, against the wishes of the canons, refused to interrupt classes and send their students to the Cathedral for all services.[14] In the 1680s, the canons protested that the Jesuits "interfered" in many areas and intentionally scheduled masses in their church that conflicted with services in the Cathedral.[15]

These minor but constant tensions clearly poisoned the relationship between the canons and the Jesuits. The fathers apparently held this grudge even during the destruction and burning of Speyer in May 1689. When they asked the Cathedral Chapter for money in November 1689, the canons responded: "During the recent fire in Speyer [we] were aware of their [the Jesuits'] poor behavior [*übles comportement*], in that they not only did nothing to save the Cathedral [which was badly damaged], but even hindered [the effort]. As a result, the chapter has no reason to do anything especially good [for the Jesuits]."[16]

11. ARSJ Rh.Sup.32, pp. 24r–24v.
12. GLAK 61/10975, pp. 27v, 32v–33r, 42v.
13. GLAK 61/10971, p. 439.
14. GLAK 61/10974a, pp. 23, 27–28. The canons wanted the students to sing during the divine office.
15. GLAK 61/10977, p. 115r.
16. GLAK 61/10979, pp. 69v–70r.

The anti-Jesuit sentiment in the Cathedral Chapter did not diminish. After 1689 the Jesuits did not return to Speyer until 1707, and they continued to receive little support from the local church. In 1708 the canons refused a series of small requests from the Jesuits. The fathers only asked for the temporary use of some vacant buildings, but the chapter rather gratuitously rebuffed them.[17] The Jesuits recognized that they were being slighted. As late as 1718, the fathers protested to the Cathedral Chapter that, although many clergymen could afford to build new residences in Speyer, the chapter continued to pay the Jesuits less than half their income.[18]

Lacking financial resources, the Jesuit college in Speyer became less active in the late seventeenth century. Fewer Jesuits were based in Speyer after 1650. Whereas between 1600 and 1620, twenty to thirty fathers lived in the college, after 1650 there were only twelve to eighteen. After 1708 only about fourteen Jesuits remained in Speyer. The decline after the destruction of Speyer in 1689 was in part the result of the transfer of the Imperial Chamber Court from Speyer to Wetzlar. The Catholic members of the Court had supported the Jesuits since their arrival. With their departure, the Jesuits lost an important and influential advocate.

The conflict with the local Church hindered the Jesuits' broader efforts to bring Tridentine Catholicism to Speyer. An exception, however, was their secondary school, which continued to flourish after 1650. All the fathers in the college taught in the school, leaving them less time for other activities. Furthermore, the number of nonordained Jesuits whose sole duty was to teach remained constant as the size of the college declined, an indication of the great importance attached to the school.[19] Of course the Jesuits also gave regular sermons in the Cathedral and held services in their own church. Their confraternities thrived, and they always managed to convert some Protestants, although not in the numbers of the 1600s and 1610s.

The Jesuits had never been very active in the countryside, preferring to work among the Catholic elite of the city of Speyer. After the Thirty Years' War they rarely ventured into the villages. The notable exception was the extensive visitation and mission of 1683. It is instructive that the two Jesuits who undertook this assignment, Wilhelm Osburg and Martin Metz, were not based in the Speyer college. As outsiders they were perhaps more acceptable to the local

17. GLAK 61/10983, p. 202r.
18. GLAK 61/10989, pp. 150–52, 172.
19. ARSJ Rh.Sup.8, pp. 17v–18r; ARSJ Rh.Sup.12, pp. 47r–48r; St.A.MZ 15/432, 15/433.

clergy. The mission was massive. The fathers visited 150 parishes, gave communion to over 30,000 people, converted 100 Protestants, taught over 300 catechism lessons, and preached almost 500 sermons, all in a period of about ten months.[20] Osburg and Metz worked very hard, cramming several masses and sermons into each one- to two-day visit in a parish. They made a strong impression in the villages, especially on the parish priests. The pfarrer in Lauterburg and Deidesheim both praised the Jesuit missionaries at great length in their parish chronicles.[21]

Yet this mission was a unique event and could have had only a limited long-term effect. It is unlikely that the fathers effected major changes in popular practice in a one day visit. In many ways, the mission of 1683 was typical of Jesuit ventures in the countryside. The fathers made an almost superhuman effort to bring the whole range of Tridentine services to the villagers—processions, catechism classes, sermons, confession, and communion—yet they could not follow up with regular missions to the rural parishes. There is, for example, little evidence of the Jesuits successfully encouraging Marian congregations in the countryside, a process Châtellier finds so important elsewhere.[22] Just as the whole Counter-Reformation had a limited effect in the villages, so it was with the Jesuit missions to the Catholic countryside.

The Capuchins

The rise of the Capuchins to prominence in the Bishopric of Speyer marks a reorientation of the Counter-Reformation away from the militancy of the Jesuits. The Capuchins were a less troublesome and forceful order than the Jesuits; their manner appealed to the conservative and hesitant in the local ecclesiastical hierarchy.[23] Furthermore, the Capuchins favored and encouraged a traditionalist religiosity that contrasted with the austere Tridentine piety of the Jesuits. The Catholic population responded positively to the Capuchin emphasis on reviving and strengthening traditional religious practices,

20. Duhr III, pp. 673–75; Ammerich, "Formen und Wege der katholischen Reform," pp. 310–12.

21. Duhr III, pp. 674–75; Sieffert, "Die Kapuziner zu Weißenburg (1684–1791)," pp. 248–51.

22. Châtellier, *Europe of the Devout*, chaps. 11, 12, and 13, and pp. 234–54.

23. In Cologne the Capuchins appear to have improved their position at the expense of the Jesuits (Birgitte Garbe, "Reformmaßnahmen und Formen der katholischen Erneuerung in der Erzdiözese Köln (1555–1648)," *Jahrbuch des kölnischen Geschichtsvereins* 47 [1976]: 154).

reinforcing the traditional aspects of Catholicism in the region.[24] In the countryside the Capuchins also became popular by providing vital pastoral services in areas where parish priests were scarce.

The Capuchin order was not new but rather the latest in a series of reformed offshoots of the Franciscans. Founded in the early sixteenth century, the Capuchins never developed the organization and discipline of the Jesuits. Capuchin fathers remained firmly in the Franciscan tradition and were renowned as popular preachers, rarely as teachers of the elite like the Jesuits. The order spread rapidly in Germany, and by 1648 there were 130 friaries in the empire. The Capuchins operated in small numbers and often as individual missionaries. Focusing their effort on the peasantry and the common people of the cities, they promoted above all the Cult of the Eucharist by organizing confraternities of the Blessed Sacrament and other eucharistic devotions.[25]

As a mendicant order that lived on alms, the Capuchins required no large outlay of capital to bring them to the bishopric. Bishop Eberhard explicitly mentioned this advantage in 1602, when he first suggested bringing the order to Speyer.[26] A further advantage of the Capuchins was that they operated in small numbers and did not need a large building. For a fraction of the cost of the Jesuit college, Capuchin friaries could be established in various places throughout the diocese.

The Capuchins did not have a reputation for anti-Protestant militancy and therefore did not provoke the same apprehension in the Protestants as the Jesuits. This also suited the local Catholics, who generally favored a nonconfrontational policy toward their Protestant neighbors. The only conflict between the Capuchins and the Protestants occurred in 1650, when the Palatinate forced the fathers

---

24. My discussion of the Capuchins in the Bishopric of Speyer is primarily based on the following works: Georg Manz, *Die Kapuziner im rechtsrheinischen Gebiet des Bistums Speyer im 17. und 18. Jahrhundert* (Bruchsal: Vorgelegt von Georg Manz, 1979); P. Arsenius Jacobs, *Die rheinischen Kapuziner, 1611–1725. Ein Beitrag zur Geschichte der katholischen Reform* (Münster: Aschendorff, 1933); P. Archange Sieffert, "Les capucins à Wissembourg sous l'Ancien Régime et la restauration catholique dans la région de la Lauter. I. La maison à Wissembourg," *Archives de l'Eglise d'Alsace*, n.s. 1 (1946):219–255; idem, "Die Kapuziner zu Weißenburg (1684–1791) und die katholische Restauration beiderseits der Lauter," pp. 248–84; idem, "Die Kapuziner zu Weißenburg (1684–1791) und die katholische Restauration beiderseits der Lauter. IV. Die Kapuziner Missionspfarreien in der Südpfalz (1684–1800)," pp. 135–78; idem, "Die katholische Pfarrei St.Johann zu Weißenburg im achtzehnten Jahrhundert," pp. 173–218.

25. Cuthbert, *The Capuchins*, esp. pp. 290–91. A second focus was on penitential practices. Some Capuchins, such as Père Joseph, Richelieu's able assistant, became important as diplomats.

26. GLAK 61/10951, pp. 435–37.

out of the church of St. Aegidius in Speyer in order to restore Calvinist services.[27] The Lutheran inhabitants of Speyer, however, found the barefoot preachers less threatening than the black-robed Jesuits.

In the southwest corner of the bishopric, the Capuchins also received the special support of the French. In 1682 the French founded the very important Capuchin house in Weißenburg, overriding the initial opposition of the vicar general in Speyer.[28] Capuchins from this establishment worked very actively in Catholic and Protestant villages under French control. The French wanted to Catholicize this largely Protestant area, and because of their poor relations with the Jesuits they turned to the Capuchins.

The Capuchins bent the rules of their order more easily than the Jesuits and frequently served as parish priests. Above all they worked as temporary priests when a parish came vacant due to the death or transfer of its priest. Furthermore, the Capuchins eagerly served in parishes in periods of crisis when the shortage of priests became acute. Consequently they were a great help in the 1690s. The villagers always appreciated the ministrations of a priest in times of trouble.[29]

The parish priests and the villagers counted on the Capuchins to assist them with special services. Thus when the villagers of Langenbrücken organized a votive procession in 1713, they asked a Capuchin father to accompany them.[30] The Capuchins also gave special services in rural parishes on major feast days, especially in the eighteenth century.[31] All these activities meant that the Capuchins were regularly seen in the villages of the bishopric. It is important then to examine the kind of Catholicism they emphasized.

The Capuchins favored and promoted those aspects of Tridentine Catholicism that were most amenable to the traditional communal religion of the rural population. These practices included votive processions and important local festivals, when the Capuchins came to the villages to assist overworked parish priests. Because they appeared in the villages either on special occasions or as temporary replacements, the Capuchins rarely had the opportunity to effect long-term changes in popular religious practice. In fact, some parish priests complained that the fathers disrupted their efforts to impose discipline on the villagers. The Capuchins, for example, visited the

27. LASp. D2/754.
28. Sieffert, "Les capucins à Wissembourg," pp. 222–27.
29. Manz, *Die Kapuziner*, pp. 90–111.
30. GLAK 229/57754, pp. 171–191.
31. Manz, *Die Kapuziner*, pp. 91–95.

sick, performed baptisms and weddings, and heard confessions in Philippsburg. Although these activities could lighten the work load of a priest, they also gave the people a way to work around the parish framework and avoid the discipline of the parish priest.[32] It was one of the central goals of the Counter-Reformation to stop this sort of irregular pastoral work.

The most important contribution of the Capuchins was the revival and promotion of local shrines. In 1602 Bishop Eberhard proposed that the Capuchins be installed at four different pilgrimage sanctuaries in the bishopric. Although Eberhard never implemented this plan, the Capuchins' first and most important friary was at the Marian shrine at Wagheusel. In Bruchsal, using pieces of the True Cross donated by the bishop, the Capuchins organized and promoted monthly services in honor of the Passion. After 1675 these ceremonies attracted processions from rural parishes.[33] By 1700 several shrines were very popular, attracting large crowds on feast days. The Capuchins preached, heard confessions, and gave communion on these occasions.

The various activities of the Capuchins did little to bring a more disciplined and individualistic piety to the countryside. Indeed, the pastoral work of the fathers, both in the villages and especially at the shrines, hindered the efforts of the parish priests to discipline their parishioners. The Capuchins, by hearing the confessions and giving communion on feast days, prevented the Church from firmly tying the population to the rural parish. Instead, the Capuchins kept alive some of the variety of traditional Catholicism.

The popularity of the Capuchins and the decline of the Jesuits after 1650 were telling signs of the changing style of the Counter-Reformation in the Bishopric of Speyer. The focus of Catholic Reform shifted further away from the emphases of the Jesuits: discipline of the common people and the education of the Catholic elite. More traditional than the Jesuits, the Capuchins had a strong preference for work with the "common people." At the same time, they were activist priests and therefore did not acquire the negative reputation of the older monastic orders such as the Cistercians and Benedictines. The Capuchins fell somewhere between the new, austere Catholicism represented by the Jesuits, and the old orders, which the population had long considered neglectful, parasitic, and useless. The Capu-

32. GLAK 61/11269, p. 9; GLAK 61/11270, pp. 136–37.
33. Manz, *Die Kapuziner,* pp. 5–9, 116–20.

chins viewed popular religion with more sympathy and understanding than the most stringent Counter-Reformers, and it was this sympathy that dominated the Catholic Church in the late seventeenth century.

The Growth of Confessional Conflict

The progress of Catholic consciousness in the Bishopric of Speyer led to an increase in conflicts with the Protestants, especially in the city of Speyer. Tensions rose after 1650, as both the clergy and the city government struggled to resolve a series of new legal problems in an effort to restore the traditional balance in the relationship between the city and the clergy.[34] This approach succeeded until the total destruction of Speyer in 1689. After 1700, however, when the city was resettled after a ten-year abandonment, confessional tensions became a serious problem. These new stresses can be traced to both a growing Catholic assertiveness and a revival of Lutheran militancy.

The new tensions reflected the desire of each confession to set itself apart from the other. This trend was not unique to Speyer. As both Paul Warmbrunn and Etienne François have emphasized, confessional lines within German cities were firmly drawn only after 1650. The peace treaties stabilized religious frontiers, and within divided imperial cities both religions gained in security. In cities such as Augsburg and Speyer, permanent religious divisions led to relatively peaceful coexistence but also a "mania for differentiation," that is, a growing desire to emphasize differences in religious practice and belief.[35] This growing confessional consciousness led to new conflicts in the city of Speyer and to a shift away from the legal and economic disputes that had traditionally divided the Catholic clergy and Lutheran citizens.[36]

The city of Speyer continued to decline in economic and political importance after the Thirty Years' War. Frequent wars and the city's position near the French frontier hastened this decline. After the French burned the city in 1689, Speyer lay uninhabited for ten years,

---

34. See Chapter 4.
35. Warmbrunn, *Zwei Konfessionen in einer Stadt,* esp. pp. 401–5; François, "De l'uniformité à la tolérance," esp. pp. 787–89; Peter Zschunke, *Konfession und Alltag in Oppenheim. Beiträge zur Geschichte von Bevölkerung und Gesellschaft einer gemischtkonfessionellen Kleinstadt in der frühen Neuzeit* (Wiesbaden: Franz Steiner Verlag, 1984), esp. chap. 2.4.
36. See Chapter 4 for more on the Imperial City of Speyer.

its citizens and clergy scattered across Germany. Yet the remarkable feature of the history of Speyer was the stability of its urban institutions, traditions, and social structures. After 1650 and again after 1700, the inhabitants rebuilt the city while avoiding major institutional or social changes.[37] This continuity characterized relations between the city and the clergy as well.

During the period from 1650 to 1689, the Catholic clergy and the Lutheran city government maintained cordial relations. In times of crisis, for example during the plague of 1666, the clergy cooperated closely with the magistrates. On this occasion the clergy agreed to help keep foreigners out of the city and made special contributions to the hospital for the victims of the plague.[38] At other times, the Cathedral Chapter tried to rein in the most combative Catholic preachers in the city in order to prevent problems with the Protestants.[39]

Of course, confrontations between the Catholics and the Protestants did occur. As before 1620, these disputes generally revolved around the long-standing issues of the legal immunities of the clergy, their economic privileges, and their right to buy and sell property in the city. Even small incidents could trigger jurisdictional or legal conflicts. In one instance in 1678, the city council complained to the Cathedral Chapter that clergymen were shooting guns in the evenings, that some canons were storing large amounts of hay in their houses, creating a fire hazard, and that one canon (perhaps under the influence of wine) had threatened a city gatekeeper with a knife.[40] Because of the clergy's immunity from the city's legal jurisdiction, the Rat had to deal with these concerns through the Cathedral Chapter. Of course the magistrates always sought to close gaps in their jurisdiction, causing further trouble with the clergy.[41]

Tensions ran especially high during the 1650s, as the city began to recover from the war.[42] There were new disputes over the Rachtung, the treaty that regulated the relationship between the city and the clergy. In 1650 and 1665, the city council proposed to amend this treaty by adding a clause that nullified any part of the agreement that

37. Wolfgang Hartwich, "Speyer von 1620 bis 1814," in *Geschichte der Stadt Speyer*, esp. p. 64.
38. GLAK 61/10974a, pp. 372, 423, 530, 534, 542, 591.
39. GLAK 61/10973, pp. 22–23.
40. GLAK 61/10975, pp. 430r–430v.
41. Some jurisdictional disputes had a religious component, such as a conflict in 1657 about the right of Catholics to light fires on St. John's night, a tradition Speyer Lutherans considered "pagan" and dangerous (GLAK 61/10973, pp. 151–54, 156, 161).
42. Refugees, often Catholic peasants from around Speyer, stayed longer in the city than the townspeople would have liked (GLAK 61/10973, pp. 241–42).

violated the Peace of Westphalia. The clergy refused to accept this *reservatio*, fearing any change in the traditional Rachtung. The matter was laid to rest only when the two sides agreed to disagree, with the clergy swearing to the Rachtung without the disputed clause.[43] Yet the signing of these two Rachtungen also demonstrates the overwhelming desire of both Protestants and Catholics to restore order and balance. Just as they had done before the Thirty Years' War, both sides sought legalistic solutions and safeguards for their position in the divided city.

During the recovery period after 1700, however, this brittle but long-standing consensus between the Protestant and Catholic elites broke down. Religious militancy among both Catholics and Protestants added a new explosive factor to confessional relations in Speyer and compounded the inevitable social and material problems associated with rebuilding the city from the ground up. The experience of exile, the construction of a large and expensive Lutheran church, and increased Catholic ritual activity all contributed to increased confessional conflict. These tensions would peak in 1716 when an "army" of Catholic peasants invaded Speyer.

The inhabitants of Speyer began returning to their city in 1699. Most of the Lutheran citizens had fled to the Protestant cities of Frankfurt and Strasbourg. The episcopal government had moved to Frankfurt and later to Kirrweiler, in the Catholic countryside near Speyer. Many of the canons resided in various episcopal cities, especially since many were members of other chapters. Both Catholics and Protestants spent the ten years in environments less diverse and more confessionally contentious than Speyer, and this factor certainly influenced them after they returned.

Catholics and Lutherans became increasingly conscious of their differences, and the distinctions were cultural as well as purely religious. Etienne François, comparing the libraries of Protestants and Catholics in Speyer in the eighteenth century, finds that over 80 percent of all books were religious, and Protestant libraries were generally larger.[44] Protestant readers had books that emphasized individual and personal religion, with a special focus on reading the scripture. Catholic reading materials were full of images and visual scenes. Catholics also decorated their houses with a variety of pious objects and pictures while Lutheran residences were bare of visible

---

43. GLAK 61/10974a, pp. 375–76, 377–82. See also GLAK 61/10977, pp. 27v–29r. This is the Rachtung negotiations of 1680.
44. François, "De l'uniformité à la tolérance," pp. 793–94.

religious articles. Two hundred years after the Reformation, a cultural gulf was developing between Protestants and Catholics; and this gulf, according to François, now overshadowed social and economic differences.

The Lutherans of Speyer demonstrated their dominance of the city by giving top priority to the construction of the first exclusively Lutheran church in Speyer, the Church of the Trinity (*Dreifaltigkeitskirche*), during the rebuilding of the city. Erected within sight of the badly damaged Cathedral and opened on the bicentennial of the Reformation, the new church was unquestionably an affront to the Catholics.[45] It was, however, the new Catholic assertiveness that caused the most trouble in Speyer.

This heightened Catholic consciousness manifested itself in religious processions, which became a growing challenge to the Lutheran rulers. The processions, especially those on Good Friday, on Corpus Christi, and during Rogation week, were also visible signs of the concurrent Catholic religious revival in the countryside around Speyer. Catholic peasants, in fact, came into the city to participate in processions, especially on Ascension Day when the inhabitants of nine surrounding villages converged on the Cathedral.[46] The presence of large numbers of peasants in the city made the processions especially tense events.

Of course Catholic processions had always taken place in Speyer.[47] After 1700, however, they became larger, more ostentatious, and more confrontational. Also, the Catholics added some new processions in this period. The Capuchins held a new procession from their friary to the convent of St. Clara because their church had been destroyed by the French and they held Easter services at the convent church. Even after the Capuchin church was repaired, the friars processed to St. Clara for Good Friday services, claiming that they liked the organ there.[48] The Rat protested this "innovation," suspecting that the Capuchins wanted to extend their influence in the city.

The Lutheran city fathers tried to restrict Catholic processions. On the Wednesday of Rogation week, 1717, the Rat ordered the town watch to close Worms gate, preventing the procession from leaving the city to go to the St. Clara convent in the suburbs. A brawl erupted at the gate, during which several canons forced the doors open.[49] The

45. Hartwich, "Speyer von 1620 bis 1814," p. 61. Before the Dreifaltigkeitskirche was built, the Lutherans had used several monastic churches in Speyer.
46. St.A.Sp. 1A/347/9.
47. St.A.Sp. 1A/347/1, 1A/347/2, 1A/347/3, 1A/347/4.
48. St.A.Sp. 1A/347/6, pp. 3r–4v.
49. LASp. D2/455. This is a Catholic pamphlet describing the events.

city fathers no doubt feared the involvement of Catholic peasants, who had gathered to join the procession at the city walls. The Catholic clergy claimed this procession was traditional, but it had probably been dormant since the Reformation. In 1718 the clergy organized seven large processions during the months of April and May alone. These culminated in three Rogation week processions, including a huge Ascension Day procession involving hundreds of Catholic villagers.[50]

The great frequency of Catholic ritual activity made the Lutherans very nervous; large gatherings of any kind threatened an early modern city. Other issues also caused tensions between Catholics and Lutherans in this period. All groups were on their guard against violations of the Rachtung during the rebuilding. The Jesuits also had some success converting Protestant citizens after 1708, and such conversions always increased tensions, as did the election in 1711 of a resident bishop, Heinrich Hartard von Rollingen.[51] The city council even objected to the pictures and statues that Catholic inhabitants built into their newly restored houses.[52]

Finally, the so-called Speyer Peasants' War of 1716 damaged confessional relations within the city. This rather pathetic conflict took place between the impoverished city and the equally poor Bishop Rollingen.[53] In violation of tradition, the octogenarian bishop wanted to be free to reside in Speyer and enter and leave the city as he pleased. At the same time, there were serious boundary disputes between the city and some neighboring Catholic villages. When a legal resolution of these two conflicts failed, several thousand peasants stormed Speyer and occupied the city on and off for two months. Some violence broke out when the peasants occupied the streets, and it is not clear how much control Rollingen had over this "army." The bishop tried unsuccessfully to use the occupation to coerce 100,000 gulden from the city, as well as the right to reside in the city. After the intervention of imperial representatives, the peasants finally left.

The meaning of the Speyer Peasants' War is a matter of some debate. Although economic and legal disputes were involved, it appears that religious issues and the long-standing conflicts between city and countryside led to the "war." The peasants around Speyer had exploited the ten-year abandonment of the city to encroach on

---

50. St.A.Sp. 1A/347/9.
51. Remling II, pp. 609–12.
52. St.A.Sp. 1A/347/7, p. 3r.
53. Remling II, pp. 612–20; Hartwich, "Speyer von 1620 bis 1814," pp. 64–65; Johan Christian Lünig, *Continuatio spicilegii Ecclesiastici des Teutschen Reichsarchivs* (Leipzig, 1720), 708–10.

the townspeople's property. Furthermore, the peasants sensed the poverty and weakness of the city in the years after 1700, and this awareness no doubt increased their resentment of the special privileges and political independence of the urban dwellers. Religion was also an important factor. The Catholic peasants around Speyer had become increasingly aware of the confessional gulf between the Lutheran city and the Catholic countryside. The elderly Bishop Rollingen was well known in the bishopric, having served as vicar general for over fifty years, and was an important symbol to the villagers. These factors all contributed to the violence in 1716.

To the extent that it was a confessional conflict, the Peasants' War demonstrates the potential for religious strife in the early 1700s. After 1716 the Lutheran city government was especially reluctant to allow Catholic peasants into the city for religious festivals and processions, and thereby further inflamed confessional passions. The peasant invasion highlighted the sad condition of the once-proud imperial city, but above all, the "war" was a sign of Catholic confidence after 1700. The Catholics were no longer on the defensive in this region.

All the disputes in Speyer are also evidence of a Catholic revival, and the focus on processions in the city indicates that the religious renewal was more traditional than Tridentine. Friction between Protestants and Catholics arose over the popular revival of the Corpus Christi, Good Friday, and Rogation week processions, and not over militant anti-Protestant sermons or aggressive efforts of the bishop to assert control in the city. This revival of traditional Catholicism and the simultaneous development of Catholic consciousness were even more marked in the countryside.

The Development of Catholic Consciousness

A vital traditional religiosity and a strong communal church constituted the foundations of Catholic consciousness in the Bishopric of Speyer. As we have seen, the weakness of the Counter-Reformation allowed these aspects of local Catholicism to remain important. Church reformers never broke the control of village communes over the rural parishes, and this failure made it difficult for ecclesiastical authorities or parish priests to bring Tridentine Catholicism—that is, tighter control over the laity, a more individually focused piety, and a rejection of many traditional practices—to the people of the bishopric.

Historians have begun to recognize the role of both traditional religion and communalism in the development of confessional consciousness. Hsia has pointed out that "Tridentine Catholicism . . . created moments of synthesis between official and popular religiosity."[54] This synthesis gave Catholicism an especially powerful tool for creating and strengthening popular attachment to the Church. Catholic authorities revived pilgrimages, encouraged eucharistic piety and the Marian cult, and reorganized traditional confraternities.[55] It was precisely these traditional aspects of baroque Catholicism that appealed to the villagers of the Bishopric of Speyer.

Part of the attraction of Catholicism was its close links to traditional religion. What gave it a strong institutional basis was its ties to the village commune.[56] In the region around Speyer, the communal church was Catholic, local, and popular. This sort of Catholic communalism was possible because of the weakness of the state, a condition that existed in much of southern and western Germany. The state and the Counter-Reformation did not coopt the communal leaders, as the Habsburg government had in Upper Austria in the 1620s and 1630s.[57] The contrast between the Bishopric of Speyer and the region around Salzburg is also instructive. In Salzburg, in the seventeenth century, the traditionalist rural communes turned to Protestantism to resist the encroachments of the archbishop's government, leading to the brutal expulsion of the Protestant population in 1731–32.[58] In Speyer, by contrast, the people did not associate Catholicism with a centralizing state, nor did they view the clergy as agents of the state. Instead, the communes controlled the village parish.

These communes, not the Church authorities or the parish priests, encouraged the development of a strong confessional consciousness among the Catholic people of the bishopric, not to resist the encroachment of a centralizing Protestant state, but to maintain communal unity during the disruptions of the second half of the seventeenth century. The identification of the village commune with Catholic practice led to the exclusion of non-Catholics from the villages. This close link between Catholicism and the commune was

54. Hsia, Social Discipline in the Reformation, p. 151.

55. Ibid., pp. 154–62; Châtellier, Tradition chrétienne et renouveau catholique, part 4, chap. 5.

56. Châtellier, Tradition chrétienne et renouveau catholique, p. 73.

57. Hsia, Social Discipline in the Reformation, pp. 146–47; Rebel, Peasant Classes, chap. 8. Rebel discusses political, social, and economic conditions, not religion.

58. Hsia, Social Discipline in the Reformation, pp. 63–69; Ortner, Reformation, katholische Reform und Gegenreformation im Erzstift Salzburg, esp. part 3.

232 The Counter-Reformation in the Villages

new after 1650. Before the Thirty Years' War, in violation of princely edicts, Protestants had lived in Catholic villages as journeymen and servants and sometimes as citizens. After 1650, however, over 90 percent of the many immigrants absorbed by the villages around Speyer came from Catholic parts of Germany.

A second indication of growing Catholic consciousness was the vitality of popular religion, especially after 1700. Traditional collective practices, especially processions and local pilgrimages, distinguished this religious revival. The nature of this revival is a clear indication of the communal and traditional nature of eighteenth-century Catholicism in the middle Rhine valley.

Confessional Consciousness in the Villages

It is difficult to document the changing mentality of the villagers. As Bernard Vogler notes "The state of [one's] soul leaves few written traces."[59] One sign, however, of a new confessional awareness is that the villagers excluded Protestants from their villages after 1650. In 1697 Johann Philipp Burckhardt, the suffragan bishop, reported to Rome that the number of Protestants in Catholic areas was declining.[60] Burckhardt could not explain this development, except to point to an episcopal ordinance forbidding Protestant pastors from entering Catholic territory. The real reason behind increasing Catholic uniformity was the unwillingness of villagers to accept Protestant immigrants.

The Bishopric of Speyer had always taken in many immigrants from poorer parts of Germany. In the period before the Thirty Years' War, most immigrants to the Rhine valley came from Swabia, Switzerland, and the neighboring Protestant territories. Between 1650 and 1720 a large number of newcomers came to the war-torn bishopric, especially in the 1650s and 1660s and again in the 1690s. In this period, the immigrants were almost all from Catholic regions of the empire.

An examination of lists of citizens (bürger) from several Speyer villages shows that after 1650 more than half of the heads of households were immigrants (see table 3). By the 1690s, after the devastating French invasion, the number of native citizens fell to less than 30 percent. Throughout the period, there were very few Protestant im-

59. Vogler, *La vie religieuse en pays rhénan*, p. 1243.
60. Hermann Tüchle, "Die Bistümer Worms und Speyer in den Nuntiaturberichten an die Propagandakongregation von 1697," *Blätter für pfälzische Kirchengeschichte und religiöse Volkskunde* 40 (1973):81.

Table 3. Number of bürger, adult heads of household, by place of origin

	Bauerbach 1683	Jölingen 1699	Wöschbach 1699	Bauerbach 1705
Natives	30 (47%)	27 (30%)	5 (22%)	13 (24%)
Immigrants from Bisophric of Speyer	7 (10%)	10 (11%)	5 (22%)	4 (7%)
Immigrants from Catholic areas	14 (22%)	32 (35%)	4 (17%)	24 (45%)
Immigrants from Protestant areas	6 (9%)	6 (6%)	1 (4%)	6 (11%)
Unknown	8 (12%)	16 (18%)	8 (35%)	7 (13%)
TOTAL	65	91	23	54

Sources: GLAK 61/5104 (Bauerbach), and GLAK 61/15542 (Jöhlingen and Wöschbach).

migrants. Even those who came to the bishopric from Swabia and Switzerland now came from the Catholic parts of those regions. Swabians, for example, were from the territories west of Augsburg rather than from nearer, but Lutheran, Württemberg.

The result was that almost all villages in the Hochstift Speyer were completely Catholic. The visitation report from 1701–2 indicates that Protestants lived in only twenty-four of the eighty-three villages visited, and in all but four villages these were isolated individuals. The visitation of 1718–21 confirms this record.[61] This situation is particularly remarkable given the intermingling of Protestant and Catholic villages in the area and the contrasting situation in the neighboring Electoral Palatinate.

By the early eighteenth century, there were large Catholic minorities in quite a few villages of the predominantly Calvinist Palatinate. The tolerant policy of Elector Karl Ludwig after the Thirty Years' War helped create religious diversity in the Palatinate, as did the pro-Catholic policy of the electors after 1685. The bishops of Speyer, by contrast, did not officially allow non-Catholics in their territory.[62] Yet the bishop's decrees were not the reason for the absence of Protestants in Catholic villages. These decrees had little effect in the sixteenth century and did not prevent small numbers of Protestants from living in the bishop's villages in the eighteenth century.[63] We have seen how ineffectual the government of the bish-

61. Concerning the visitation of 1701–2 see GLAK 61/11267. Concerning the visitation of 1718–21 see GLAK 61/11271 and LASp. D/2/306/6.
62. Stamer III/2, p. 37; *Sammlung der Hochfürstlich-Speierischen Gesetze und Landesverordnungen*, part 1, pp. 66–67, 71.
63. Stamer III/2, pp. 37–39.

opric was in enforcing ordinances opposed by the villagers. The exclusion of non-Catholics in the late seventeenth century was possible only with the support of village communes.

Catholicism became a vital part of the group identity of the villagers. This identity meant loyalty to certain religious practices as well as exclusion and dislike of non-Catholics. The popularity of one such practice, pilgrimages to the shrines at Wagheusel and St. Michaelsberg, grew in the first decades of the eighteenth century. These pilgrimages were community oriented, in that the villagers proceeded to the shrines as a group, carrying crosses and flags.[64] Processions, which were often an affront to neighboring Protestants, served the purpose of reinforcing communal unity and asserting the village's loyalty to Catholic practices.

The connection between Catholic consciousness and communal unity was an important one. The turnover in population in the wake of the wars put a strain on rural society. In order to assimilate large numbers of immigrants, the communes turned to Catholicism as a common tradition, especially after 1689, when a majority of the population was of "foreign" origin. At times communal leaders explicitly articulated the need for religious unity and discipline. As early as 1680, the gemeinde of Riedseltz worried that it needed a good priest because there were so many immigrants and children in the village.[65] Like many princes in this period, the local peasant leaders considered religion an effective device for integrating and socializing newcomers.

The influx of newcomers from all over Catholic Germany had a profound effect on life in the villages. The immigrants brought different customs with them and undoubtedly widened the horizons of local Catholics. Part of the growing confidence of Catholics in the Bishopric of Speyer can probably be traced to the immigrants from other, more militantly Catholic regions of Germany. The natives, however, kept control of the commune and perpetuated local institutions and religious traditions. In Jöhlingen in 1699, for example, seven of the twelve members of the village council were natives, including the four senior councilors.[66] This urge to promote village unity combined with the strong traditional Catholicism of the region to bring about a period of active popular Catholicism.

64. Schaab, "Die Wiederherstellung des Katholizismus," p. 202; Manz, *Die Kapuziner*, pp. 121–22.
65. ADBR 19 J 396, no. 7.
66. GLAK 61/15542.

The Vitality of Traditional Catholicism

Catholicism as practiced by the inhabitants of the Bishopric of Speyer remained strongly traditional at the turn of the eighteenth century. Tridentine reforms had effected some changes but were most successful when they involved revitalizing and encouraging traditional practices. Meanwhile, Church authorities made feeble attempts to discipline the laity, abolish popular practices, or wipe out "superstitions." Ironically, it was the inability of episcopal officials and parish priests to enforce Tridentine decrees against popular religious "abuses" that made it possible for the local Church to avoid alienating the population and helped keep rural Catholicism vital.

Although bishops published some general ordinances designed to keep public order in their territory, these regulations had little impact on local religion. It is instructive that the *Polizei-Ordnung* of 1653 did not regulate the religious practice of the bishop's subjects.[67] In 1703 a new ordinance included five clauses ordering catechism classes, yearly communion, respect for Sundays and holidays, and restrictions on dancing among the youth.[68] Only at this late date did Catholic authorities bring secular power to bear on the religious practice of the villagers.

An edict promulgated for the district around Lauterburg in 1700 indicates the failure of official measures. The edict stated that there was "great disorder" in religious practice and ordered punishments for those who worked on Sundays, drank during processions, danced without the priest's permission, and failed to send their children to catechism class. Special fines were instituted for wedding parties who arrived late and/or drunk at the church and for women who gave birth without confessing and taking communion beforehand.[69] The author lamented the widespread nature of these problems. The Counter-Reformation had not changed lay behavior significantly, even in the basic areas.

The inability of the Church to regulate behavior in the villages was in part the result of wartime disruption. During the period of peace between 1650 and 1674, some disciplinary measures were actually enforced. At the Jöhlingen Vogtsgericht in 1652, 1659, and 1662, officials of the Cathedral Chapter fined villagers for blasphemy, ab-

67. *Sammlung der Hochfürstlich-Speierischen Gesetze und Landesverordnungen*, part 1, pp. 41–45.
68. GLAK 78/734.
69. ADBR G5813, 24 April 1700.

sence from services, and working on forbidden days.[70] As visitation reports show, however, these measures were sporadic and ineffective.

The episcopal visitors focused their attention on two areas of lay behavior. The first was the population's firm belief in the power of blessings (*Segen*), magical cures, and other "old customs," all labeled "superstitions" by the visitors. The second was a general lack of discipline and morality among the villagers, characterized by regular drunkenness and frequent violation of the sanctity of holy days.

The struggle against what Delumeau has called "the world of witchcraft" was a significant aspect of the Counter-Reformation.[71] The records of the visitations indicate that the people of the Bishopric of Speyer continued to believe in a variety of magical practices into the eighteenth century. The Jesuits reported that the bishopric was especially "fertile" in such practices.[72] In some villages in 1683, the peasants demanded that the priest bless crops and animals.[73] The Jesuit visitors disapproved of this practice but were even more distressed to find cunning folk and healers in many areas. These people were often old women known for their knowledge of medicinal plants as well as special blessings and prayers. The visitors warned the women to avoid any practice of "magic."[74] Most shocking of all was a traditional cure in Untergrombach, which required that the patient say a sacrilegious prayer and walk around the church altar naked.[75]

Although such "paganism" concerned the visitors, who hoped the priests would teach the catechism so the peasants "might forget their rustic customs and forest morals," their greatest concern was with the widespread immoral behavior of the population.[76] This emphasis reflected the focus of the Tridentine Church on the behavior of the faithful and the effort of reformers of all confessions to encourage self-discipline among the laity.[77] Excessive drinking was an enduring and almost universal problem in the bishopric, especially in the villages along the Palatinate *Weinstraße*. Even the experienced Jesuit

70. GLAK 61/15539, 61/15541.
71. Delumeau, *Catholicism between Luther and Voltaire*, pp. 161–75. See also Keith Thomas, *Religion and the Decline of Magic.*
72. Duhr III, p. 673; ARSJ Rh.Sup.34 I, p. 169v.
73. GLAK 61/11263, p. 26.
74. Ibid., pp. 16, 18, 33, 36.
75. Ibid., p. 7.
76. Ibid., p. 29: "Rusticam illam contumaciam ac sylvestres mores dediscant." The fathers made this comment in reference to the villagers of Forst. The pun "sylvestres mores" was probably intentional.
77. Bossy, *Christianity in the West, 1400–1700*, chap. 7; Delumeau, *Catholicism between Luther and Voltaire*, p. 179.

visitors of 1683, Wilhelm Osburg and Martin Metz, appeared surprised at the frequency of drinking parties in the villages. The visitors found regular gambling, occasional cases of adultery, and other evidence of sexual misconduct. The young men and women of Odenheim, for example, met secretly in the forest near the village.[78] These timeless abuses, however, did not upset the visitors as much as some local customs.

The *Weiberfastnacht* (women's carnival) took place on Ash Wednesday, that is, on the first day of Lent after Carnival itself had ended. On this day women controlled the village, chased after men, and drank heavily. In 1719 the gemeinde of Rauenberg subsidized this tradition by providing three *ohm* of wine (about 360 liters), which the women consumed. During the "disorder" that followed, the women badly beat one male villager.[79] In the village of Wiesental, the women sold a tree from the community woods and drank the proceeds. In some places, women continued carousing on the following Thursday and organized a feast on the first Sunday of Lent.[80]

The *Weiberfastnacht* was firmly in the carnival tradition of "world turned upside down" and fits the pattern of what Natalie Davis has called "women on top."[81] Sexual roles were reversed, and women temporarily dominated the village. Communes in the Bishopric of Speyer supported this tradition and, whatever disruption of normal relations it caused, there were never any requests from the villages to change or forbid the "women's carnival." The episcopal visitors, however, were appalled at the "insolent," "perverse," and "frenzied" behavior of the women.[82] The general moral indulgence and especially the sexual license accorded women at this event had a special resonance for these clerics at a time when the Church emphasized the dangers of sexual permissiveness.

Of course the visitors also focused on *Weiberfastnacht* because it violated the sanctity of Lent; the attempt to abolish this tradition was part of the general effort to enforce the sanctity of Sundays and holidays. Like all endeavors to instill discipline in the population, it was only partially successful. By the early eighteenth century, few Catholics worked in the fields on Sundays and holidays. Other officially forbidden practices, however, were quite common. The vil-

---

78. GLAK 61/11263, p. 23.
79. GLAK 61/11271, p. 69.
80. Ibid., pp. 74, 80; GLAK 61/11263, pp. 30, 32, 33, 34, 36, 37, 42; GLAK 61/11265/2, pp. 178, 229–30.
81. Natalie Davis, "Women on Top," in her *Popular Culture in Early Modern France*. See also Burke, *Popular Culture in Early Modern Europe*, esp. chap. 7.
82. GLAK 61/11263, pp. 37, 41.

lagers often continued Saturday night drinking parties into Sunday morning, dances continued to be held on Sundays, and some people ate meat on Fridays and during Lent.

Secular and ecclesiastic authorities in Speyer remained concerned with disciplining the laity but took little effective action. The *Weiberfastnacht*, for example, was as entrenched in the region in 1720 as it had been in 1683. Ineffective against and perhaps tolerant of many aspects of popular culture, Catholic authorities in fact supported much of popular religion. Parish priests, the Capuchins, and the episcopal hierarchy participated in and encouraged processions, pilgrimages to local shrines, and the Eucharistic cult.

Although such practices had the support of the official Church, the village communes organized and controlled them. In the villages of Rheinhausen and Oberhausen, for example, the parish priest complained that the villagers held unlicensed processions on four different occasions during the year. Even officially sanctioned events, such as the yearly procession to the cathedral in Speyer on Ascension Day, included drinking and a general lack of order.[83] Villagers organized their own votive processions, which received varying degrees of support from the Church. Some of these were one-time events, arranged in response to the plague, drought, crop failure, and so on. Others, such as the St. Sebastian procession in Langenbrücken, were regular festivals undertaken despite the opposition of the parish priest. Still others, like the St. Urban festival in Ostringen, which included a procession of children carrying a statue of the saint to bless the village well, were labeled "superstitious" by the authorities.[84]

Such traditional, collective religious practices were very prominent in the villages. If one of the goals of the Counter-Reformation was, as John Bossy argues, to change the focus of Catholicism away from popular ritual, it failed completely in Speyer. Regular Catholic rituals were also very popular, and the most important of these were processions.[85] By the time of the visitation of 1683, the disruption to processions caused by the Protestant Reformation had been overcome, and Catholics participated frequently in these events. The most significant procession took place at Corpus Christi and went around the boundaries of the village. More than any other liturgical

83. GLAK 61/11265/2, pp. 176–77.
84. GLAK 61/11271, pp. 44–45, 67.
85. Bossy, *Christianity in the West, 1400–1700*, esp. the conclusion; A. D. Wright, *The Counter-Reformation: Catholic Europe and the Non-Christian World* (London: Weidenfeld and Nicolson, 1982), 15, 271.

practice, this procession linked the village commune to Catholic traditions and distinguished a Catholic from a Protestant village. By carrying the Host through the village, the Corpus Christi procession reinforced the importance of the Mass and of transubstantiation, both of which the villagers recognized as distinctively Catholic practices and beliefs. The participation of the community in these processions strengthened the villagers' Catholic identity.[86]

The popularity of the Corpus Christi processions is not the only sign of the importance of the cult of the Eucharist. Villagers always wanted a resident priest and regular services that included the Mass. The centrality of the Mass in weekly Church services was traditional, although perhaps reinforced by the stress put on it by Catholic reformers.[87] Weekly services remained, of course, vital community affairs. Baptisms, marriages, and deaths were announced, as were edicts and decrees of the bishop and his officials. Seating arrangements in the church also affirmed social divisions within the village, with the schultheiß and members of the village council sitting in the front and non-citizens standing in the back.[88]

Processions were an excellent means of joining Catholic villages together as well as of asserting the Catholic identity of each individual village. A network of regular yearly processions linked the Catholic villages of the bishopric. During Rogation week the faithful from four or five neighboring villages processed to a series of parish churches to attend services together. On the feast of St. Mark, there were often processions to neighboring churches for services as well. The processions between villages had the effect of creating and strengthening bonds between Catholic villages, sometimes at the expense of traditional ties between neighboring villages of different confessions.

These extended ties between villages are another indication of the affinity between village communes and traditional Catholicism. The loyalty of the people was to Catholic practices and the Catholic Church, not just to the local parish regardless of religion. The popularity of local shrines in the years after 1700 is a further sign of the growing Catholic consciousness. Shrines and pilgrimages had been an important aspect of medieval Christianity, especially in much of

---

86. Tackett, *Priest and Parish in 18th Century France*, pp. 202–4.

87. For traditional views of the Mass, see Chapter one. For the cult of the Eucharist see Veit and Lenhart, *Kirche und Volksfrömmigkeit*, section 2, chap. 3.

88. There were seats in churches beginning in the 1660s, and the first conflicts over seating arrangements begin in this period. Before this everyone stood during services and this problem did not exist. See GLAK 61/10974a, pp. 679v–680r, GLAK 229/57754, pp. 13r–13v.

South Germany, particularly Bavaria. The Bishopric of Speyer, however, was the home of few medieval shrines and had no ostentatious pilgrimage churches.[89] Many late medieval shrines and rural chapels fell into disuse in the early sixteenth century and remained forgotten until the Thirty Years' War. Even after 1700, most remained very local, attracting worshipers from a few surrounding villages. This was the case, for example, of the Schweinheimer Kirchel near Jockgrim. This chapel, originally dedicated to a wine saint, became in the eighteenth century a center of the Marian cult for the people of Jockgrim and a few neighboring villages.[90] Similarly, the chapels in Rülzheim and Königsbach, the latter dedicated to the wine saint Cyriacus, both attracted increasing numbers of local Catholics after the 1690s.[91]

Two shrines, however, became pilgrimage centers of some regional importance. The first of these was the chapel at St. Michaelsberg, perched on a hill overlooking the Rhine valley near the village of Untergrombach. On the feast of St. Michael, processions from all the villages in the Bruhrein region came to the chapel. After 1699 the popularity of these processions increased, as did the donations left at the chapel. In 1720 these donations had become so substantial that episcopal visitors began to examine the records of the chapel's administrators.[92]

The shrine at Wagheusel was even more popular. Wagheusel had become a customary pilgrimage destination in the fifteenth century when a miraculous picture of Mary was found in a nearby tree. The shrine declined in importance in the sixteenth century but revived after 1616, when the Capuchins took it over. Although the shrine received a steady flow of pilgrims in the seventeenth century, like St. Michaelsberg it boomed after 1700.[93] In 1704 the Capuchins reported that villagers from at least fourteen parishes had converged on the shrine on Whitsun Monday (Pfingstmontag), overwhelming the fathers and leading to general disorder.[94] In the 1720s, it became necessary to assign different groups of parishes a day during the week of Whitsun to come to Wagheusel. Despite these measures, the size of

89. Fred Weinman, *Kapellen im Bistum Speyer* (Speyer: Pilger Verlag, 1975), Foreword. On shrines and pilgrimage piety, see Lionel Rothkrug, "Popular Religion and Holy Shrines. Their Influence on the Origins of the German Reformation and Their Role in German Cultural Development," in James Obelkevich, ed., *Religion and the People, 800–1700* (Chapel Hill: University of North Carolina Press, 1979).

90. Weinman, *Kapellen im Bistum Speyer.*

91. GLAK 61/11267, pp. 50v–51v, 164r.

92. GLAK 61/11269, pp. 19–26.

93. Manz, *Die Kapuziner,* pp. 7–8, 11–17.

94. GLAK 229/108453.

crowds remained a problem.[95] The pilgrims gave extensive donations to the shrine and the Capuchin house, enabling the fathers to make a large number of loans in the villages around Wagheusel.[96]

The popularity of these shrines has several important aspects. First, the shrines remained local. Even Wagheusel and St. Michaelsberg attracted Catholics only from a radius of perhaps thirty kilometers, reflecting the parochial nature of Catholicism in the Bishopric of Speyer. Second, the shrines grew in favor in the period of crisis after the French invasion of 1688–89. In the decades from 1690 to 1720, the local population struggled first to recover from the invasion and then to absorb large numbers of immigrants. Group pilgrimages to local shrines for the purpose of prayer and appeal for divine support provided considerable impetus to this process and to the development of Catholic consciousness. Finally, although most people went to the shrines in fairly raucous village processions, the chapels also offered the individual pilgrim the opportunity for private prayer, confession, and communion. Pilgrimage sites could be used to encourage the individualist piety of the Tridentine Church as well as the communal religion of traditional Catholicism.[97]

Counter-Reformation piety, however, had little resonance in the countryside of the Bishopric of Speyer before 1720. The visitations from the early eighteenth century make it clear that catechism classes remained unpopular and neglected in many villages. In the absence of regular catechism classes, it was difficult to break the hold of traditional Catholicism and transform the lay religious practice. The history of the sacrament of confession in the bishopric shows the failure of the Counter-Reformation in this area. It was a major goal of the Tridentine Church to encourage frequent confession and communion. Yet almost all villagers confessed and took communion only once a year, at Easter as the law required. Because so many people confessed during the last days of Lent, this rite was often perfunctory.[98] Most parishioners in fact preferred short, formal confessions; the villagers of Maikammer, for example, worried that the appointment of a local man as priest might lead to prying questions about their personal lives.[99]

Whereas the Catholicism of most villagers remained traditional,

---

95. Manz, *Die Kapuziner,* pp. 121–23.
96. GLAK 61/11269. The loans were valued at over 8000 gulden in 1721, bringing an income (at 5%) of 400 gulden.
97. See the intelligent discussion of this issue in Châtellier, *Tradition chrétienne et renouveau catholique,* book 1, part 4, chap. 5.
98. ADBR G5813, 24 April 1700.
99. LASp. D2/412/3.

new Tridentine attitudes may have penetrated to a small minority. Just such a group in the village of Ubstadt complained about the conduct of the pfarrer in that village, Sebastian Sterberich. In January 1721, a special episcopal commission went to Ubstadt to investigate the charges that Sterberich neglected services, had allowed a woman to die without last rites, and, above all, frequented the inn.[100] The commission questioned each adult male about the pfarrer. The first four witnesses, the schultheiß and three members of the village council, all testified that Sterberich was indifferent to his pastoral duties and drank frequently and excessively. The other ninety-three citizens found the priest diligent in his job and appropriate in his drinking. One villager commented that Sterberich, like everyone, ought to be allowed to enjoy an occasional glass of wine.

The vast majority of the villagers, then, responded as their ancestors had done in the late sixteenth century to similar questions. They expected the priest to obey the same basic moral rules they did. Those rules certainly did not forbid moderate drinking. Yet there was a small group in Ubstadt, dare we call it an elite, that had absorbed some of the ideals of the Tridentine reform. These men held their priest, and perhaps themselves, to higher standards of behavior than those of their other neighbors. We do not know, of course, if Sterberich's enemies might have cynically accused him of abuses that would attract the attention of episcopal officials. In any case, if the villagers did not follow a Tridentine model of behavior, at least they knew what that model was.

There are a few other indications that some new forms of piety were gaining acceptance. In 1704 the priest in Malsch, Sebastian Wolff, organized a new confraternity of the Rosary in his parish.[101] One year before, a 150-year-old confraternity in Herxheim was revived and rededicated to the Passion of Christ.[102] The use of the Rosary was an important part of the personal and practical piety encouraged by the Counter-Reformation, and meditative practices focusing on the life and passion of Christ were an integral part of reformed Catholic spirituality.[103] These two new confraternities are evidence of the penetration of this spirituality to the countryside, or at least of the effort of the priests to encourage it. It was probably effective to promote new forms of piety through traditional corporate institutions like confraternities.

100. GLAK 61/11271, pp. 111–33.
101. GLAK 229/63964.
102. LASp. D2/381/4.
103. H. Outram Evennett, *The Spirit of the Counter-Reformation* (Cambridge: Cambridge University Press, 1968), chap. 2.

Yet the dominant forms of Catholic piety remained traditional. Catholicism as it was historically practiced and organized in the Bishopric of Speyer was closely tied to the rural communes, and it was these communes that supported and spurred the Catholic revival in the first decades of the eighteenth century. Traditional communal practices such as processions were central to this revival and helped to integrate new immigrants and restore political and social stability in the villages. Village leaders, just like princes and city magistrates, understood the value of religion as an instrument of integration and, perhaps, as a means of domination.

Three central developments altered religious life in the Bishopric of Speyer in the first two decades of the eighteenth century. The first was the installation of a Tridentine clergy in the rural parishes. The second was the revival and vitality of traditional Catholicism in both the city of Speyer and the villages of the bishopric. The last major development was the rise of a Catholic consciousness in the population.

These three trends were by no means contradictory; indeed, they reinforced one another. Certainly the identification of the Catholic Church with traditional customs and rituals, and the close links between the village communes and these time-honored religious practices, were decisive in the development of confessional loyalty. The "new" priests, who often came to the bishopric intent on reforming traditional piety and introducing new rituals and devotions, usually found local religious practices firmly entrenched. The priests sometimes quarreled with their parishioners, but more often they turned their energies to promoting those traditional practices that offered the best opportunity to deepen and strengthen the faith of their flock. By cooperating with the villagers and by diligently and faithfully performing their duties as parish priests, these men did much to strengthen the loyalty of the villagers to the Catholic Church.

Conclusion: Local Religion, Traditional Catholicism, and the Counter-Reformation

Damian Hugo von Schönborn, bishop of Speyer from 1719 to 1743, a cardinal and member of the leading ecclesiastical family in Germany, realized early in his episcopate that the decrees of the Council of Trent were unknown to many in his bishopric.[1] In 1724 he asked Graf von Seinsheim, a Cathedral canon, to translate the reform decrees into German and comment on the extent to which they were obeyed in the Bishopric of Speyer. A fragment, with comments from Seinsheim and the cardinal, has survived.[2]

This document, titled "What, according to Trent, still needs to be reformed," reflects the view of Tridentine-minded clerics like Schönborn. For them, Catholic reform had barely touched Speyer. Schönborn was upset with the behavior of the clergy in his bishopric, the weakness of episcopal authority, the lack of regular visitations or a seminary, and the resistance of the population to Tridentine reforms. He also lamented the organizational problems of the bishopric. Full visitations were too expensive, and he wondered how other bishops accomplished them. No diocesan synod had been held in eighteen years. Without a seminary it was difficult to find good priests, and

1. Damian Hugo was the nephew of Lothar Franz von Schönborn, archbishop-elector of Mainz and the leading ecclesiastic of the late seventeenth century. Three of Damian Hugo's brothers were bishops, a fourth was a canon in five Cathedral Chapters. See Remling II, pp. 625–26.
2. GLAK 78/906 ("Was vi Tridenti annoch zu reformiren were").

because the bishop had patronage of only a fraction of the parishes, he had limited control of appointments.

The overriding theme of Schönborn's comments was the weakness of episcopal authority. The bishop, he felt, should have exclusive power to grant dispensations and absolution for major ecclesiastical crimes, to inspect nunneries and examine all novices in convents, to absolve heretics, and to decide who was permitted to preach and hear confessions in his bishopric. Episcopal authority was frail in all these matters.

Schönborn recognized that the chapters, monasteries, neighboring princes, and village communes all restricted episcopal authority. He pointed out that all the church accounts were kept by local secular officials. Even the priests appealed directly to these officials when they needed money. The bishop also understood the powerful pull of village life on the rural priests. Too many of them drank and danced at baptisms and funerals, gambled regularly, and failed to dress in clerical garb.

A churchman with international connections and broad experience, but a newcomer to Speyer, Schönborn was surprised by the situation in the bishopric. Although his judgment is a bit harsh on some matters, especially in criticizing the clergy, it provides contemporary confirmation that the impact of the Counter-Reformation was limited in this part of Germany. In Schönborn's informed opinion, Speyer compared unfavorably with other bishoprics.

Local Church historians have shared Schönborn's focus on Church reform in the Bishopric of Speyer. The history of the early modern Church in Germany is usually the story of the progress of Tridentine reform. These historians trace the failure of late fifteenth-century reform, the problems caused by the Reformation, the sad state of Catholicism in the countryside in the middle of the sixteenth century, and the gradual success of Catholic reform in the seventeenth and especially eighteenth centuries.[3] Like Schönborn, this school assesses the popularity of local Catholicism by analyzing the extent to which it met the standards of the Tridentine Church. In this view, the weakness of Tridentine reform hurt Catholicism in Speyer.

My conclusions are different. The rural population's loyalty to the Catholic Church resulted from the success of traditional Catholicism, which gave rural communes control of the local Church. The Counter-Reformation had brought changes to Speyer in the 160 years

3. Ludwig Stamer's *Kirchengeschichte der Pfalz* is the best example of this. See Stamer II, III/1, III/2.

after 1560, but the continuities in Catholic practice and Church organization were more important. In the deeply traditionalist and conservative society of early modern Germany, it was good policy to avoid rapid change. The moderation of the Counter-Reformation was, however, more than judicious strategy. Tridentine Catholicism had no social basis in this region. There was no important Catholic state that needed the organization and discipline the reformed Church could provide, nor were there any influential Catholic urban centers with an elite that favored a more personal and individual Catholicism.[4] Village life remained corporate, focused on the village, commune, and parish. The upper clergy was aristocratic and never absorbed the ideals of Tridentine Catholicism, which had threatened their autonomy and privileges. The Counter-Reformation did remake the parish clergy; but without the support of strong episcopal or state structures, the priests could not dramatically change religious life in the countryside.

The particular trajectory of Catholicism in the Bishopric of Speyer from traditional Christianity in the mid-sixteenth century to confessionally conscious Catholicism in the eighteenth century challenges some current assumptions in the field. Most important, it pulls apart several themes that are often closely linked. Perhaps least surprising is the separation of the Counter-Reformation and the state. Historians have long recognized the different interests and goals of the international Church and the national or territorial states. If some authorities have focused on the close links between church reform and state-building, others, such as Jürgen Bücking and Joachim Köhler, emphasize the tensions in this relationship.[5] In Speyer, churchmen self-consciously pursued Tridentine reform in the absence of a strong state. The lack of state support limited the progress of reform, but the Counter-Reformation also succeeded in important ways, especially by transforming the rural clergy.

More important for German history, the story of Catholicism in Speyer shows that confessionalism was not necessarily the consequence of either state policy or church reform. Instead, Catholic consciousness in the countryside around Speyer was rooted in village communalism and traditional religion. Confessionalization could,

4. It might be argued that a "Catholic elite" did exist in the city of Speyer among the members of the Imperial Chamber Court and the episcopal administration. After the court was transferred to Wetzlar in 1689, this was a tiny group. Their influence, however, probably grew in the eighteenth century, especially after the episcopal government was shifted to Bruchsal. See Hoffman, *Church and Community in the Diocese of Lyon*. He argues that the Counter-Reformation had much more appeal in the city of Lyon than in the rural parishes.

5. Köhler, *Obrigkeitliche Konfessionsänderung in Kondominaten*; Schilling, "Die Konfessionalisierung im Reich." pp. 1–45; Köhler, *Das Ringen um die tridentinische Erneuerung im Bistum Breslau*; Bücking, *Fruhabsolutismus und Kirchenreform in Tirol*.

and did, take place without the support of a centralizing state. It was a long-term process, one that took more than a century to complete. Furthermore, popular confessionalism did not develop out of the political conflicts of the period from 1555 to 1648. Distinct confessional cultures evolved slowly in the decades after the Thirty Years' War and involved persuasion as much as coercion.[6]

French historical models and methods of religious sociology have caused German historians to recognize the gradual nature of religious change at the popular level. In the first place, the mass of French diocesan studies, all of which emphasize the slow reception of Tridentine reforms, have forced German Reformation historians to look to the late sixteenth century for the permanent consequences of the Reformation.[7] Historians now recognize the importance of the "late Reformation," "second Reformation," and the Catholic Reformation—all of which contributed as much, or more, to the creation of the confessional cultures of early modern and modern Germany as did the Reformation itself.

Studies of the Counter-Reformation, especially, have drawn on French examples and the older German tradition associated with Ludwig Veit to examine the long-term impact of Tridentine reforms. Here, however, there is a danger of making church reform the exclusive cause of confessionalization. It is important to recognize instead that the relationship between popular and elite religion and traditional and reformed Catholicism was complex and dynamic. The Catholic population also participated in confessionalization, and not only to resist it. Could it be that modern historians are reluctant to find the roots of religious intolerance in the common people?

In the eighteenth century, the Catholic people of the Bishopric of Speyer did not accept elite religion, but they did not tolerate Protestants in their villages either. Instead, they promoted a popular, traditional Catholicism in the countryside, making Catholicism part of their communal identity while simultaneously defending their local autonomy against outside forces. This self-conscious defense of local autonomy makes it clear that the peasants of the Bishopric of Speyer were neither passive "subjects" (*Untertanen*) of the rising state, nor simply objects of Church policy, but rather active and decisive participants in the development of local Catholicism.

6. Hsia, *Social Discipline in the Reformation*, p. 89.
7. For French studies, see the Introduction. Other useful Reformation studies include the following: Strauss, *Luther's House of Learning* and Abray, *The People's Reformation*. See also James Kittelson, "The Confessional Age: The Late Reformation in Germany," in Steven Ozment, ed. *Reformation Europe, A Guide to Research* (St. Louis, 1982), pp. 361–81.

Bibliography

Unpublished Sources

*Archives Departementales du Bas-Rhin,
Strasbourg (ADRB)*

Serie G
   Rural Chapter of Weißenburg: G5812 to G5819, G5847 to G5854.
Serie J
   19 J: Ordre Teutonique (Village of Riedseltz): 19 J 365, 19 J 395 to 19 J 399, 19 J
   405 to 19 J 409, 19 J 429, 19 J 435.
   12 J: Exchanges with GLAK (Weißenburg, City and Chapter): 12 J 1648, 12 J
   1656.

Archivum Romanum Societas Jesu, Rome (ARSJ)

Fondo Gesuitico-Collegio
   Speyer College: Busta N.222/1608
Fondo Vecchio Compagna
   Prov. Rheni et Rheni Inferioris
      Rh.Inf.1–4 (Epistolae Generalium, 1576–1610).
      Rh.Inf.37 (Catalogi Brevis, 1565–1639).
      Rh.Inf.48 (Historia, 1578–1631).
   Prov. Rheni Superioris
      Rh.Sup.2 (Epistolae Generalium, 1646–64).
      Rh.Sup.8 (Catalogi Trienales, 1661, 1669).
      Rh.Sup.12 (Catalogi Trienales, 1685).
      Rh.Sup.26 (Catalogi Brevis, 1641–1740).
      Rh.Sup.29–35 (Historia, 1575–1716).

Badisches Generallandesarchiv Karlsruhe (GLAK)

Abteilung 42: Urkunden
Specialia: Rohrbach (no. 4736), Bruchsal (no. 2491).
Abteilung 61: Protokolle
Minutes of the *Vogtsgericht* in Bauerbach, 1621–1756: 61/5104.
Minutes of the *Ritterstift* in Bruchsal, 1595–1710: 61/5341 to 61/5346.
Minutes of the *Vogtsgericht* in Oberöwisheim, 1657–1705: 61/8508.
Minutes of the Cathedral Chapter, 1565–1720: 61/10941 to 61/10989.
Minutes of the Allerheiligen Chapter, 1696–1727: 61/11095.
Minutes of the St. Guido Chapter, 1573–1692: 61/11104 to 61/11112.
Minutes of the St. German and Mauritius Chapter, 1704–15: 61/11127.
Minutes of the *Fiscus*, 1553–1586: 61/11139, 61/11140.
Minutes of the Visitation of the Rural Chapter of Weißenburg, 1584: 61/11262.
Minutes of the Visitation of 1683: 61/11263 to 61/11265.
Minutes of the Visitation of 1701: 61/11266, 61/11267.
Minutes of the Visitation of 1718–21: 61/11269 to 61/11273.
Minutes of the Bishop's Council (*Hofratsprotokolle*), 1564–1669: 61/11494 to 61/11507.
Minutes of the *Vogtsgericht* in Jöhlingen, 1535–1712: 61/6981, 61/15534 to 61/15544.
Abteilung 65: Handschriften
Jesuits: 65/261 to 65/265.
Chronicles of the Bishopric of Speyer: 65/624 to 65/627.
Ritterstift Bruchsal: 65/11583, 65/11584, 65/11604, 65/11605.
Abteilung 66: Beraine
Amt Kißlau: 66/4456, 66/4457.
Abteilung 67: Kopialbücher
Libri Spiritualium, 1552–1736: 67/421, 67/422, 67/425 to 67/428.
Urfehden (Oaths), 1560–1616: 67/423, 67/424.
Missivbücher, 1568–1703: 67/381 to 67/403.
Fruchtspeicherrechnungen, 1577–78: 67/484.
Abteilung 74: Akten Baden Generalia
74/4116, 74/4259 to 74/4262, 74/4267, 74/4490.
Abteilung 78: Akten Bruchsal Generalia
Parishes, 1603: 78/615.
Description of Clerical Property, 18th Century: 78/618.
Patronage Parishes of the Cathedral Chapter: 78/619.
Rural Chapter Bruchsal, 1699–1719: 78/629, 78/712.
Visitations: 78/703, 78/711.
Ordinance (*Polizei-Ordnung*), 1703: 78/734.
Council of Trent: 78/906.
Missions, Jesuits and Capuchins: 78/1008.
Visitatio Limina: 78/1052.
St. German Chapter: 78/1190, 78/1723.
Allerheiligen Chapter: 78/1552.
St. Guido Chapter: 78/1814, 78/1773, 78/1816.
Jesuits: 78/1947, 78/2013.
Monasteries: 78/1964, 78/2015, 78/2016.
Chapter in Weißenburg: 78/2778.

Abteilung 88: Akten Frauenalb
  88/389 to 88/391, 88/398 to 88/402, 88/406, 88/820.
Abteilung 94: Akten *Ritterstift* Odenheim/Bruchsal
  Wills: 94/32 to 94/40.
  Visitations: 94/271, 94/273, 94/274.
  Relations with Village Communes: 94/390 to 94/392, 94/639.
  Conflicts with Bishops: 94/439.
Abteilung 133: Akten Bruchsal Amt und Stadt
  Capuchins: 133/418, 133/803.
  Parishes: 133/445 to 133/463.
Abteilung 153: Akten Kißlau Amt
  153/148, 153/149, 153/157, 153/161.
Abteilung 218: Akten Philippsburg Stadt
  Parish: 218/234 to 218/237, 218/240 to 218/244, 218/246, 218/485, 218/671
  to 218/673.
Abteilung 229: Akten der Landgemeinden
  Balzfeld, Bauerbach, Brühl, Büchig, Forst, Grombach, Jöhlingen, Kronau,
  Landshausen, Langenbrücken, Malsch, Mingolsheim, Neipsheim, Neu-
  hausen, Neutart, Ober- und Rheinhausen, Oberöwisheim, Odenheim,
  Rauenberg, Rheinsheim, Rohrbach, Stettfeld, Tiefenbronn, Ubstadt,
  Wagheusel, Waibstadt, Weyer b. Bruchsal, Zeutern.

Hauptstaatsarchiv Stuttgart (HStA.St.)

Abteilung A151: Relations of Weil der Stadt with Württemberg
  Religious disputes: Bü.15 to Bü.17.
Abteilung A208: Oberrat-Reichsstädte
  Weil der Stadt: 655 to 661.

Landesarchiv Speyer (LASp.)

Bestand D2: Akten Hochstift Speyer
  Report on Parishes in Amt Guttenberg, 1707: D2/306/5.
  Minutes of the Visitation of 1718: D2/306/6.
  Report on Monasteries, Parishes, and Schools, Amt Germersheim, 1556:
  D2/306/8.
  Minutes of the Visitation of 1583: D2/306/10.
  Records of the Rural Chapters: D2/310 to D2/313, D2/315.
  Parishes in Speyer: D2/455 to D2/462.
  Monasteries: D2/746 to D2/765.
  Jesuits: D2/905.
  Records of the Rural Parishes: Dahn, Deidesheim, Diedesfeld, Edesheim, Hain-
  feld, Hambach, Herxheim, Maikammer, Otterstadt, Rödersheim, Rupperts-
  berg, Schaidt.
Bestand D4: Kirchenrechnungen
  Rheinzabern, St. Katharina Pfrunde: D4/74, D4/75.
  Lauterburg, Armenstiftung: D4/114 to D4/116.
Bestand D21: Urkunden Domstift Speyer
Bestand D22: Urkunden Allerheiligenstift
Bestand D23: Urkunden St.Germanstift

Bestand D24: Urkunden St.Guidostift
Bestand D25: Speyerer Kloster
Bestand D27: Weißenburg Stift
Bestand F1: Kopialbücher
  Chronicle of St. Guido Chapter, 1565–1681: F1/77b.
Bestand F6: Kirchenbücher
  Diedesfeld: F6/38.
  Maikammer: F6/175, F6/176.

Parish Register Collection, Church of Jesus
Christ of Latter-Day Saints
0367712 Hochdorf
1049306 Waibstadt
1052127 Jöhlingen
1052129 Jöhlingen

Stadtarchiv Mainz (St.A.MZ)

Abteilung 15: Archiv der Oberrheinischen Jesuitenprovinz
  Speyer College: 170.
  Missions: 350.
  Litterae Annuae, 1543–1619: 400–2.
  Catalogi Triennales, 1597–1720: 431–39.

Stadtarchiv Speyer (St.A.Sp.)

Abteilung 1A: City-Clergy Relations
  Processions: 1A/347.
  Catholic Clergy: 1A/360.
  Capuchins: 1A/405.
  Jesuits: 1A/408/1 to 1A/408/8.
  "Reformation": 1A/450/4, 1A/450/11.

Published Primary Sources

Collectio processuum synodalium et constitutionum ecclesiarum diocesis Spirensis ab anno 1396 ad annum 1720. Bruchsal: 1786.

Hansen, Josef, ed. *Rheinische Akten zur Geschichte des Jesuitenordens (1542–1582).* Bonn: Hermann Behrendt, 1896.

Krebs, Manfred, ed. *Die Protokolle des Speyerer Domkapitels.* Stuttgart: Veröffentlichung der Kommission für geschichtliche Landeskunde in Baden-Württemberg, Reihe A, Quellen, Vol. 17, 21, 1968–69.

Lünig, Johan Christian. *Continuatio spicilegii Ecclesiastici des Teutschen Reichsarchivs* Leipzig: 1720.

Remling, Franz, ed. *Urkundenbuch zur Geschichte der Bischöfe zu Speyer.* Vol. II. Mainz: Franz Kirchheim, 1853.

Sammlung der Hochfürstlich-Speierischen Gesetze und Landesverordnungen, 4 vols. Bruchsal: 1789.

Schroeder, Rev. H.J., O.P., ed. *Canons and Decrees of the Council of Trent*. Rockford, Ill.: Tan Books, 1978.

Atlases

Alter, Willi, ed. *Pfalzatlas*. Im Auftrag der pfälzischen Gesellschaft zur Förderung der Wissenschaften. Speyer: Eigenverlag der Gesellschaft, 1963–   .
Kommission für geschichtliche Landeskunde in Baden-Württemberg. *Historischer Atlas von Baden-Württemberg*. Stuttgart: Die Kommission, 1972–

Secondary Works

Abray, Lorna Jane. *The People's Reformation: Magistrates, Clergy, and Commons in Strasbourg, 1500–1598*. Ithaca: Cornell University Press, 1985.
Albrecht, Dieter. "Die Barockzeit." In Max Spindler, ed., *Handbuch der bayerischen Geschichte*, vol. 2, pp. 730–35.
———. "Gegenreformation und katholische Reform." In Max Spindler, ed., *Handbuch der bayerischen Geschichte*, vol. 2, pp. 714–30.
Alter, Willi. "Von der konradinischen Rachtung bis zum letzten Reichstag in Speyer (1420/22–1570)." In *Geschichte der Stadt Speyer*, vol. 1, pp. 363–570.
Ammerich, Hans. "Formen und Wege der katholischen Reform in den Diözesen Speyer und Straßburg. Klerusreform und Seelsorgerreform." In Volker Press et al., eds., *Barock am Oberrhein*, pp. 290–327.
Bader, Karl Siegfried. *Dorfgenossenschaft und Dorfgemeinde*. Teil II, *Studien zur Rechtsgeschichte des mittelalterlichen Dorfes*. Cologne: Bohlau Verlag, 1962.
Bartmann, Horst. "Die Kirchenpolitik der Markgrafen von Baden-Baden im Zeitalter der Glaubenskämpfe, 1535–1622." *Freiburger Diözesan-Archiv* 81 (1961): 289–333.
Baur, Joseph. "Das Fürstbistum Speyer in den Jahren 1635 bis 1652." *Mitteilungen des historischen Vereins der Pfalz* 24 (1900): 1–163.
Bechberger, Werner. "St. Leon und seine Bevölkerung 1707–1757: Beiträge zur demographischen und sozialen Entwicklung einer dorflichen Gemeinde im Hochstift Speyer." *Zeitschrift für Geschichte des Oberrheins* 134 (1986): 129–93.
Becker, Thomas Paul. *Konfessionalisierung in Kurköln. Untersuchung zur Durchsetzung der katholischen Reform in den Dekanten Ahrgau und Bonn anhand von Visitationsprotokollen 1583–1761*. Bonn: Edition Röhrscheid, 1989.
Becker-Huberti, Manfred. *Die tridentinische Reform im Bistum Münster unter Fürstbischof Christoph Bernhard v. Galen 1650 bis 1678*. Münster: Aschendorff, 1978.
Benrath, Gustav. "Die Kurpfälzischen Kirchenvisitationen im 16. Jahrhundert." *Blätter für Pfälzische Kirchengeschichte* 42 (1975): 17–24.
Birely, Robert, S.J. "Early Modern Germany." In John O'Malley, ed., *Catholicism in Early Modern Europe: A Guide to Research*, pp. 11–30.
———. *Maximilian von Bayern, Adam Contzen, S.J. und die Gegenreformation in Deutschland 1624–35*. Göttingen: Vandenhoeck und Ruprecht, 1975.

——. *Religion and Politics in the Age of the Counterreformation. Emperor Ferdinand II, William Lamormaini, S.J., and the Formation of Imperial Policy.* Chapel Hill: University of North Carolina Press, 1981.

Blickle, Peter. *Deutsche Untertanen. Ein Widerspruch.* Munich: C. H. Beck, 1981.

——. *Gemeindereformation. Die Menschen des 16. Jahrhunderts auf dem Weg zum Heil.* Munich: R. Oldenbourg Verlag, 1985.

——. *Landschaften im alten Reich: Die staatliche Funktion des gemeinen Mannes in Oberdeutschland.* Munich: C. H. Beck, 1973.

——. *The Revolution of 1525. The German Peasants' War from a New Perspective.* Baltimore: Johns Hopkins University Press, 1981.

——, ed. *Zugänge zur bäuerlichen Reformation.* Zurich: Chronos, 1987.

Bohlender, Rolf, ed. *Dom und Bistum Speyer: Eine Bibliographie.* Speyer: Pfälzische Landesbibliothek, 1963.

Boos, Heinrich. *Geschichte der rheinischen Städtekultur.* 4 Vols. Berlin: Verlag von J. A. Stargardt, 1901.

Bossy, John. *Christianity in the West, 1400–1700.* London: Oxford University Press, 1985.

——. "The Counter-Reformation and the People of Catholic Europe." *Past and Present* 47 (1970):51–70.

Breuer, Dieter. *Oberdeutsche Literatur, 1565–1650. Deutsche Literaturgeschichte und Territorialgeschichte in frühabsolutistischer Zeit.* Munich: C. H. Beck, 1979.

Bücking, Jürgen. *Frühabsolutismus und Kirchenreform in Tirol 1565–1665. Ein Beitrag zum Ringen zwischen "Staat" und "Kirche" in der frühen Neuzeit.* Wiesbaden: Franz Steiner Verlag, 1972.

Bull, Karl-Otto. "Die erste 'Volkszählung' des deutschen Südwestens—Die Bevölkerung des Bistums Speyer in 1530." *Zeitschrift für Geschichte des Oberrheins* 133 (1985):337–62.

Burke, Peter. *Popular Culture in Early Modern Europe.* New York: Harper and Row, 1978.

Châtellier, Louis. *The Europe of the Devout. The Catholic Reformation and the Formation of a New Society.* Cambridge: Cambridge University Press, 1989.

——. *Tradition chrétienne et renouveau catholique dans le cadre de l'ancien Diocèse de Strasbourg (1650–1770).* Paris: Ophrys, 1981.

Clasen, Claus-Peter. *The Palatinate in European History, 1555–1618.* Oxford: Basil Blackwell, 1966.

Cohn, Henry. *The Government of the Rhine Palatinate in the 15th Century.* Oxford: Oxford University Press, 1965.

Conrad, Franziska. *Reformation in der bäuerlichen Gesellschaft: Zur Rezeption reformatorischer Theologie im Elsaß.* Stuttgart: Franz Steiner Verlag Wiesbaden, 1984.

Croix, Alain. *La Bretagne aux 16e et 17e siècles. La vie, la mort, la foi.* Paris: Maloine SA, 1981.

Cuthbert, Father, O.S.F.C. *The Capuchins: A Contribution to the History of the Counterreformation.* 2 Vols. New York: Longmans, Green, 1929.

Davis, Natalie Z. *Society and Culture in Early Modern France.* Stanford: Stanford University Press, 1975.

Delumeau, Jean. *Catholicism between Luther and Voltaire: A New View of the Counter-Reformation.* London: Burns and Oates, 1977.

Dickens, Arthur. *The Counter-Reformation*. New York: Harcourt, Brace, and World, 1969.

Drollinger, Kuno. *Kleine Städte Südwestdeutschlands. Studien zur Sozial- und Wirtschaftsgeschichte der Städte im rechtsrheinischen Teil des Hochstifts Speyer bis zur Mitte des 17. Jahrhunderts*. Stuttgart: Kohlhammer Verlag, 1968.

Duggan, Lawrence. *Bishop and Chapter. The Governance of the Bishopric of Speyer to 1552*. New Brunswick: Rutgers University Press, 1978.

Duhr, Bernhard. *Geschichte der Jesuiten in den Ländern deutsche Zunge vom 16. bis 18. Jahrhundert*. 4 Vols. Freiburg im Breisgau: Herdersche Verlagshandlung, 1907–21.

Egler, Anna. *Die Spanier in der linksrheinischen Pfalz, 1620–1632. Invasion, Verwaltung, Rekatholisierung*. Mainz: Selbstverlag der Gesellschaft für mittelrheinische Kirchengeschichte, 1971.

Evennett, H. Outram. *The Spirit of the Counter-Reformation*. Cambridge: Cambridge University Press, 1968.

Feigenbutz, Leopold. *Kurzer Abriß der Geschichte von Odenheim und seiner Benedictinerabtei, dem nachmaligen Ritterstift Odenheim im Kraichgau*. Bühl: Konkordia, 1886.

Ferté, Jeanne. *La vie religieuse dans les campagnes parisiennes, 1622–1695*. Paris: Librarie Philosophique J. Vrin, 1962.

Finkel, Klaus. *Die Speyerer Domkapelle im 17. und 18. Jahrhundert*. Speyer: Schriften des Diözesanarchivs Speyer 2, 1975.

François, Etienne. "De l'uniformité à la tolérance: Confession et société urbaine en Allemagne, 1650–1800." *Annales E.S.C.* 37, no. 4 (1982):783–800.

———. "Die Volksbildung am Mittelrhein im ausgehenden 18. Jahrhundert. Eine Untersuchung über den vermeintlichen Bildungsrückstand der katholischen Bevölkerung Deutschlands im Ancien Régime." *Jahrbuch für Westdeutsche Landesgeschichte* 3 (1977):277–304.

Franz, Günther. *Der dreißigjährige Krieg und das deutsche Volk. Untersuchung zur Bevölkerungs- und Agrargeschichte*. 1940. Reprint. Stuttgart: Gustav Fischer Verlag, 1979.

Fuhrmann, Rosi. "Die Kirche im Dorf. Kommunale Initiativen zur Organisation von Seelsorge vor der Reformation." In Peter Blickle, ed., *Zugänge zur bäuerlichen Reformation*, 147–86.

Garbe, Birgitte. "Reformmaßnahmen und Formen der katholischen Erneuerung in der Erzdiözese Köln (1555–1648)." *Jahrbuch des kölnischen Geschichtsvereins* 47 (1976):136–75.

Geschichte der Stadt Speyer. 2 vols. Stuttgart: Kohlhammer Verlag, 1982.

Ginzburg, Carlo. *The Cheese and the Worms: The Cosmos of a Sixteenth Century Miller*. Baltimore: Johns Hopkins University Press, 1980.

Greyerz, Kaspar von, ed. *Religion and Society in Early Modern Europe*. London: George Allen and Unwin, 1984.

Harster, Wilhelm. *Der Güterbesitz des Klosters Weißenburg i.E.* Speyer: Jägersche Buchdruckerei, 1893, 1894.

———. "Speierer Flurplan von 1715 und der sog. Speierer Bauernkrieg." *Mitteilungen des historischen Vereins der Pfalz* 13 (1888):93–123.

Hartwich, Wolfgang. *Bevölkerungsstruktur und Wiederbesiedlung Speyers nach der Zerstörung von 1689*. Heidelberg: Carl Winter Universitätsverlag, 1965.

———. "Speyer von 1620 bis 1814." In *Geschichte der Stadt Speyer*, vol. 2, pp. 1–113.

Häusser, Ludwig. *Geschichte der rheinischen Pfalz.* 2 Vols. 1856. Reprint. Primasens: Buchhandlung Johann Richter, 1970.

Heckel, Martin. *Deutschland im konfessionellen Zeitalter.* Göttingen: Vandenhoeck und Ruprecht, 1983.

Hersche, Peter. *Die deutschen Domkapitel im 17. und 18. Jahrhundert.* 3 Vols. Bern: Selbstverlag, 1984.

——. "Intendierte Rückständigkeit: Zur Charakteristik des geistlichen Staates im alten Reich." In Georg Schmidt, ed., *Stände und Gesellschaft im Alten Reich.* Stuttgart: Franz Steiner Verlag Wiesbaden, 1989.

Hoffman, Philip T. *Church and Community in the Diocese of Lyon, 1500–1789.* New Haven: Yale University Press, 1984.

Hsia, R. Po-chia. *Social Discipline in the Reformation: Central Europe, 1550–1750.* New York: Routledge and Kegan Paul, 1989.

——. *Society and Religion in Münster: 1535–1618.* New Haven: Yale University Press, 1984.

Jacobs, P. Arsenius. *Die rheinischen Kapuziner, 1611–1725. Ein Beitrag zur Geschichte der katholischen Reform.* Münster: Aschendorff, 1933.

Jedin Hubert, ed. *Handbuch der Kirchengeschichte.* Vol. 5. Freiburg: Herder, 1970.

——. "Die Reichskirche der Schönbornzeit." In Hubert Jedin, *Kirche des Glaubens, Kirche der Geschichte.* Freiburg: Herder, 1966.

Kammerer, Louis. *Repertoire du clergé d'Alsace sous l'ancien régime, 1648–1792.* 2 vols. Typescript, Strasbourg, 1985.

Karant-Nunn, Suzanne. *Zwickau in Transition, 1500–1547: The Reformation as an Agent of Change.* Columbus: Ohio University Press, 1987.

Keyser, Erich, ed. *Badisches Städtebuch.* Stuttgart: Kohlhammer Verlag, 1959.

——. *Städtebuch Rheinland-Pfalz und Saarland.* Stuttgart: Kohlhammer Verlag, 1964

——. *Württembergisches Städtebuch.* Stuttgart: Kohlhammer Verlag, 1962.

Kittelson, James. "The Confessional Age: The Late Reformation in Germany." In Steven Ozment, ed., *Reformation Europe, A Guide to Research,* pp. 361–81.

——. "Successes and Failures in the German Reformation: The Report from Strasbourg." *Archiv für Reformationsgeschichte* 73 (1982):153–75.

Kloe, Karl. *Die Wahlkapitulation der Bischöfe zu Speyer, 1272–1802.* Speyer: Verlag der Jaegerischen Buchhandlung, 1928.

Köhler, Hans-Joachim. *Obrigkeitliche Konfessionsänderung in Kondominaten. Eine Fallstudie über ihre Bedingungen und Methoden am Beispiel der baden-badischen Religionspolitik unter der Regierung Markgraf Wilhelms (1622–1677).* Münster: Aschendorff, 1975.

Köhler, Joachim. *Das Ringen um die tridentinische Erneuerung im Bistum Breslau. Vom Abschluß des Konzils bis zur Schlacht am Weißen Berg.* Cologne: Böhlau Verlag, 1973.

Kolb, J. V. *Historisch-Statistisch-Topographisches Lexicon von dem Großherzogs-thum Baden.* Karlsruhe: 1816.

Krebs, Manfred, ed. "Das Dienerbuch des Bistums Speyer, 1464–1768." *Zeitschrift für Geschichte des Oberrheins* 96 (1948):55–195.

Lamott, Alois. *Das Speyerer Diözesanritual von 1512 bis 1932. Seine Geschichte und seine Ordines zur Sakramentliturgie.* Speyer: Verlag der Jaegerschen Buchdruckerei, 1961.

Lang, Peter Thaddäus. "Die tridentinischen Reform im Landkapitel Mergentheim bis zum Einfall der Schweden 1631." *Rottenburger Jahrbuch für Kirchengeschichte* 1 (1982):143–67.

Lind, Emil. *Speyer und der Protestantismus.* Heidelberg: Evangelischer Verlag, 1929.

Lottin, Alain. *Lille, Citadelle de la Contre-Réform, 1598–1668.* Lille: Westhoeck, 1984.

Lutz, Heinrich. *Das Ringen um deutsche Einheit und kirchliche Erneuerung: Von Maximilian I bis zum Westfälischen Frieden 1490 bis 1648.* Berlin: Propyläen Verlag, 1983.

Lutz, Karl. "Fürstbischöfliche und kaiserliche, österreichische und französische Rekatholisierung im südlichen Speiergau 1622–1632, und ihre reichs- und kirchenrechtlichen Begründungen." *Archiv für mittelrheinische Kirchengeschichte* 20 (1968):275–95.

Manz, Georg. *Die Kapuziner im rechtsrheinischen Gebiet des Bistums Speyer im 17. und 18. Jahrhundert.* Bruchsal: Vorgelegt von Georg Manz, 1979.

Marigold, William. "Jesuitentheater in Speyer. Zu zwei Programmheften im GLA Karlsruhe." *Zeitschrift für Geschichte des Oberrheins* 127 (1979):263–80.

Mayer, Johan Georg. *Das Konzil von Trent und die Gegenreformation in der Schweiz.* 2 vols. Stans: Hans und Matt, 1901.

Meier, Johannes. "Die katholische Erneuerung des Würzburger Landkapitels Karlstadt im Spiegel der Landkapitelversammlungen und Pfarreivisitationen, 1549 bis 1624." *Würzburger Diözesangeschichtsblätter* 33 (1971):51–125.

Mentz, Georg. *Joh. Philipp von Schönborn, Kurfürst v. Mainz und Bischof von Würzburg und Worms.* 2 vols. Jena: Verlag von Gustav Fischer, 1896/1899.

Midelfort, H. C. Erik. *Witchhunting in Southwestern Germany, 1562–1684: The Social and Intellectual Foundations.* Stanford: Stanford University Press, 1972.

Mielke, Heinz-Peter. "Schwenkfeldianer im Hofstaat Bischof Marquards von Speyer (1560–1581)." *Archiv für mittelrheinische Kirchengeschichte* 28 (1976): 77–82.

Molitor, Hansgeorg. *Kirchliche Reformversuche der Kurfürsten und Erzbischöfe von Trier im Zeitalter der Gegenreformation.* Wiesbaden: Franz Steiner Verlag, 1967.

Mone, Franz. "Schulwesen vom 13. bis 16. Jahrhundert." *Zeitschrift für Geschichte des Oberrheins* 1 (1850):257–302.

Münch, Paul. *Zucht und Ordnung. Reformierte Kirchenverfassungen im 16. und 17. Jahrhundert. (Nassau-Dillenberg, Kurpfalz, Hessen-Kassel).* Stuttgart: Klett-Cotta, 1978.

Musall, Heinz. *Die Entwicklung der Kulturlandschaft der Rheinniederung zwischen Karlsruhe und Speyer vom Ende des 16. bis zum Ende des 19. Jahrhunderts.* Heidelberg: Selbstverlag des Geographischen Instituts der Universität Heidelberg, 1969.

Neumaier, Helmut. *Reformation und Gegenreformation im Bauland unter besonderer Berücksichtigung der Ritterschaft.* Würzburg: Bohler Verlag, 1977.

O'Malley, John, ed. *Catholicism in Early Modern Europe. A Guide to Research.* St. Louis: Center for Reformation Research, 1988.

Ohler, Norbert. "Alltag in einer Zeit des Friedens (1570–1620)." In *Geschichte der Stadt Speyer,* pp. 571–655.

Ortner, Franz. *Reformation, katholische Reform, und Gegenreformation im Erz-stift Salzburg.* Salzburg: Universitätsverlag Anton Pustet, 1981.

Ozment, Steven, ed. *Reformation Europe. A Guide to Research.* St. Louis: Center for Reformation Research, 1982.

Parker, Geoffrey. *Europe in Crisis, 1598–1648.* Fontana History of Europe. Ithaca: Cornell University Press, 1980.

——, et al. *The Thirty Years' War.* London: Routledge and Kegan Paul, 1984.

Pérouas, Louis. *Le diocèse de la Rochelle de 1648 à 1724: Sociologie et pastorale.* Paris: S.E.V.P.E.N., 1964.

Press, Volker. *Calvinismus und Territorialstaat. Regierung und Zentralbehörden der Kurpfalz, 1559–1619.* Stuttgart: Ernst Klett, 1970.

——. "Das Hochstift Speyer im Reich des späten Mittelalters und der frühen Neuzeit-Portrait eines geistlichen Staates." In Volker Press et al., eds., *Barock am Oberrhein,* pp. 251–90. Karlsruhe: Kommissionsverlag G. Braun, 1985.

——. "Kurfürst Maximilian I. von Bayern, die Jesuiten und die Universität Hei-delberg im dreißigjährigen Krieg 1622–1649." In *Semper Apertus. Sechshun-dert Jahre Ruprecht-Karls-Universität Heidelberg 1386–1986.* Berlin: Springer Verlag, 1986.

——. "Zwischen Versailles und Wien. Die Pfälzer Kurfürsten in der deutschen Geschichte der Barockzeit." *Zeitschrift für Geschichte des Oberrheins* 130 (1982):207–62.

Press, Volker, Eugen Reinhard, and Hansmartin Schwarzmaier, ed. *Barock am Oberrhein.* Karlsruhe: Kommissionsverlag G. Braun, 1985.

Raab, Heribert. "Die oberdeutschen Hochstifte zwischen Habsburg und Wittels-bach in der frühen Neuzeit." *Blätter für deutsche Landesgeschichte* 109 (1973): 69–101.

Rapp, Francis. *Réformes et Réformation à Strasbourg. Eglise et société dans le Diocèse de Strasbourg (1450–1525).* Paris: Ophrys, 1974.

Raumer, Kurt von. *Die Zerstörung der Pfalz von 1689 im Zusammenhang der französischen Rheinpolitik.* 1930. Reprint. Bad Neustadt a.d. Saale: Verlag Dietrich Pfaeler, 1982.

Rebel, Hermann. *Peasant Classes: The Bureaucratization of Property and Fam-ily Relations under Early Hapsburg Absolutism, 1511–1636.* Princeton: Princeton University Press, 1983.

Reinhard, Wolfgang. "Gegenreformation als Modernisierung? Prolegomena zu einer Theorie des konfessionellen Zeitalters." *Archiv für Reformationsge-schichte* 68 (1977):226–52.

——. "Konfession und Konfessionalisierung in Europa." In Wolfgang Reinhard et al., eds., *Bekenntnis und Geschichte. Die Confessio Augustana in histori-schem Zusammenhang.* Munich: Verlag Ernst Vogel, 1981.

Reinhardt, Rudolf. *Restauration, Visitation, Inspiration. Die Reformbestrebun-gen in der Benediktinerabtei Weingarten von 1567–1627.* Stuttgart: Kohlham-mer Verlag, 1960.

Remling, Franz. *Geschichte der Bischöfe zu Speyer.* 2 vols. Mainz: Franz Kirch-heim, 1854.

——. *Urkundliche Geschichte der ehemaligen Abteien und Klöster im jetzigen Rheinbayern.* 2 vols. 1836. Reprint. Pirmasens: Verlag der Buchhandlung Johann Richter, 1973.

Robisheaux, Thomas. *Rural Society and the Search for Order in Early Modern Germany.* Cambridge: Cambridge University Press, 1989.

Roth, F. W. E. "Geschichte der Verlagsgeschäfte, der Buchdruckereien und des Buchhandels zu Speyer im 17. Jahrhundert bis 1689." *Mitteilungen des historischen Vereins der Pfalz* 20 (1896):259–341.

——. "Geschichte und Bibliographie der Buchdruckereien zu Speyer im 15. und 16. Jahrhundert." *Mitteilungen des historischen Vereins der Pfalz* 18 (1894):1–112.

Rothkrug, Lionel. "Popular Religion and Holy Shrines. Their Influence on the Origins of the German Reformation and Their Role in German Cultural Development." In James Obelkevich, ed., *Religion and the People 800–1700*. Chapel Hill: University of North Carolina Press, 1979.

Rublack, Hans-Christoph. *Gescheiterte Reformation. Frühreformatorische und protestantische Bewegungen in süd- und westdeutschen geistlichen Residenzen*. Stuttgart: Klett-Cotta, 1978.

Sabean, David. *Power in the Blood: Popular Culture and Village Discourse in Early Modern Germany*. Cambridge: Cambridge University Press, 1984.

Schaab, Meinrad. "Pfälzische Klöster vor und nach der Reformation." *Blätter für deutsche Landesgeschichte* 109 (1973):253–58.

——. "Die Wiederherstellung des Katholizismus in der Kurpfalz im 17. und 18. Jahrhundert." *Zeitschrift für Geschichte des Oberrheins* 114 (1966):146–205.

Schaab, Meinrad, and Kurt Andermann. "Leibeigenschaft der Einwohner des Hochstifts Speyer, 1530." Erläuterung zu *Historischer Atlas von Baden-Württemberg*, map IX, 4.

Schilling, Heinz. "Die Konfessionalisierung im Reich. Religiöser und gesellschaftlicher Wandel in Deutschland zwischen 1555 und 1620." *Historische Zeitschrift* 246 (1988):1–45.

Schmidlin, Joseph. *Die kirchlichen Zustände in Deutschland vor dem dreißigjährigen Kriege nach den bischöflichen Diözesanberichten an den heiligen Stuhl*. 3 vols. Freiburg in Breisgau: Herdersche Verlag, 1908–10.

Schmidt, Peter. *Das Collegium Germanicum in Rom und die Germaniker. Zur Funktion eines römischen Ausländerseminars (1552–1914)*. Tübingen: Max Neumeyer Verlag, 1984.

Schreiber, Georg, ed. "Tridentinische Reformdekrete in deutschen Bistümern." In Remigius Bäumer, ed., *Concilium Tridentinum*, pp. 462–521. Darmstadt: Wissenschaftliche Buchgesellschaft, 1979.

Scribner, Robert W. "Ritual and Popular Religion in Catholic Germany at the Time of the Reformation." *Journal of Ecclesiastical History* 35 (1984):47–77.

Seifert, Arno. *Weltlicher Staat und Kirchenreform. Die Seminarpolitik Bayerns im 16. Jahrhundert*. Münster: Aschendorff, 1978.

Sieffert, P. Archange. "Les capucins à Wissembourg sous l'Ancien Régime et la restauration catholique dans la région de la Lauter. I. La maison à Wissembourg." *Archives de l'Eglise d'Alsace*, n.s. 1 (1946):219–55.

——. "Die Kapuziner zu Weißenburg (1684–1791) und die katholische Restauration beiderseits der Lauter." *Archives de l'Eglise d'Alsace*, n.s. 3 (1949–50):248–84.

——. "Die Kapuziner zu Weißenburg (1684–1791) und die katholische Restauration beiderseits der Lauter. IV. Die Kapuziner Missionspfarreien in der Südpfalz (1684–1800)." *Archives de l'Eglise d'Alsace*, n.s. 5 (1953–54):135–78.

——. "Die katholische Pfarrei St. Johann zu Weißenburg im achtzenten Jahrhundert." *Archiv für elsässische Kirchengeschichte* 4 (1929):173–218.

Speyerer Buchdruck in fünfhundert Jahren. Speyer: Pfälzische Landesbibliotek, 1981.

Spindler, Max, ed. *Handbuch der bayerischen Geschichte.* Vol. 2. Munich: C. H. Beck, 1988.

Stamer, Ludwig. "Die ersten tridentinischen Priesterseminare des Bistums Speyer im 16. und 17. Jahrhundert." In Alphons Kloos, ed., *St. German in Stadt und Bistum Speyer,* pp. 103–9. Speyer: Verlag des Priesterseminars, 1957.

———. *Kirchengeschichte der Pfalz.* 3 vols. Speyer: Pilger-Verlag, 1949–55.

Strauss, Gerald. *Luther's House of Learning: Indoctrination of the Young in the German Reformation.* Baltimore: Johns Hopkins University Press, 1978.

Tackett, Timothy. *Priest and Parish in 18th Century France. A Social and Political Study of the Curés in the Diocese of Dauphiné, 1750–1791.* Princeton: Princeton University Press, 1977.

Thomas, Keith. *Religion and the Decline of Magic.* New York: Charles Scribner's Sons, 1971.

Tüchle, Hermann. "Die Bistümer Worms und Speyer in den Nuntiaturberichten an die Propagandakongregation von 1697." *Blätter für pfälzische Kirchengeschichte und religiöse Volkskunde* 40 (1973):78–85.

Ulbrich, Claudia. *Leibherrschaft am Oberrhein im Spätmittelalter.* Göttingen: Vandenhoeck und Ruprecht, 1979.

Veit, Andreas Ludwig. *Kirche und Kirchenreform in der Erzdiözese Mainz, 1517–1618.* Freiburg: Herdersche Verlagshandlung, 1920.

Veit, Andreas Ludwig, and Ludwig Lenhart. *Kirche und Volksfrömmigkeit im Zeitalter des Barock.* Freiburg: Verlag Herder, 1956.

Vierhaus, Rudolf. *Deutschland im Zeitalter des Absolutismus (1648–1763).* Göttingen: Vandenhoeck und Ruprecht, 1978.

———. *Staaten und Stände. Vom westfälischen bis zum Hubertusburger Frieden, 1648 bis 1763.* Berlin: Propyläen Verlag, 1984.

Vogler, Bernard. "Die Ausbildung des Konfessionsbewußtseins in den pfälzischen Territorien zwischen 1555 und 1619." In Horst Rabe et al., eds. *Festgabe für Ernst Zeeden zum 60. Geburtstag.* Münster: Aschendorff, 1976.

———. *Le clergé protestant rhénan au siècle de la Réforme (1555–1619).* Paris: Ophrys, 1976.

———. "Die Entstehung der protestantischen Volksfrömmigkeit in der rheinischen Pfalz zwischen 1555 und 1619." *Archiv für Reformationsgeschichte* 72 (1981): 158–96.

———. "Les inspecteurs écclésiastiques protestants en territoire rhénan (1555–1619)." *Revue d'histoire et de philologie religieuse.* 54 (1974):89–101.

———. "La politique scolaire entre Rhin et Moselle." *Francia* 3 (1975):235–320 and *Francia* 4 (1976):287–364.

———. *La vie religieuse en pays rhénan dans la seconde moitié du XVIe siècle (1556–1619).* 3 vols. Lille: Service des reproductions des thèses, 1974.

———. "Les visites pastorales protestants dans les pays rhénans du XVIe siècle." *Revue d'histoire de l'Eglise de France* 57 (1971):315–19.

Vogler, Bernard, and Janine Estèbe. "La genèse d'une société protestante: Etude comparée de quelques registres consistoriaux Langoduciens et Palatins vers 1600." *Annales, E. S. C.* 31, no.2 (1976):362–88.

Walker, Mack. *German Home Towns: Community, State, and General Estate, 1648–1871.* Ithaca: Cornell University Press, 1971.

Warmbrunn, Paul. *Zwei Konfessionen in einer Stadt: Das Zusammenleben von*

Katholiken und Protestanten in den paritätischen Reichstädten Augsburg, Biberach, Ravensburg, und Dinkelsbühl von 1548–1648. Wiesbaden: Franz Steiner Verlag, 1983.

Weber, Hermann. *Frankreich, Kurtrier, der Rhein, und das Reich, 1623–1635.* Bonn: Ludwig Röhrscheid Verlag, 1969.

Weinman, Fred. *Kapellen im Bistum Speyer.* Speyer: Pilger Verlag, 1975.

Wetterer, Anton. "Geistliche Verlassenschaften in Bruchsal im 16. Jahrhundert." *Freiburger Diözesan-Archiv* 37 (1909):204–18.

——. "Die Jesuiten in Bruchsal, 1616–1632." *Freiburger Diözesan-Archiv* 65 (1937):218–25.

Wille, Jakob. *Bruchsal. Bilder aus einem geistlichen Staat im 18. Jahrhundert.* Heidelberg: Carl Winters Universitätsbuchhandlung, 1900.

Wright, A. D. *The Counter-Reformation: Catholic Europe and the Non-Christian World.* London: Weidenfeld and Nicolson, 1982.

Wunder, Heide. *Die bäuerliche Gemeinde in Deutschland.* Göttingen: Vandenhoeck und Ruprecht, 1986.

Zeeden, Ernst W. *Die Entstehung der Konfessionen: Grundlagen und Formen der Konfessionsbildung im Zeitalter der Glaubenskämpfe.* Munich: R. Oldenbourg Verlag, 1965.

——, ed. *Gegenreformation.* Darmstadt: Wissenschaftliche Buchgesellschaft, 1973.

——. "Grundlagen und Wege der Konfessionsbildung in Deutschland im Zeitalter der Glaubenskämpfe." *Historische Zeitschrift* 185 (1958):249–99.

——. *Kleine Reformationsgeschichte von Baden-Durlach und Kurpfalz.* Karlsruhe: Badenia, 1956.

Zeeden, Ernst W., and Hans-Georg Molitor, eds. *Die Visitation im Dienste der kirchlichen Reform.* Münster: Aschendorff, 1967.

Zschunke, Peter. *Konfession und Alltag in Oppenheim. Beiträge zur Geschichte von Bevölkerung und Gesellschaft einer gemischtkonfessionellen Kleinstadt in der frühen Neuzeit.* Wiesbaden: Franz Steiner Verlag, 1984.

Index

Library of Congress Cataloging-in-Publication Data

Forster, Marc.
    The Counter-Reformation in the villages : religion and reform in
the Bishopric of Speyer, 1560–1720 / Marc Forster.
      p. cm.
    Includes bibliographical references and index.
    ISBN 0-8014-2566-2 (alk. paper)
    1. Speyer (Ecclesiastical principality)—History. 2. Counter—
Reformation—Germany—Speyer Region. 3. Catholics—Germany—Speyer
Region—History. 4. Speyer Region (Germany)—Church history.
I. Title.
BX1538.S6F67   1992
282'.43435—dc20   91-55564